D0049541

# IN THE SHADOWS
# OF THE DIAMOND:

# HARD TIMES IN THE
# NATIONAL PASTIME

# IN THE SHADOWS OF THE DIAMOND:
## HARD TIMES IN THE NATIONAL PASTIME

by

Michael Santa Maria
James Costello

The Elysian Fields Press
Brown & Benchmark
A Division of Wm. C. Brown Communications, Inc.

Library of Congress Cataloging in Publication Data:
    SANTA MARIA, MICHAEL 1954-
    IN THE SHADOWS OF THE DIAMOND:
    HARD TIMES IN THE NATIONAL PASTIME

Library of Congress Catalog Card Number: 91-73708
ISBN: 0-697-15031-3

Printed in the United States of America by The Elysian Fields Press, 2460 Kerper Boulevard, Dubuque, IA 52001.
10 9 8 7 6 5 4 3 2 1

### Mission Statement of The Elysian Fields Press Imprint

The purpose and philosophy of The Elysian Fields Press is grounded in an appreciation of baseball as a central mythology of American culture. We wish to explore in print, via periodicals and books of essay, history, fiction, biography, poetry and anthology, the unifying romance of baseball as it connects us with our larger heritage and the natural cycles of generation.

# Dedication

To the memory of my father
MSM

For Laura, Willie and Anna
"the heart of the order"
JC

# CONTENTS

# FOREWORD

Like the larger world around it, baseball loves its myths, sometimes even more than it loves its truths. We often need myths more than truths, and as a result we cling to them steadfastly. Murders have been committed for them. Wars have been fought over them. Eventually, the myths become more real than reality.

Jim Costello and Michael Santa Maria are quintessential SABR (Society for American Baseball Research) men, probing the record to separate the myths from the reality. It's a hard job, and my hat is off to them.

The stories they tell here—of goats who were not goats—go a long way to set the records straight.

My own favorite story is of Johnny Pesky, who definitely did *not* hold the ball. A study of the official game film makes that clear. If anyone can watch the film and honestly say that John held the ball, Pesky and I will buy that person a steak dinner for two; and if that person cannot honestly say it, of course, he or she will buy us each a steak.

The news accounts of the play the next morning are revealing. Jack Hand of the Associated Press was emphatic that Pesky held the ball. Most other writers fudged it and mentioned it low in their stories—many didn't mention it at all.

My theory is that everyone in the press box was watching Enos Slaughter dashing to the plate. Hand may have shouted, "Did you see that! Did you see that! Pesky held the ball!" No one had seen that (including the camera), but all were too sheepish to admit they hadn't, so they fudged their stories in case their editors demanded to know why they had missed the key play of the Series. Some writers didn't mention the incident at all. Of the others, most buried the angle low in their stories, and the details they offer of what they say they saw are contradictory. A good defense attorney could call all the eyewitness reporters to Johnny's trial—plus the tell-tale movie film—and no jury would convict.

Yet, forty-five years later, we still read in stories by men who never saw the game at all (or weren't even born) that "Pesky held the ball."

The cruel myth, plus World War II, has kept Pesky out of the Hall of Fame. Without the war, he would probably have collected 200 hits in his first six seasons, rivaled only by Wade Boggs, and would have ended with a lifetime batting average of about .315, which would put him up among the three top-hitting shortstops of all time.

I've always thought the real goat of the 1946 Series was Red Sox reliever Bob Klinger, who gave up the winning hits, or manager Joe Cronin, who left Klinger in after they began hitting him, and did not call—as Cardinal skipper Eddie Dyer did—on his ace starter, Tex Hughson, to put out the fire. But neither Klinger nor Cronin ever spoke up in Johnny's defense, relieved perhaps that he had directed the fire away from them.

Oddly, two other shortstops did hold the ball in clutch World Series situations—Johnny Evers in 1914 and Dick Bartell in 1940—but neither of them were stigmatized as Pesky was. Evers escaped goat horns because of Hank Gowdy's game-winning homer, which Costello and Santa Maria describe with such drama.

In the same game that Gowdy tripped on his mask in 1924, the Giants' eighteen-year-old third baseman, Freddie Lindstrom, was the victim of a freak pebble-bounce that tied the game and set up the Gowdy play that led to the loss on another freak pebble-bounce over Lindstrom's head. Yet, far from suffering as a goat, Lindstrom probably took advantage of a strong sympathy vote that carried him into the Hall of Fame. History deals differently with players who wear an "NY" on their hats.

Nathaniel Hawthorne's heroine, Hester Prynne, was stigmatized by wearing a scarlet "A" on her blouse. I've often thought that another great shortstop, Cecil Travis, carried the equally heavy stigma of a white "W" on his cap. "W" for Washington.

That, plus World War II. Travis was the second highest-hitting shortstop of all time when he was called into the army in 1942. He lost four years, suffered frost-bitten toes in the Battle of the Bulge, and his average took a dive when he returned. Even so, he's still the third-highest batting shortstop in history. With no war—and with an "NY" on his cap—Travis would have been in Cooperstown decades ago.

The authors also describe another shortstop's travail, that of Roger Peckinpaugh, who made eight errors in the 1925 Series. To add to the poignancy, in 1941, Peckinpaugh, then manager of the Indians, would invent the Williams Shift. He never got credit for it. The Indians' sophomore shortstop Lou Boudreau quietly made a mental note of Peck's move and in 1946 unveiled it as his own invention.

I've always felt that one of the great myths of baseball history was that Branch Rickey freed the slaves. He didn't free them, he stole them from their Negro League owners—and then stole the credit for stealing them.

The new commissioner, Happy Chandler, had actually made the courageous decision to give Rickey the green light to end apartheid. Then, when the 15 other club owners voted against the move, Chandler announced in effect that "I vote aye, and the ayes have it." He lost his job for his courage.

The Joe DiMaggio hitting streak is another myth. At least four pitchers actually stopped Joe that summer: a sore-armed minor leaguer named Jimmy Halperin shut him out in an exhibition 11 games into the streak; Boston's Mickey Harris would have shut him out after 13 if the right fielder hadn't lost an easy fly ball in the sun; Johnny Rigney and Thornton Lee stopped Joe in games 30 and 31 except for two eyebrow-raising calls by the New York official scorer on easy ground balls booted by Luke Appling.

One could add the names of Willie Keeler, Ty Cobb, George Sisler, and George McQuinn, all of whom ran up long hitting streaks and got no publicity for them. Sisler ended his streak with his useless right arm hanging limp—and the newspapers, which had barely reported his streak, forgot even to mention the end of it. That would not have happened in New York.

Among the pitchers, if space permitted, one could recount the story of Mace Brown of the 1938 Pittsburgh Pirates. As night fell fast, Brown fired a pitch to Chicago's Gabby Hartnett, who probably literally couldn't see it. But Gabby swung and, *mirabile dictu*, hit it into the bleachers to ice the pennant. Brown was so disconsolate that his teammates kept a worried watch on him for days for fear he might try to harm himself.

The story of Don Newcombe is made more poignant by the fact that he lost two years in the army during the Korean war.

The missing seasons may have cost him 50 victories, enough to give him 200 lifetime wins and a possible plaque in Cooperstown. Newk, a victim of alcoholism, licked the disease and went on to counsel others afflicted with it.

Ralph Branca, who served the Shot Heard 'Round the World to Bobby Thomson in 1951, also devoted his late years to service to others; he's a leading executive of BATS, baseball's fund to help former players and their families in need of aid.

Ralph is a particularly tragic figure. Carl Erskine was the first choice to come in in relief that day, but just as manager Charlie Dressen phoned the bullpen, Erskine broke a curve into the dirt. "Erskine's bouncing his curve," the coach said. "Give me Branca," Dressen replied. The rest, as they say, is history.

When Boston's Mike Torrez gave up Bucky Dent's home run in 1978, was he the victim of an illegal corked bat? After Dent fouled a pitch off his foot and hopped around in pain, on-deck hitter Mickey Rivers ordered the batboy to shove a new bat into Bucky's hand. Years later Rivers told Torrez that the bat was cork-filled, though Mickey later tried to laugh it off.

If one adds the old Negro leaguers to the litany, the first name would be Louis Santop, slugging catcher for the Philadelphia Hilldales. In the 1924 black World Series, Frank Duncan of the Monarchs lifted a routine foul behind the plate. 'Top tapped his glove and waited—and dropped the ball. Duncan then drilled a grounder to Biz Mackey, a great defensive catcher playing third base—and it went right through Mackey's legs. The Monarchs rallied to win the game and Series.

Two other Negro leaguers, Claude "Red" Grier and Luther "Red" Farrell, pitched World Series home runs in 1926 and 1927, some three decades before Don Larsen. While Larsen is a legend, Grier and Farrell are unknown.

Josh Gibson may have been the most powerful slugger in baseball history. When the major leagues passed him by in favor of the then unknown rookie, Jackie Robinson, it broke Gibson's heart. In 1946, Jack's first year at Montreal, the newspaper headlines were all for Robinson. Not even the black papers cared that Josh was hitting more home runs—some in the 550-foot range—than he ever had in his life. It was as though Gibson was crying out, "Look at me, somebody!" Instead, they ignored him.

Heavily into drugs and alcohol, within six months Josh was dead at the age of 35.

Or take Ray Dandridge, the Brooks Robinson of the black leagues. Other Negro leaguers were too old to go into the majors after Jackie Robinson and never got their hopes up. Others were young enough to make the bigs themselves. Ray was just young enough to dream and old enough to have his dreams dashed. If Cleveland's Bill Veeck had given him a bonus in 1949, Ray might have helped the Indians win a second straight pennant. If the Giants had called Dandridge from their Minneapolis farm in 1950, pitcher Sal Maglie feels sure, the Giants could have won the pennant that year. Instead, Ray watched his roommate Willie Mays go up in 1951, while Ray stayed down on the farm.

Fame is often an accidental thing. It is bestowed by writers and taken away by writers. And the permanent record is written by the historians—and repeated by other historians—until the myth is almost impossible to dislodge. Usually there is no appeal from their judgment.

But thanks to historians Costello and Santa Maria, the historical mis-records can be corrected and justice can be done, belatedly but, let us hope, effectively.

John B. Holway

# PREFACE

We wrote this book for a simple reason. We love baseball. We love the lore of the game and the stories behind the players and plays that comprise its rich history.

But history is not always kind or just. Its light is often distorted or obscured by the harsh shadows of fate. It happens in baseball as it happens in life. The noble strides alongside the crass, the favored with the doomed, the hero with the goat. For every triumphant story like Ruth's, there is a tragic tale like Gehrig's; for every Go-Go Sox pennant, there is a Black Sox series; for every Kirk Gibson jubilant trot around the bases, there is a Dennis Eckersley dejected walk off the mound. And so a player's career is lost in the glare of one unfortunate play or denied its chance to fully shine. One is remembered too well; the other, not well enough.

This book takes a look at this darker and often ignored underside of baseball. Its cast of characters places scapegoats and victims in starring roles—instead of the usual heroes. The forty player profiles presented here range over 100 years of baseball, from the 1880s through the 1980s. They touch on five major leagues, the Negro leagues, several minor leagues, and even a barnstorming team in drag. They cover every position, every decade, and every type of player—some famous, some infamous, some forgotten. The result is a sweeping, panoramic look at baseball—how it has changed and how it has stayed the same—from a perspective you do not often see.

The players examined here were stigmatized in such a way that they were denied a full development and fair assessment of their careers. Our intention was not only to revisit the notorious events but to place them within the greater context of the players' history and the history of the game. And so the stories are varied despite their common thread. Some are tragic, some comical, some poignant, some pitiful, some inspiring, some harrowing. Most combine several of these traits.

We were deliberate in our choices of whom to include. The first half of the book looks at the game's most famous goats, those players immortalized for one momentous misplay or mistaken pitch—the Merkles and Brancas of baseball. But we wanted to look beyond the shadows of those plays and recall more about the players' careers, what they were like apart from those plays and how they were affected by them. The attempt is not to save anyone from obscurity, for most of these players are remembered often to their own chagrin. We just wanted to remember them better.

The second half looks at victims of another sort—players whose careers were dramatically cut short by illness, injury, or the letter of the law. This group offers hundreds of candidates, for a long career is more the exception than the rule. But we narrowed the field in two ways. We restricted it to players of exceptional talent, those who were league leaders, All-Stars, and in several cases Hall of Famers. And among them, we focus on those who were stopped by events that verged on the bizarre or who responded to personal adversity in unexpected ways. Unlike the goats, many of these victims have faded into obscurity or at least shine less brightly than they should. But our intention was not to imagine what might have been. We just wanted a reminder of what was.

There are obvious exclusions too: Lou Gehrig, Dizzy Dean, Thurman Munson, Roy Campanella, Shoeless Joe Jackson, to name a few. In some cases, we felt their stories were told well enough already, and there was little we could add to the discussion. Where possible, however, we tried to get at them in other ways. You won't find Gehrig in these pages, but you will find Babe Dahlgren and Wally Pipp. Don't bother looking for Shoeless Joe; try Benny Kauff instead.

The most obvious exclusion is one that has cast the largest and bleakest shadow across the game: baseball's refusal to allow black men to play. We touch on this stigma briefly in the pieces on Don Newcombe, Lyman Bostock, and Curt Flood, but within a different setting. Baseball's apartheid is a shadow of another order, one deeper and more deliberate than the casual context of this book. And so we leave those stories for another book.

The sun shines on the game's greatest and most beloved players. This book is written about and for the others. The ones who have had to play, live, and sometimes even die in the shadows of the diamond.

# Acknowledgements

Obviously no book, especially one like this, is written without a great deal of assistance and support. We owe our greatest debt in this regard to the resources and staff of the National Baseball Library in Cooperstown, N.Y., especially Jon Blomquist, who fielded our requests flawlessly. This book truly would not have happened without them.

And there were others. The Albany Public Library and the William K. Sanford Library in Colonie, N.Y.—particularly Mrs. Aida Stevens—were invaluable for searching out books and microfilm. The Society for American Baseball Research was also invaluable, particularly Mark Alvarez of its microfilm lending library; and Jim Kaplan and John Holway, the editors of its *Baseball Research Journal*.

Several individuals enriched our research with their knowledge and information, among them Scott McKinstry of *Old Tyme Baseball News*, Joseph Overfield, Vinnie Cannamela, Steven Alexander, Phil Agganis, Robert K. Wood, Charlie Gehringer, Edsall Walker, Quincy Trouppe, and Leon Day.

Alvin Hall and everyone associated with the "Baseball and the American Culture" symposium in Cooperstown, N.Y. gave the project a needed boost. Others such as Rick Kelly, Bruce Eaton, Steve Schultz and Vernon Newton encouraged us in various ways.

Most importantly, we have our personal acknowledgements. Michael wishes to thank his children, Elizabeth, Ciaran, and Robbie, and especially his wife, Kathleen, whose inspiration and guidance were indispensible throughout the writing of this book. Jim has already acknowledged his wife and children in the dedication, but if that's not enough (and it's not), thanks again.

And last but not least, we thank our mothers and fathers, brothers and sisters, and all our family and friends who helped in ways too numinous and subtle to mention.

# Shadows Cast Forward: Branded by One Event

# 1

# A TURN
# FOR THE WORSE

THE "MERKLE INCIDENT" of 1908 is the grandfather of baseball blunders. Whatever colossal mistakes were committed previously have been lost in oblivion. For over eighty years, the
name of Frederick Charles Merkle has been synonymous with
"Bonehead," a name unjustly thrust upon one of the most intelligent players of an era of very intelligent players. The play that
made him famous came at the most inopportune time not only
of the 1908 pennant drive but of Fred Merkle's career and life.
Imagine having your life defined, once and forever, with no
chance of reprieve, at the age of nineteen. As Fred Lieb wrote,
"Fred Merkle was a veritable martyr to the game he loved."

Even casual fans have heard the story of that single play
that "Bonehead" Merkle could never complete. Lee Allen, the
eminent historian of the Baseball Hall of Fame, said the play
sparked "the greatest controversy the game has ever known."
But few have heard the whole story: that Merkle was hardly responsible for a lost pennant; that he had a significant career in
spite of the incident; and most of all, that he spent the rest of
his life in the shadow of one moment.

Fred Merkle was born in Watertown, Wis., in December
1888. While he was very young, his family moved to Toledo,
Ohio, which at the turn of the century was a baseball-crazed
town. He got his start playing for local semi-pro teams, and he
was signed by Newark of the International League in 1907. In
August of that year, his contract was purchased by the mighty

3

New York Giants for an unknown sum between $700 and $2500, a healthy amount for a minor leaguer of the time. He played in 15 games that September, all at first base, and "aroused the enthusiasm of local fans." Unfortunately for Merkle, the Giants had a solid starter at first, Fred Tenney. *The New York American* wrote in December of 1907, "While Fred Tenney at present seems assured of holding down first base for the Giants next season, he will have to play up to a high mark to hold the place, for he has a young, ambitious rival in Fred Merkle, the Toledo High School boy." The article went on to say, "Best of all, he [Merkle] has plenty of nerve and a cool head." Merkle made the club in 1908 as the "general utility man."

As it turned out, six rookies made the Giants in the spring camp of 1908: Larry Doyle, Art Fletcher, Buck Herzog, Otis Crandall, Fred Snodgrass, and Fred Merkle. Merkle played infrequently, filling in for Tenney in late innings of blowouts and pinch hitting. Most of his season was spent on the bench with the other young substitutes, learning the game and the ways of their volatile but beloved manager, John McGraw.

It was an era when runs were extremely hard to come by, and games often hinged on the intelligence of every player on the field. Hence, young players served long apprenticeships. In the few opportunities he was given, Merkle responded well, including a pinch-hit three-run homer in a game against the Braves in June.

The 1908 pennant races rightly have been called the greatest of all time. In the American League a three-team race between the Detroit Tigers, Chicago White Sox and Cleveland "Naps" would go down to the final game of the season. The National League matched the AL race for drama. It also included three teams: the New York Giants, the Chicago Cubs, and the Pittsburgh Pirates, and that race was decided one day *after* the season ended. The Cubs got off to the best start, with the Giants struggling to play .500 ball in the first two months of the season. But by July, the teams were separated by only one-and-a-half games. The Giants swept the Pirates in a doubleheader on August 25 to gain first place for the first time in the season. They would not relinquish the hold until September 30.

The second most important game of the 1908 season, and of Fred Merkle's life, was played on September 4 in Pittsburgh, and the Giants weren't even involved. With two outs and the bases loaded in the bottom of the tenth inning of a scoreless game, Pittsburgh's Owen Wilson, who in 1912 would set the still-standing record for triples in one season, smashed a clean single to center, ostensibly beating the Cubs, 1-0. But sharp-thinking Johnny Evers, the Cubs' second baseman, noticed that Warren Gill, the runner at first, only traveled about halfway to second and then headed to the clubhouse. Evers screamed for the ball from center fielder Jimmy "The Human Mosquito" Slagle, got the throw and touched second, and turned to show umpire Hank O'Day. But O'Day was already leaving the field, and he only said over his shoulder that "Clarke was over the plate so his run counted anyway." Of course, O'Day's interpretation of the rule, by that reasoning, was incorrect, for a run cannot score on the third out of an inning if it is a force out. Chicago protested to NL president Harry C. Pulliam, who refused the protest in no uncertain terms by saying that Chicago's complaint was "far-fetched." He added, "I think the baseball public prefers to see games settled on the field and not in this office."

The race remained tight until the pivotal game of the season, the September 23 contest between the Cubs and the Giants at the Polo Grounds. The Cubs had closed the gap and only trailed the Giants by one-and-a-half games heading into the game. Fred Merkle was making his first start of the season at first base only because regular Fred Tenney woke up with a touch of lumbago. Chicago's pitcher was Jack Pfiester, and the Giants countered with Christy Mathewson. It was a classic pitchers' duel, with the Cubs drawing first blood on a Joe Tinker inside-the-park home run in the fifth. The Giants tied the game in the sixth on two singles, a sacrifice and an error. It remained 1-1 until the bottom of the ninth.

Cy Seymour led off what would become the most controversial inning in the history of baseball in a remarkably ordinary way, grounding out to second. Artie Devlin followed with a single, but he was forced by Moose McCormick, and the Giants had only one out left to win in regulation. Since darkness was descending, the game probably would have been called after the ninth inning, and the tie would have been made up the following afternoon. But the Giants did not go quietly. Fred Merkle came through with an opposite field line drive down the right field line. He said later, "It was an easy double but in that situation, why risk it?" So he stayed at first, and McCormick, the winning run, was at third.

Up stepped shortstop Al Bridwell, who lined Pfiester's first pitch through the middle with such force that umpire Bob Emslie fell down to get out of the way. McCormick scored easily, and the Giants won 2-1. Or so they thought. As soon as the ball went through the infield, Merkle turned and headed for the clubhouse, much like Warren Gill had three weeks earlier. Johnny Evers yelled to centerfielder Solly Hofman, who alertly retrieved the ball in the midst of thousands of jubilant Giants' fans who had swarmed onto the field in celebration. His throw to Evers was wild, however, and Joe McGinnity, who was coaching third, got the ball instead. Although McGinnity was unsure of what the Cubs were up to, he knew it meant no good for the Giants, so he did what any honest ballplayer would do—he heaved the ball into the now emptying stands.

Even that did not stop the Cubs. Shortstop Joe Tinker and third baseman Harry Steinfeldt went over the railings, found the ball and threw it to Evers. According to some sources, Hank O'Day, the home plate umpire who made the incorrect call in Pittsburgh on September 4, was near second and watching with interest. Others say that O'Day had to be brought back from the umpire's dressing room. In any event, when Evers finally touched second, he and manager Frank Chance appealed to O'Day to call Merkle out. O'Day asked Emslie for assistance, but Emslie was flat on his back at the time of the play, and he said he was watching to make sure that Bridwell touched first. To the horror of the Polo Grounds' crowd, O'Day did indeed call Merkle out, and the umpire was promptly attacked and rather soundly beaten. Luckily, he still had his gear on. As he left the field he said, "Merkle didn't run to second; the last run don't count; it's a tie game." The Giants' fans rioted well into the night.

Why did Merkle head for the clubhouse before touching second? The best answer is supplied by Fred Snodgrass who explained in *The Glory of Their Times* that the Giants' benchwarmers would always dash for the clubhouse beyond right field when a game was over. Merkle, as one of the benchwarmers all season, did what he always had. At the end of this game, Snodgrass said, "The crowd began to come on the field, we bench sitters sprinted out through right center field for our clubhouse, as usual, along with Merkle and everybody else." At another time, John McGraw said, "O'Day was wrong because it had become customary for the runner on first to dash to the clubhouse. If the custom was wrong, it should have been stopped by the umpires." One could say that the umpires effectively stopped the custom that day.

The incident was now in the hands of President Pulliam, who on September 24 agreed with O'Day and declared the game a 1-1 tie, evidently forgetting his statement of only three weeks before that games should be settled on the field and not in his office. Pulliam's ruling hardly ended the controversy. New York Giants' president John T. Brush appealed the ruling to the National League Board of Directors, while Chicago Cubs' president Charles Murphy demanded that the Cubs be awarded a 9-0 forfeit because the Giants had not shown up to play off the tie on September 24. The board of directors met on October 5, with the Cubs in first place and the Pirates and Giants tied for second only one game behind.

The board consisted of Garry Herrmann, president of Cincinnati, Charles Ebbets of Brooklyn, George Dovey of Boston, Barney Dreyfuss of Pittsburgh, Charles Murphy of Chicago, and Pulliam. Pulliam ruled that Dreyfuss and Murphy could not vote because of a conflict of interest, and Pulliam also abstained. Herrmann supported the Giants, stating, "I don't think a team should lose a game because a man did not run to second base on a clean hit when there was no chance to get him out." Ebbets agreed in principle, but he voted for a tie because he felt it was not his place to overrule the league president. Dovey sided with Pulliam as well, and the game was declared a tie.

In their ruling, the board wrote, "There can be no question but that the game should have been won by New York had it not been for the reckless, careless, inexcusable blunder of one player, Merkle." Merkle was already used to such disparagement. On September 24, the day after the game, The *New York Times* wrote, "Censurable stupidity on the part of player Merkle in yesterday's game at the Polo Grounds between the Giants and Chicago placed the New York team's chances of winning the pennant in jeopardy." The same day *The New York Herald* wrote,

"In fact, all our boys did rather well if Fred Merkle could gather the idea into his noodle that baseball custom does not permit a runner to take a shower and some light lunch in the clubhouse on the way to second." *The Chicago Tribune* called Merkle "fat-headed," but the word "bonehead" was not used until September 25. Gym Bagley of *The New York Evening Mail* in writing of Fred Tenney's return to the lineup even though he was still feeling poorly, said, "A one-legged man with a noodle is better than a bonehead." When Tenney was replaced by Merkle again on the 25th, Jack Ryder of *The Cincinnati Enquirer* wrote, "No plays came up in which Merkle had to think, so he got by."

To Fred Merkle's everlasting dismay, the Giants and the Cubs ended the season in a flat-footed tie. The playoff game was scheduled for October 7 at the Polo Grounds. Each team sent its ace to the mound: "Three-Finger" Mordecai Brown for the Cubs, and Christy Mathewson for the Giants. The Cubs beat Matty, 4-2, and went on to win the World Series. The gods of baseball may have been angered by the Cubs' method of victory and the subsequent unjust treatment of Merkle—the Cubs have not won the World Series since 1908.

John McGraw was livid that the Giants "were jobbed out of the pennant." He was convinced that the board of directors was not gunning for Merkle, but instead was trying to put the hugely successful John J. McGraw in his place. Instead of blaming Merkle, McGraw and the rest of the Giants stuck steadfastly behind him. "Why should Merkle have been blamed for losing a pennant?" asked Fred Snodgrass. "We lost a doubleheader to Cincinnati and three to Philadelphia after the Merkle incident. Then we beat Boston four straight and that ends us up in a tie, but all through Fred Merkle's life he was blamed for losing the pennant. Why go back over five games and pick out one play and blame that guy for losing the pennant?"

Merkle's first name was changed from "Fred" to "Bonehead," but he did not allow his ignominy to deter him from becoming a fine ballplayer. He was known as the second fastest big man of his day, after Honus Wagner. After he won the starting first base job in 1910, he averaged 73 runs scored, 72 runs batted in, 32 stolen bases, and batted .283 over a six-year period. He hit either fifth or fourth in a Giants' lineup that won pennants in 1911, 1912, and 1913. In the 1912 Series, Merkle was involved in the second most famous blunder of all time, "Snodgrass's Muff." When the Giants traded him to Brooklyn in 1916, Merkle contributed to the Dodgers' first pennant of the twentieth century, and he was a member of the Chicago Cubs pennant-winning team of 1918.

In the waning days of this fine career, Merkle joined the Babe Ruth-led New York Yankees in 1926. He rode the bench, just as he had some 18 years earlier, and only appeared in one game. During one game, a rowdy fan teased Merkle about his "bonehead" play. Yankee manager Miller Huggins yelled at the fan, "Fred Merkle has more brains in his little finger than you have in your whole head."

Huggins was not alone in his estimation of Merkle. Chief Meyers said "the smartest man on the club was the 'bonehead,' Mr. Merkle . . . One of the smartest men in baseball, Fred Merkle." In 1915, Heywood Broun called him "One of the finest first basemen in the league." Dan Daniel wrote, "Fred was not a Hall of Fame first baseman. But he was a fine player, entitled to his niche in the game's annals." Many years later, Jim "Mudcat" Grant, a talented pitcher for Cleveland, was signed by scout Fred Merkle. "He was anything but a bonehead," Grant said. "He was one of the nicest men I ever met. He deserved to get something out of baseball. He sure gave it a lot."

But all Merkle ever got out of baseball was heartache. He was still not allowed to forget the incident as late as 1949. "Past sins should be forgiven," he said. "I've been paying for 40 years." And not only Merkle was haunted by the play. Al Bridwell told Lawrence Ritter, "For Fred's sake, I wish it had never happened, it caused him so much grief." He went on, "I wish I'd never gotten that hit that set off the whole Merkle incident. I wish I'd struck out instead."

Perhaps the most eloquent defense for Merkle was told to Red Barber by Hall of Fame umpire Bill Klem. "That boy has really had to suffer over the black thing they put on him," said Klem, thought by many to be the greatest arbiter the game has known. "He was broken and he never should have been. Fred Merkle never pulled a bonehead play. He wasn't out in that game, and he wasn't out until this day . . . On a clean hit ball to the outfield it couldn't have been anything else," Klem continued. "They ruined as promising and as nice and as clean and as smart a young player as we ever had."

Fred Merkle went to his grave, in 1956, still remembered almost exclusively as "Bonehead." His hometown Daytona Beach newspaper obituary had this headline: " 'Bonehead Play' Over at Last: Fred Merkle dies in Florida." Every time since 1908, when a man has made a costly error at a pivotal moment, Merkle's blunder has appeared in comparison in the next day's papers. But the truth is that it was hardly a blunder at all. Merkle's following of custom, the Giants' five other losses, and the NL Board of Directors' vindictiveness toward John McGraw conspired to make Fred Merkle a supposed bonehead. Most eyewitnesses before and after September 23, 1908, agree that Merkle was the antithesis of a bonehead, and indeed was one of the most intelligent players of his time. Once again, Bill Klem made the right call. "Why, he isn't out yet."

# 2

# MUFF OF A LIFETIME

FRED SNODGRASS and Fred Merkle shared much more than a first name. The two came up to the big leagues with the same team in the same season. That rookie year, Snodgrass was a twenty-year-old, third-string catcher, and Merkle was a nineteen-year-old, backup first baseman. Snodgrass had a ringside seat when Merkle committed his so-called "boner" in late September of 1908. Then, when Snodgrass committed his infamous "muff" in the 1912 World Series, Merkle saw it clearly from his position at first base. If Merkle's blunder is "the most famous play in baseball history," as ex-Giant Al Bridwell has stated, Snodgrass's play ranks a close second in baseball's hall of infamy. Both men had otherwise respectable careers obliterated in a matter of seconds. Both were branded as scapegoats and had to carry that burden to their graves. And most similarly, Snodgrass, like Merkle before him, was hardly guilty of anything at all.

Before that World Series, Fred Snodgrass was not well known. He was a solid center fielder, respected mostly for his defense. Although his career was relatively short, spanning only eight seasons, six and one-half of them were with the New York Giants in their glory years of 1908-1914. During his tenure as the everyday center fielder for the Giants, New York won three pennants and came in second twice.

Snodgrass arrived in the major leagues in storybook fashion. John McGraw had first seen him in 1906, when Snodgrass's Los Angeles semi-pro team, the Hoagy Flags, played the Giants in three exhibition games. When McGraw made a side trip to a race track in L.A. in 1907, he was told Snodgrass had developed into the finest prospect in Southern California, and McGraw gave him a closer look. He signed Snodgrass on the spot as a backup catcher to Roger Bresnahan and Chief Meyers for the 1908 campaign. Throughout the 1908 season Snodgrass saw limited action, appearing in only six games. But he was only twenty years old, and just being in the major leagues and a member of the Giants was more than enough.

The next year, McGraw began an experiment with Snodgrass, putting him in center field every now and then. By the first road trip of the 1910 season, McGraw offered Snodgrass the center field job permanently. He remained a fixture in the Giants' outfield until he was traded in late 1915.

Snodgrass credited most of his defensive prowess not to innate talent but to baseball intelligence. "I never was a sensational ballplayer," he said, "but I used my head out there. I used to study hitters and I figured when the man came to bat I knew exactly where to play him." Although he was superior in the field, Snodgrass was a fine offensive player as well. His primary value at bat rested in his ability to score runs, and he batted third in the Giants' lineup. "I used to pride myself on my ability to get on base," he said. In Snodgrass's four best seasons his on-base percentage ranged from a low of .354 to a peak of .424. And this is discounting the numerous times he was hit by pitched balls. He said, "I wore a baggy uniform and I got hit an awful lot."

Snodgrass's many talents did not go unnoticed by his skipper. "It makes me very happy," Snodgrass once said, "that John McGraw picked me on his all-time, all-star Giant team." Considering the talent McGraw had at his command over his thirty-three-year career as Giants' manager, this is no mean feat.

But of course, the kind of ballplayer Snodgrass was before and after 1912 goes for naught. No one cares to remember any of that. The reason Snodgrass still retains a place in our collective baseball memory is that undying moment in the tenth inning of the last game of the 1912 World Series.

And what a thrilling Series it was, one of the handful that rightly can be called the greatest of all time. First of all, the two best teams, without doubt, were facing each other. The Giants had won the National League by ten games; the Red Sox had won the American League by fourteen. Both teams had great pitching. New York was led by the nearly mythic tandem of Christy Mathewson and Rube Marquard. Mathewson had an off year by his standards—he won a measly twenty-three games. Marquard won twenty-six, including the still standing record of nineteen games in a row. Boston had three pitchers who won more than twenty games—Buck O'Brien, Hugh Bedient, and Smoky Joe Wood. Wood's miraculous season was 1912 when he won 34, lost 5, compiled an earned run average of 1.91, struck out 258, hurled 10 shutouts, and completed 35 games.

The first game of the Series was played in New York with visiting Boston winning, 4-3, behind Wood's eleven-strikeout, complete-game effort. Game two was a veritable slugfest for 1912, but after eleven innings it was called because of darkness and the teams settled for a 6-6 tie. Marquard evened the Series by besting the Red Sox in newly opened Fenway Park, but the Sox came right back as Wood won his second game of the series, this time striking out eight Giants.

After Bedient outduelled Mathewson in game five, the New Yorkers found their backs to the wall, down three games to one. But the Giants scored five big runs in the first inning of game six and coasted to a victory that left them one game shy of a Series tie. Of course, the Giants had the unenviable task of having to beat Wood to stave off defeat. The Giants rose to the challenge, knocking Wood out of the box in the very first inning with a six-run outburst. The 1912 World Series came down to one game, played on October 16 in Boston.

The starting pitchers were a rematch of game five: Bedient for Boston and Mathewson for New York. Both pitched courageously. Fred Merkle endeared himself to Giants' fans by knocking in the first run of the game in the fourth, but the Red Sox rallied to tie in the seventh. Included in that rally was a single by Olaf Henriksen, who knocked in the tying run pinch hitting for Bedient. To the dismay of the Giants, Smoky Joe Wood came on to relieve. The score was 1-1 after seven, and the Series was in the hands of each team's best pitcher.

The score remained knotted through the regulation nine, but in the top of the tenth, the Giants squeezed across the go-ahead run. With one out, Red Murray doubled and Fred Merkle promptly singled him home. The bonehead of 1908 was about to become the hero of 1912. Wood then got out of the jam by striking out Buck Herzog and throwing out Chief Meyers after knocking down his line smash with his pitching hand. All Mathewson had to do was get three outs and New York would be champions.

Leading off in the bottom of the tenth was Clyde Engle, pinch hitting for the injured Joe Wood. Engle lifted a lazy pop fly to right center, and in the time it takes for a ball to drop from the sky, Fred Snodgrass's life changed immeasurably. As Snodgrass camped under it, right fielder Jack Murray cheered him on: "Squeeze it, Snod!" The ball landed in Snodgrass's mitt, but then popped out, falling safely in right center. The hustling Engle had been running all the way, and he was standing on second with the potential tying run.

Talking about the play many years later, Snodgrass said, "Now that was a matter that could have happened one thousand times, one million times. It was a fly ball. Because of over-eagerness, over-confidence, or carelessness, I dropped it. It's something I'll never forget." Snodgrass's muff had put Engle on second with no one out instead of getting the Giants to within two outs of the championship.

The next batter for Boston was Harry Hooper. The entire Giants' defense was poised for a sacrifice attempt, and Snodgrass was essentially playing backup to second base. But Hooper crossed the Giants up by swinging away and smashed a long liner to center field. Snodgrass told Lawrence Ritter, "I made one of the greatest plays of my life on it, catching the ball over my shoulder on the run out in deep left center. They always forget about that play when they write about that inning." Snodgrass nearly redeemed himself completely, as his throw to second just missed doubling Engle, who was convinced that Hooper's liner was at least a triple. But the hustling Engle made it back into second safely. Snodgrass's brilliant catch has been all but forgotten by the play that preceded it and the bizarre events that followed.

Boston now had Steve Yerkes at the plate. Mathewson, who over his career walked just over one-and-a-half batters every nine innings, chose this crucial moment to walk Yerkes, putting the potential winning run aboard. What was perhaps worse was that

Mathewson now had to contend with Boston's greatest hitter, Tris Speaker, who walked to the plate amid deafening cheers from the nearly hysterical Boston crowd. Imagine the tension and drama of that moment—Mathewson vs. Speaker with the World Championship on the line.

It seemed as if Mathewson would win this classic confrontation, as he induced Speaker to pop up feebly about seventy feet down the first-base line in foul territory. Mathewson, catcher Chief Meyers, and first baseman Fred Merkle converged on the pop. Although Merkle clearly had the best chance. Mathewson inexplicably called for Meyers to make the play. "I could have made the catch any time, but Mathewson kept calling for the Chief to take it," Merkle later recalled. "We were both big men. I wanted no collision. I kept the way clear for Meyers, but he too stopped at the last moment, thinking I would take it, and the ball fell safe." Snodgrass watched the tragic scene from center. "I can see Matty yet yelling 'Come on, Chief! Come on Chief!' "

Speaker took full advantage of the new life tendered him. He smashed a line drive single to the gap in right center, scoring Engle to tie the game and sending Yerkes around to third. The Giants decided to walk Duffy Lewis intentionally and take their chances with Larry Gardner. With one out and the bases filled, Gardner lifted a high fly to left fielder Josh Devore, who caught the ball and made a valiant attempt to nab Yerkes at the plate, but to no avail. The Boston Red Sox, behind Wood's third victory, were the World Champions of 1912.

On the very next day, Snodgrass got an inkling of what was in store for him for the rest of his life. The *New York Times* reported that Snodgrass's error was "the rankest sort of muff, one that would have shamed a schoolboy." The *Times* went on to blame others for the debacle, singling out Fred Merkle for his role in Speaker's pop fly, which the paper referred to as the Giants' version of "the Alphonse-Gaston act." A few days later, when each team received their World Series' shares, the play was renamed the "$30,000 Muff," for that was the total difference between the winning and losing shares. As Bill James has remarked, "Every baseball headline of the entire decade [of the teens] has a dollar sign attached to it." None was so infamous as this one.

As was the case with Fred Merkle, John McGraw stood staunchly behind his player. He wrote in his book, *My Thirty Years in Baseball*, "Often I have been asked to tell what I did to Fred Snodgrass after he dropped that fly ball in the World Series of 1912, eleven years ago. Well, I will tell you exactly what I did: I raised his salary $1,000."

But Snodgrass was never allowed to forget the play. In Boston, on Labor Day of 1914 as the Braves were making their "miracle" run for the pennant, opposing pitcher George Tyler mimicked the Snodgrass Muff, tossing the ball in the air and dropping it, to the delight of the Boston crowd. Snodgrass thumbed his nose at Tyler, inciting the crowd to razz and boo Snodgrass unmercifully. On his way back to the dugout, Snodgrass thumbed his nose at the stands, which included Mayor James M. Curley. Immediately, Curley jumped onto the field and demanded Snodgrass's removal from the game for insulting the good people of Boston. Umpire Bob Emslie removed Mayor Curley instead and allowed Snodgrass to remain in the game.

Ironically, Snodgrass was traded to the Boston Braves late in the following season, and thereby ended his career in the town of his disgrace. The end came quickly: after a little less than a year, Snodgrass was released by the Braves in July, 1916. At the age of twenty-eight, Fred Snodgrass's career was over.

His notoriety never ebbed, however. For the rest of his life Snodgrass tried desperately to clear his name, but to no avail. In 1942, thirty years after the events, Snodgrass said, "Hardly a day in my life, hardly an hour goes by that in some manner or other the dropping of that fly ball doesn't come up." At other times he would state tersely, "I didn't lose any World Series." In spite of all of it, though, Snodgrass never turned bitter toward the game he loved. "Those were wonderful years," he said in *The Glory of Their Times*, "and if I had the chance I'd gladly do it all over again, every bit of it."

Even in death, Snodgrass could not escape his ignominy. The headline of his now famous obituary in the *New York Times* of April 6, 1974, read, "Fred Snodgrass Dies: Ballplayer Muffed 1912 Fly." The obituary began, "Fred Carlisle Snodgrass, who muffed an easy fly ball that helped cost the New York Giants the 1912 World Series, died Friday at the age of 86." Sixty-one-and-a-half years had passed.

Fred Snodgrass had a workmanlike and undistinguished career. He was good enough to be a regular on championship teams but not good enough to stand out on those teams. He was through before he was thirty. We probably would have no occasion to mention his name if not for his "muff."

Perhaps infamy is better than oblivion. Some famous scapegoats, Mickey Owen and Tracy Stallard among them, say they prefer being remembered at all, even if only for a mistake. But Fred Snodgrass never enjoyed his undeserved notoriety for as much as one second. A dropped fly ball, yes; a lost World Series, hardly. Yet, as Snodgrass himself poignantly phrased it, "The facts don't seem to matter."

# 3

# MONKEY BUSINESS

IN THE SPACE of a dozen years, John McGraw saw four World Championships slip away due to unusual occurrences. Merkle's boner in 1908, Snodgrass's muff in 1912, Zimmerman's chase in 1917, and Gowdy's stumble in 1924 all snatched defeat from the jaws of victory. In only one case did McGraw suspect any monkey business and that was with Heinie Zimmerman in 1917. For years afterward, Zimmerman complained about being classed as a goat, and with good justification. He was really closer to a weasel or a jackal. As such, he was unofficially but effectively banned from baseball in 1920.

Zimmerman's early history did not forebode his untimely and unsavory exit from the game. He entered major league baseball as a twenty-year-old backup second baseman to Johnny Evers of the Cubs. For his first four years, his playing was limited to a reserve status, but it did increase steadily. His major break came in 1911 when illness forced Evers to sit out most of the season. Given full-time status at second base and 553 at-bats, Zimmerman responded with a .307 batting average to pace his club and also knocked in and scored 85 runs.

The next year, Evers returned to his regular spot at second base. Jim Doyle, the Cubs rookie third baseman in 1911, died in the off-season so Zimmerman moved over to take that position. He had already proven he could fill the shoes of a sick man; he would now have to show how well he could fill those of a dead one. He did it by winning the Triple Crown in 1912 with 14 home runs, 103 RBI and a .372 batting average. (Though

Zimmerman was long credited with a Triple Crown season, later research revealed an error in his RBI total. *Total Baseball*, for example, gives him credit for only 99 RBI which places him third behind Honus Wagner and Bill Sweeney, rather than first.) He also led the league in hits (207), doubles (41) and slugging percentage. His fielding was below that of an average third baseman, but his bat was good enough to make up for that deficiency.

He never enjoyed another season like his Triple Crown year. In fact, his offensive production declined steadily in the three years that followed it, bringing him down to a .265 average with only 62 RBI in 1915. Still he was only twenty-seven years old as the 1916 season began, which promised at least the possibility of some productive years ahead.

John McGraw, who was known to place an occasional bet, decided to take a chance on that possibility. His New York Giants acquired Zimmerman near the end of August 1916, in exchange for Larry Doyle, the Giant second baseman for the previous ten years, who had won the batting crown in 1915. When he was a rookie, Doyle immortalized himself with the phrase, "It's great to be young and a New York Giant." Having just passed his thirtieth birthday, he was discovering it wasn't as great to be an old Giant. On their side, the Cubs were disillusioned with the performance and attitude of "The Great Zim," as he liked to call himself. He was under a ten-game suspension when the trade came.

Zimmerman was batting .291 at the time of the trade and after adjusting to the new environment finished the season at .286. The average was less than fantastic, but his 83 RBI led the league, inching out Hal Chase of Cincinnati by one. The next year, his average climbed to .297 and his 102 RBI again led the league, this time sixteen runs better than Hal Chase in second place. More importantly, the Giants won the National League pennant and earned the right to face the Chicago White Sox (when their socks were still white) in the World Series.

It was the fourth World Series appearance in seven years for McGraw's Giants, but McGraw had not been enjoying much success in post-season play during this decade. His team lost to Connie Mack's Athletics in 1911 and 1913. In 1912, he watched his team bobble away certain victory against the Red Sox; 1917 would not be much different.

Chicago won the first two games at home, but then the Giants took the next two at the Polo Grounds. Nothing unusual so far, but then strange things started to happen near the end of game five with the Giants leading 5-2. In the bottom of the seventh, with the bases loaded and two outs, a fly ball dropped untouched between three Giants. Dave Robertson in right field picked up the ball and relayed it to the second baseman, Buck Herzog. But Herzog could not catch the ball either. All three runs scored. In the next inning, Zimmerman threw a ball past Herzog on second to right field allowing a run to score. Four singles later, two more runs scored and the White Sox won 8-5.

The teams returned to the Polo Grounds for game six. In the top of the fourth, with a scoreless tie in progress, Zimmerman made his way into baseball immortality. He helped set it up when he took Eddie Collins' lead-off grounder and threw the ball into the seats behind first base, with Collins advancing to second. The next batter, Joe Jackson, hit a fly ball to right field, but Robertson dropped it putting runners on first and third. For McGraw, it may have seemed too reminiscent of the final game of the 1912 Series. But he was about to see something not even he could have expected.

Happy Felsch stepped to the plate and bounced one back to the mound. Rube Benton, the Giants' pitcher, caught Collins halfway between third and home. Benton ran Collins back toward third and tossed the ball to Zimmerman. In the meantime, Bill Rariden, the Giants' catcher, moved up the line for the rundown—way up the line. When Collins turned back towards home, he probably could not believe what he saw. No one was covering home. Collins dashed past Rariden for the plate, and Zimmerman, stuck with the ball, chased him all the way, a few steps behind.

With Zimmerman in futile pursuit of Collins, the other two runners advanced to third and second. Chick Gandil followed with a single to score both runs and give the White Sox the margin of victory in a 4-2 win. The Great Zim was instantly hailed as the goat. As was his custom, McGraw deflected blame from the players, as he had with Merkle in 1908 and Snodgrass in 1912. Uncharacteristically, however, McGraw did cast a shadow of suspicion over one of his players. He suspected that Buck Herzog had been trying to help the opposition. In the off-season, McGraw traded him to the Boston Braves and brought Larry Doyle back to the Giants in exchange.

McGraw never could prove that Herzog had performed dishonestly, but the suspicion would spread in the next few years. McGraw was probably wise in ridding his team of Herzog, whose career finally ended in 1920 under a cloud of allegations about fixed games. But one could hardly call McGraw principled or consistent on the issues. His acquisition of Hal Chase from Cincinnati in 1919 (for Bill Rariden) certainly proved that McGraw at least kept an open mind. That acquisition would prove to be the unravelling of at least three players on the 1917 Giants (Zimmerman, Benton and Kauff), eight of their White Sox opponents in the World Series, and almost all of baseball.

If McGraw hesitated to blame Zimmerman in 1917, he was not nearly so reticent about making accusations in 1919. Late in that season, Zimmerman was suspended from the Giants, presumably for breaking curfew. Hal Chase lasted until nearly the last game of the season, but then he left the team too. Neither ever played major league baseball again.

A year later, a different reason for Zimmerman's dismissal surfaced. Testifying before the Chicago grand jury investigating the fixing of the 1919 World Series, John McGraw stated "that he had dropped Zimmerman from the Giants last year because he offered Benny Kauff $500 to throw a game." Supposedly Chase and Zimmerman had offered Kauff, the Giants' centerfielder, $125 to throw a September game against St. Louis. Apparently, it was not Zim's only attempt at finding some pocket money for his teammates. He allegedly made a similar offer to Giants' pitchers Fred Toney and Rube Benton. All three players would subsequently testify against Zimmerman to the Chicago grand jury.

In March 1921, Zimmerman came to his own defense in a sworn statement he made to the *New York American* newspaper. "I am being made the goat for John McGraw," he said. "To keep his own team, the Giants, intact, he is persecuting me." But even in attempting to exonerate himself, Zimmerman raised the specter of his guilt: "During the last western trip of the Giants in 1919, a man came to me in Chicago and gave me a message to deliver to Benny Kauff, Fred Toney and Rube Benton. His offer was $100 to each of these three players if the

Giants were beaten. He made me no personal offer, but asked me to deliver this message to those three men. Here is where I made my mistake.''

Zimmerman goes on in his affidavit to state that all three players went along with the scheme quite happily. He then proceeds to attack McGraw for trying to lay all the blame on him and deflect it from the other players in order to keep his team intact. The false accusations, according to Zim, even went back before 1919: ''Since McGraw had me banished from baseball he has accused me of throwing the 1917 World's Series to the White Sox. He has declared that I deliberately chased Eddie Collins home with the winning run in the final game. However, in the clubhouse after the game, McGraw said that he did not blame me for the play. . . . He absolutely cleansed me of all blame.''

In his own mind, Zimmerman was blameless on both counts. But it was a time of shadowy morals. He even accused McGraw of being in league with thiefs. Saying that the Giants owed him a $500 bonus for finishing second in 1918, Zimmerman said they reneged on paying him. When he brought the matter up to Mc-Graw, McGraw sent him to ''a certain man'' for his money, a gambler according to Zimmerman. Zim refused, but not because he objected to associating with gamblers. He just wanted the team to pay.

Despite his protests, the case against Zimmerman was too strong. Even if the testimony against him was not as convincing as it was, his association with Chase was enough to indict any man. Chase had been involved in fixing games for at least a decade and was a major player in the 1919 fix. But then Zimmerman's strength was never in making subtle moral distinctions or in selecting friends. His record did not improve much after being banned from baseball. In 1935, his name cropped up again in conjunction with gangsters. This time he was named as an unindicted conspirator when Dutch Schultz was brought before a federal grand jury on tax evasion charges. The Great Zim had been a partner of Schultz in a speakeasy in 1929-1930.

Despite these unsavory connections, Zimmerman lived a long and relatively quiet life working as a steam fitter. He died in 1969 in the Bronx at the age of eighty-two. In its obituary for Zimmerman, the New York Times quoted one of its own stories written shortly after the 1917 series: "Zim's notorious bonehead play will be known in every corner of the earth. If Zim lives to be 100 years old, he will never be able to live down that awful foot race."

Just two years after that awful foot race, Zimmerman would be out of baseball for trying to fix games, and Eddie Collins would be one of the few honest players in a fixed World Series. The picture from two years earlier could serve as an emblem for that era of baseball, the "decade wrapped in greed" as Bill James called it: Heinie Zimmerman, the bag man, caught red-handed with the ball and futilely chasing two steps too slow behind honest Eddie Collins, safe at home.

# 4

# THE HERO CAN'T
# WEAR HORNS

HANK GOWDY stepped on his mask in the twelfth inning of the seventh game of the 1924 World Series. Like Merkle's boner and Snodgrass's muff, it would help another pennant slip away from John McGraw's Giants. It was a singular and costly blunder (Christy Mathewson remarked: "I've been in baseball thirty years and that's the first time I ever saw a catcher step into his own mask."), but Gowdy's act would not be immortalized as Merkle's or Snodgrass's. It would not be indexed as Gowdy's goof. He would not be branded by that one play. When he's remembered now, it's more often as a hero than a goat and perhaps that's as it should be. He wore the goat's horns but once; he played the hero's role twice.

Through seventeen years of major league service stretching from 1910-1930, Hank Gowdy was a first-rate though not Hall of Fame-caliber catcher. He was a capable hitter, better than most catchers of his day, but never among the league leaders in any category. For much of his career he was used only in a backup role. But three separate incidents—one at the start of his career, one at its peak, one near its end—were remarkable enough to ensure that he would be recognized in his time and still be remembered today.

Hank Gowdy first came into public notice during the 1914 World Series as a member of the miracle Boston Braves. That year was Hank's first as a full-time starting catcher in the major leagues. (He originally came up as a backup first baseman to

24

Fred Merkle of the Giants in 1911.) As the Braves made their all-time record pennant drive, moving from last place on July 19 and winning 60 of their final 76 games to win the pennant by 10 1/2 games, Gowdy received his share of the credit for handling the pitching trio of Dick Rudolph, Bill James, and Lefty Tyler (27, 26, and 16 wins). It was in the World Series, however, that the real miracle occurred.

The underdog Braves swept Connie Mack's Athletics and its vaunted "million dollar infield" of Stuffy McInnis, Eddie Collins, Jack Barry, and Home Run Baker in four games with Gowdy leading the charge. He batted .545 in that Series with six hits (a homer, a triple, three doubles and a single) and five walks in 16 plate appearances. The Braves won the first game 7-1, and "Gowdy, the slender, auburn-haired catcher, gave a marvelous exhibition of heavy batting. Four times he faced the Philadelphia boxmen and the net result was a base on balls, a single, a double and a triple. No Cobb or Delahanty, no Jackson or Wagner, no slugger of the present or of times gone by, could better that record."

It was not only the most solid thrashing of an A's team in their World Series appearances but was also the first time that Chief Bender or any A's pitcher was chased from the mound in a Series game.

But Gowdy's best performance was still to come in the pivotal third game at Fenway Park on October 12. This game went into extra innings, and the A's were desperate for a win. In the top of the tenth, they scored twice. Gowdy came to bat in the bottom of the inning and hit a solo home run into the center field bleachers. The Braves scored again on a walk, a single, and a sacrifice fly to tie it up. In the bottom of the twelfth, Gowdy led off with a double to left. Outfielder Les Mann came in to run for him. The next batter was intentionally walked to set up the force play at third. Outfielder Herbie Moran then stepped to the plate and bunted. The A's pitcher, Bullet Joe Bush, fielded the bunt but threw it past Frank Baker at third, and Mann sped home with the winning run.

Hank Gowdy became an instant celebrity, although at least one person was less than enamored with his fame. In January 1915, it was reported that Miss Ethel Clark of Chicago broke off her engagement to Gowdy due to the "unwelcome notoriety"

from a World Series story that she had promised to marry
Gowdy if he distinguished himself in the games.

Philadelphia and Boston appeared in the World Series again
in 1915, except this time it was the Phillies and the Red Sox.
The Boston Braves moved down to second and then third in
1916, as Gowdy withdrew from the limelight to his less illus-
trious role as their dependable, but hardly remarkable, first-string
catcher.

Then in 1917, at the outbreak of World War I, he found
himself in the news once again when he enlisted in the army "in
a day when most professional athletes were holding back to the
last hour and then seeking the shipyards." On June 2 of that
year he became the first major league player to enlist and by October was in France.

The singularity of his action did not pass unrecognized. The
Honorable John K. Tener, president of the National League,
praised the unselfish valor of his enlistment: "There is no detail,
no item, no mitigating circumstance which can detract in the
slightest degree from the appreciation due Gowdy for his personal sacrifice . . . He was a player in his prime . . . He enjoyed the benefits of a good salary . . . Even a single season in
the army might ruin his subsequent career as a player. But he
didn't hesitate . . . Hank Gowdy stepped forward . . . He entered a department of service which would inevitably be among
the first to be called to the battle scarred fields of France . . .
The National League is proud to give full credit to the man who
in so signal a way has done honor to his league and to his
country."

There were rumors that Gowdy was killed in action shortly
before the Armistice was signed, but he returned unharmed. The
Braves held "Gowdy Day" on his first game back on May 24,
1919, and Hank responded by hitting the first pitch thrown to
him for a single. But Gowdy only saw part-time duty behind the
plate for the rest of his career. Though he reached the highest
batting averages of his career during the years 1919-1925, most
of that increase can be attributed to baseball's general increase
in offensive production after 1920 and Gowdy's fewer at bats.

But his heroism was never forgotten. In August 1924, the
United States Army honored Gowdy with a pre-game ceremony
at the Polo Grounds (Gowdy was traded from Boston to the

Giants the year before). The reason for the official visit was to announce that the large baseball field at Camp Benning, Ga., was being named "Gowdy Field." The war had been over for almost five years, but Gowdy was still being honored as baseball's first enlistee. The game gloried in his presence: "Baseball has its Shibe Park, named after the late venerable 'Uncle Ben' Shibe, of Philadelphia; Ebbets Field, named after the goodly squire of Flatbush; Navin Field, in Detroit, and Comiskey Field in Chicago; but the one from which it can take greatest pride is Gowdy Field, located in the sun-baked red clay of old Georgia."

Two months after being honored at the Polo Grounds, he would again catch every game in a World Series for his team. This time, however, there would be no .545 batting average and no final victory for his team. Even the sentiment was leaning in another direction—toward the thirty-six-year-old Walter Johnson, appearing with the Senators in his first World Series after eighteen years and 376 victories. Johnson went twelve innings in the first game, struck out twelve, but lost on a bases-loaded single and sacrifice fly. In the fifth game, Johnson lost again allowing the Giants to take a 3-2 Series lead.

The seventh and deciding game also went into twelve innings. Walter Johnson had come on in relief for the Senators to start the ninth and pitched four shutout innings to keep the score at 3-3 entering the bottom of the twelfth. He was still looking for his first World Series victory. With one out, Washington's catcher, Muddy Ruel, popped up behind the plate. Gowdy "hardly had to move from his tracks," according to the *New York Times'* account of the game, but that did not stop him from moving considerably within them. "He stepped this way and that, circling around and throwing his glove uncertainly before him. At the last minute he made a furious lunge to his right, but stumbled over his mask, nearly fell to one knee and dropped the ball." Given a second chance, Ruel doubled to left.

John McGraw, the Giants manager, had seen pennants and championships taken away from his team in 1908, 1912, and 1917, on freak plays and bad luck. He was about to see it happen again. Earl McNeely, a reserve outfielder for the Senators, followed Ruel's double with an infield grounder that should have been the third out of the inning (if Gowdy had avoided his mask). Instead, the ball hit a pebble and bounced over third baseman Fred Lindstrom's head (the second time that had happened during the game!). Ruel scored, the Senators won the pennant, and Johnson got his victory.

Gowdy, however, was never blamed or branded as a goat. He was a hero and would a hero remain. The *New York Tribune* at the time portrayed Gowdy not as a blundering fool, but as a worthy field marshall to baseball's most honored commander-in-chief, the "little Napolean," John McGraw: "Hank stepped on his mask in a crisis of the seventh game . . . but this miscue cannot dim the old scout's record. Marshall Ney was beaten at Waterloo, but a century afterward he was still called 'The Bravest of the Brave.' "

Over a decade later, Hank Gowdy was back coaching with the Boston Braves when Babe Ruth was traded to that team by the Yankees. The Braves had not even ordered a uniform for Ruth when he showed up March 5, 1935. So when the Babe first took the field for his new team, he was wearing a pair of Hank Gowdy's pants. It was a hero's welcome for Ruth. He could not have been more honored.

# 5

# BEHIND THE
# EIGHT BALLS

ROGER PECKINPAUGH set a record in the 1925 World Series by committing eight errors at shortstop for the Washington Senators. The final error set up the deciding runs which gave the Pittsburgh Pirates the victory in game seven. Over fifty years later and only months before his death, a reporter asked the eighty-six-year-old Peckinpaugh about those errors. Roger, who had been called the calmest man in baseball, lashed out: "What do you want to know about that goddamn record? I played in three World Series. I was the Most Valuable Player and I was a major leaguer for 18 [sic] years when there were only 16 major league teams in the world. And all you want to know about is that goddamn record for errors." His outburst was a lament that could have been echoed by any player who was ever hung with the goat label and suddenly found a career reduced to a single unforgettable occurrence. Peckinpaugh handled over 10,000 chances in his career at shortstop; eight that he fumbled in a nine-day stretch in October 1925 are hardly indicative of a career.

If Peckinpaugh wasn't the greatest shortstop of his time (and he wasn't, though many have said differently), it was no detraction from his talent. He played in an era of several great shortstops. He came to the major leagues in 1910 as a nineteen-year-old with the Cleveland Indians but only appeared in 15 games. In 1912, he became the Indians' primary shortstop, playing in 67 games, but he only batted .212. When Ray Chapman arrived near season's end and batted .312 in 31 games, Peckinpaugh's days in Cleveland looked to be numbered. The next year, Chapman played in 138 games at short, and Peckinpaugh was traded after only one game with Cleveland to the New York Yankees.

Peckinpaugh found a home in New York. After playing 94 games as shortstop for the Yankees (and batting .268) in 1913, he suddenly found himself named manager of the team for the 1914 season. At the age of twenty-three, it made him the youngest manager in the history of the game. He penciled his name into the lineup 157 times that year and for the next eleven years was a full-time regular shortstop. While his hitting steadily improved, it never advanced past adequate. His value was in the field.

From 1916 through 1919, he led his league in assists three times, in double plays twice and in total chances per game twice. However, in those years the Yankees were a poor-to-mediocre team. John McGraw's Giants were still the main show in town. Peckinpaugh's talents were appreciated, but hardly celebrated.

By the early twenties, that situation had begun to change. McGraw still fielded the best team in town (in any town) as they appeared in four straight World Series from 1921 to 1924 and won two of them. But the Yankees had undergone a transformation, thanks largely to the theatrical setbacks of the Red Sox owner, Harry Frazee, who sent players like Babe Ruth, Carl Mays, Herb Pennock, and Duffy Lewis to the Yankees. These new Yankees appeared in three World Series against the Giants from 1921 to 1923.

In 1921, the Yankees took the first two games of the World Series, which was played under the best-of-nine format, but the Giants quickly evened it at two games apiece. The Yankees came back to win game five, but it would be their last victory of 1921. The deciding run in the final game seemed almost harmless when it happened. A ground ball passed through the legs of Roger Peckinpaugh in the first inning of game eight. The Giants' shortstop, Dave Bancroft, scored on the error—the only run in a 1-0 game.

Colonel Tillinghast L'Hommedieu Huston, one of the title-bearing owners of the Yankees (along with Colonel Jacob Ruppert), did not find the play harmless. He faulted Peck not only for the error but for his subsequent "paralysis" in failing to follow the ball into the outfield, retrieve it, and possibly hold off the run. He questioned Peck's ability and desire to win. In the off-season he shipped him to the Senators via Boston and received another slick-fielding shortstop (apparently one more to his liking), Everett Scott, in exchange.

Roger could not have been feeling too well as he entered the 1922 season. Dumped from the Yankees and their budding dynasty, he found himself with the hapless Senators. At thirty-one years old, the word around the league was that his best years were behind him. He was suspected of losing a step or two and maybe some of his competitive edge.

If this were true, he seemed to regain both with the move to Washington. Teamed with second baseman Bucky Harris (who would himself become a boy wonder manager in 1924 at the age of twenty-seven), Peckinpaugh found himself on one of the best double-play combinations of all time. For three straight years, 1922-1924, Harris and Peckinpaugh led their league in double plays. Peckinpaugh also saw his other fielding statistics improve, particularly assists when he again led the league with 510 in 1923 and placed second in 1922 and 1924. His batting average and run production also increased steadily through these years, though they lagged behind his big batting years of 1919-1921. The Senators also saw their own fortunes rising during this period, culminating in a first-place finish with a 92-62 record in 1924.

Peckinpaugh missed much of the 1924 World Series but still played a vital role, if only by example, in the Senators' seven-game victory. His .417 batting average in only four games led the Senators. He was forced out of the Series in the third game due to a leg injury, but returned in game six on "grit and courage." A newspaper account of the time proclaimed his return this way: "He played when common sense caution would have kept him on the sideline. More than that, he played brilliantly, effective in defense and effective at the bat. He helped tighten up the Washington infield, he reached first base every time he came to bat, and his single in the fifth inning started the short rally that enabled the Senators to beat the Giants and even up the series."

The Senators would win game seven and the Series the next day without Peckinpaugh and with a fair amount of luck. Peck's valiant return in game six led to a second injury which knocked him out of the Series for good. It also threatened his ability to play the next year. But Peck did come back the next year. As he had done before, he rose when everyone expected him to fall and enjoyed perhaps his finest season as he won the MVP award and led the Senators to their second consecutive World Series.

Peckinpaugh batted .294 in 1925 but played in only 126 games. He won the MVP award that year probably in recognition of long-time consistent performance over the years. His character, which had been called into question only four years earlier, probably won him a few votes as well. As sportswriter Nat Fleisher reported it in October 1925: "The selection of Peckinpaugh was a triumph for moral conduct on and off the field, a victory for the clean living and well behaved ballplayers, a strong blow against bluster and defiance."

He was given the award not so much for an outstanding individual performance, but in recognition of his exemplary role as a team player. Peckinpaugh himself believed he won the award on the basis of a crucial defensive play that benefitted his team. In a "pennant series against the A's," as Peckinpaugh remembered it, "with two men on and one out, I dived full length over second base to snare a liner with one hand and made a double play." The MVP award, which was announced before the World Series, seemed a great honor at the time but would soon come to haunt him.

The Senators defended their championship against the Pittsburgh Pirates. In the first game, which the Senators won 4-1, Peckinpaugh made a throwing error in the fifth inning which put a man on first, but no runs ensued. An error in the second game proved more costly. With the score tied 1-1 in the eighth, Peckinpaugh juggled Eddie Moore's grounder for an error. Max Carey then forced Moore at second with a ground out but was safe at first himself. Kiki Cuyler then hit a two-run homer that gave the Pirates the final margin of victory for the game which they won 3-2.

Peck made throwing errors in games three and five, but they didn't affect the final outcome of either game. In game six, with Eddie Moore on first in the third inning, Peckinpaugh fielded Max Carey's grounder too late to get the force out at second. The Pirates then went on to score twice and tie the game 2-2. Four innings later, Peckinpaugh made still another throwing error but the Pirates did not score. The Pirates still won the game 3-2 to force a seventh and deciding contest.

The Senators held a 6-4 lead entering the seventh inning of the final game. Walter Johnson, who had picked up victories in games one and four, was on the mound. Eddie Moore popped up to lead off the bottom of the seventh for Pittsburgh, but Peckinpaugh "lost the fly in the darkness" and dropped the ball, allowing Moore to reach second. The next batter doubled, and the Pirates went on to score two runs in the inning and tie the game at 6-6.

In the top of the eighth, Peckinpaugh homered (his only World Series homer, and the forty-eighth of the forty-nine he hit in his career) to put the Senators back on top 7-6. If it had ended there, it would have been a fitting end to an MVP year, and all would have been forgiven. But the Pirates got a chance to hit again in their half of the inning. It looked at first like it would not be much of a chance as Johnson retired the first two batters. Then back-to-back doubles tied the score at 7-7. Eddie Moore followed with a walk. Peckinpaugh had found it unusually difficult to force Moore out during the Series, and this time would prove no easier. When Max Carey grounded to Roger, the inning should have ended. But Peckinpaugh threw high trying to force Moore at second, and the Pirates wound up with runners at each base. It was Peckinpaugh's eighth error of the Series (a record), and it would prove costly. Cuyler doubled to score two, and the Pirates held on to win 9-7 and take the Series four games to three, becoming the first team to come back from a three-games-to-one deficit to win.

There was no denying that Roger Peckinpaugh was the goat. He was even handed a tongue-in-cheek award naming him the Goat of the Series, an award he would later laugh about. If nothing else, it prompted the MVP committee to decide to never announce the MVP award winner before the World Series, and that practice still holds today.

Peckinpaugh would never fully escape the memory of that fateful World Series. When his obituary appeared in the paper in 1977, it noted that many people believed those Series errors kept Peckinpaugh out of the Hall of Fame. That's doubtful. Though he was an exceptional ballplayer, he was still somewhat short of true Hall of Fame quality.

In the eyes of his peers, however, he was considered Hall of Fame. Eddie Collins called him the best all-around shortstop of his time. Ty Cobb agreed and went further to say that "his real worth is appreciated only by his co-workers." When asked whom he considered the best double-play combination, Babe Ruth responded quickly: "That's easy. Stanley Harris and Roger Peckinpaugh."

These players remembered Peckinpaugh more for the thousands of balls he played cleanly than the few he missed. They were the greatest players of their time, and they considered Roger Peckinpaugh to be the same.

# 6

# IN THE SHADOW
# OF GIANTS

THE NEW YORK YANKEES DYNASTY of the twenties, thirties, forties, fifties, and sixties began with their acquisition of a home-run hitting left-hander in 1915. He led the league in home runs in 1916 and 1917, but it would take another three years and the arrival of another home-run hitting left-hander before the Yankees would contend for the pennant. By 1921, they won their first American League pennant and would go on to win twenty-seven times in the next forty-three years. Babe Ruth, of course, is the slugger who everyone remembers for starting the Yankee dynasty. His predecessor (the player who really began the trend) is also remembered, but not for that. He's remembered as probably the best-known trivia answer in baseball: Who did Lou Gehrig replace at first base to start his streak of 2,130 consecutive games played? Answer: Wally Pipp. The truth is, Pipp is remembered, mistakenly, for starting that streak. But that's only a small part of his story and by no means the beginning or end of it.

In 1914, the Yankees ended up in seventh place in an eight-team league. It was their fourth straight second-division finish. Since joining the American League, they had lost more games than they won (937 to 861), twice lost more than 100 games in a season (1908 and 1912), and gave no hint of the dynasty they were to become. They began the change in January 1915 by acquiring Wally Pipp at the waiver price from Detroit. At that point, Pipp was only twenty-one years old and had appeared in only twelve major league games, and those nearly two years before. Six months later, they acquired pitcher Bob Shawkey from the cash-hungry Philadelphia Athletics for $18,000. For the next ten years, these two players would anchor the Yankees in defense, hitting, and pitching. During those years, the team made even more significant additions. Home Run Baker in 1916; Del Pratt in 1918; Carl Mays and Muddy Ruel in 1919; Babe Ruth and Bob Meusel in 1920; and Wally Schang and Waite Hoyt in 1921 (traded for Pratt and Ruel). The Yankees, as we know them, had been formed.

During those ten formative years of the Yankee dynasty (1915-1924), Wally Pipp played in nearly every game and appeared in more games than any other Yankee player. Not counting his war-shortened year of 1918, he led American League first basemen in at least one defensive category every season but two. He frequently led in several categories: 1915 (putouts, assists, double plays, and percentage), 1916 (double plays), 1917 (assists and double plays), 1919 (putouts and total chances per game), 1920 (putouts, double plays and total chances per game), 1922 (putouts and total chances per game), 1924 (fielding average).

He also swung a pretty fair bat. Along with teammates Home Run Baker, Duffy Lewis, Ping Bodie, and Roger Peckinpaugh, Pipp formed the original Yankee Murderers' Row in the years before Ruth arrived. With the Yankees in 1915, he drove in sixty runs to lead his team. Through the next nine years, the Yankees would come to depend on him to drive in runs as he regularly placed second or third on the team in RBI, including the years following the advent of Ruth and Meusel. From 1921 to 1924, he averaged over 100 RBI per year (97, 90, 108, and 113) and led his team in batting average with a .329 mark in 1922. He was, in other words, an indispensible player on an exceptionally talented team.

Of course, Pipp is not remembered for that. Instead, he has become the personification of dispensibility. It happened on June 2, 1925. There are several versions of the story (some conflicting ones propogated in later years by Pipp himself), but the most popular one (and probably the most accurate) is that Wally begged out of the lineup that day due to a headache. Lou Gehrig, just short of his twenty-second birthday, took Pipp's place in the lineup—and did not leave it for another fourteen years. Legend has it that Gehrig started his consecutive game playing streak that day, but that is not exactly true. Actually, the streak began the day before when Gehrig pinch-hit for shortstop Pee Wee Wanninger in the eighth inning. Coincidentally, Wanninger had replaced Everett Scott as the Yankee shortstop in a game just a few weeks earlier. At that point, Scott held the consecutive game playing mark at 1,307 games. Years later, following the death of Gehrig, Pipp would remark, "The breakdown of Gehrig reminds me of the total collapse of Scott. . . . playing day after day for a record in the book. It takes too much out of a man."

Actually, whether or not the headache story is true, the fact is the Yankees were in bad shape early in 1925. Babe Ruth was consigned to the bench in April and May due to a serious intestinal ailment. The team was practically in the cellar as June began, and Pipp's batting was showing rapid decline. Manager Huggins started juggling his lineup to get his team back on track. It made little difference as the team could never recover that year and ended up in seventh place sixteen games under .500.

It made all the difference to Pipp. One month after Gehrig took his place in the lineup, Wally was beaned above the right ear in batting practice by Charlie Caldwell, a hard-thrower who had just finished his college career at Princeton. He suffered a serious concussion, was hospitalized for over a week, and very nearly died. As the papers reported it, "Pipp had a narrow escape from the fate that overtook Chapman five years ago." Though he returned to the Yankees that year, they sold him to Cincinnati for $7,500 before the 1926 season. He played for the Reds for three years before retiring in 1928.

Legend has it that Pipp sat down one day and never got back in, but that's not exactly true either. In fact, Pipp played in 155 games for the Reds in 1926. Once again he led all first basemen in his league in putouts, double plays, and total chances per game. His 99 RBI paced his team and placed him fourth in the league. Once again he posted those numbers on a pretty fair team which finished second, only two games behind St. Louis.

After his playing career ended, Pipp tried his hand at several ventures, mainly in writing, speaking, and sales. His connection to the Yankee legends would endure as he became Babe Ruth's ghostwriter and appeared regularly at Yankee Old-Timers' games. Yet Gehrig was the name his would be inextricably linked to and perhaps that is as it should be.

The connection began as early as 1922 when Pipp first scouted Gehrig at Columbia for the Indianapolis ball club. In 1923, Pipp sprained his ankle late in the year, and the Yankees called up Gehrig from Hartford to take his place in the final weeks. One day early in the 1939 season, Pipp bumped into Gehrig in the Book-Cadillac Hotel in Detroit. Gehrig mentioned that he did not feel well and might not play that day. He didn't. It ended his consecutive playing streak. Two years later Gehrig would be dead. He died on June 2, 1941—sixteen years to the day since Wally Pipp came to the ballpark with a headache and stepped aside and into the shadow of the Iron Horse.

# 7

# GEHRIG'S SHADOW

FOR A WHILE THERE, 2,130 games to be exact, it seemed that perhaps no one would ever have to replace Lou Gehrig. For fourteen seasons, Gehrig defied more than mere odds; his consecutive game streak laughed in the face of human frailty and our shared mortality. That, of course, is why his untimely death has been so much more deeply felt than the death of any other ballplayer: We see in Gehrig's unbelievably rapid demise the tragic nature of our human condition. Even supermen must die.

But before he died, Gehrig had to first be taken out of the New York Yankee lineup. And the man who took his place will never be forgotten. That man's nickname, ironically, was Babe. Ellsworth "Babe" Dahlgren certainly had difficult billing; Gehrig was the one act in baseball impossible to follow. No matter what Dahlgren accomplished, whether he reached greatness or fell flat on his face, his career would always be evaluated in terms of that one day in May 1939.

He did have a past, however. Dahlgren was born in San Francisco on June 15, 1912, and his early years were marred by the tragic loss of his father. "When I was three years old," Dahlgren told *Herald Tribune* writer Arthur E. Patterson in 1939, "my father was scalded to death on the Coast. He was a steam-fitter and a big pipe burst. It must have been terrible." Dahlgren's mother remarried, and it was to his stepfather that Dahlgren always gave the credit for his ballplaying abilities. "He would hit me grounder after grounder, fly after fly, and the one thing he told me most often was that I must never be afraid of being hurt by a baseball. It was those many hours spent each night which were the foundation for my fielding ability in later years."

Dahlgren played for San Francisco's Boys Clubs and sand-lot teams until he reached high school. He was a six-letter man at Mission High School, graduating in 1930. Shortly afterward, he played minor league ball in Tuscon, hitting .347 in 1931. He was then signed by Bobby Coltrin, a scout for the Pacific Coast League team known as the Missions. From 1932 throughout 1934, Dahlgren played every single game of the Missions' sched-ule, earning the nickname, coincidentally, of "Iron Man of the PCL." His best season was 1933, when he hit .305 with 97 runs batted in while fielding .987 at first base. Even with these im-pressive offensive numbers, Dahlgren already had earned a "good-field, no-hit" label that he never would be able to shake.

His much-travelled major league career began in 1935 with the Boston Red Sox. Red Sox general manager Eddie Collins paid a substantial $50,000 for his contract from the Missions. After seeing Dahlgren play only a few games, writer John Lard-ner was already comparing Babe to some of the best defensive first basemen to have played the game. He was "not as graceful and rhythmic as [George] Sisler in action," wrote Lardner, but he was the "best first sacker in a Red Sox uniform since John 'Stuffy' McInnis." But the Red Sox were not pleased with his hitting. He especially lacked power; here was a six-foot, 190-pound, right-handed hitter who could only manage nine home runs in 149 games, many of them played in Fenway Park. Tom Yawkey had seen enough, and after the 1935 season, Yawkey traded for the second-greatest first baseman of the time, Jimmie Foxx. Dahlgren was sent to Syracuse where he spent almost the entire 1936 season, hitting .318 with 121 RBI.

And then Dahlgren got his big break, if that's what one wishes to call it. Lou Gehrig and Yankee owners Col. Jacob Rup-pert and Ed Barrow could not agree on a contract, and Gehrig threatened a holdout heading into the 1937 season. Barrow pur-chased Dahlgren from the Red Sox as "insurance" against a long holdout, and also as a tangible threat to Gehrig's job. But the holdout was short-lived, and once Lou returned, it was Dahlgren who no longer had a position or even a place on the roster. Yankees' manager Joe McCarthy sent Dahlgren to the Newark

Bears of the International League and instructed Bears' manager Charlie Vitt to play Dahlgren at third base. "I guess Joe saw in me the future Yankee utility man," Dahlgren said.

The 1937 Newark Bears were possibly the greatest minor league team of all time, and their exploits have been recorded in a fine book by Ronald A. Mayer. Besides Dahlgren, who hit .340 with 86 RBI and played a sparkling third base, the Bears had future Yankee stars Charlie "King Kong" Keller, Joe Gordon, Atley Donald, and Spud Chandler. This conglomeration won 109 and lost only 43, for a .717 winning percentage. Montreal came in second—twenty-five-and-a-half games behind. In the Little World Series, the Bears fell behind Columbus three games to none, with those first three games played in Newark's Ruppert Stadium. On the road in Columbus, the Bears promptly swept the next four games to win the championship. They were, as one writer put it, a "Wonder Team" indeed.

Nineteen thirty-eight was not nearly as much fun for Dahlgren. He spent the entire season with the Yankees, but he appeared in a scant 29 games and hit a paltry .186 in just 43 at bats. In spring training of 1939, though, Gehrig was having difficulty getting in shape, and his hitting was far below his usual capability. McCarthy saw Dahlgren in a new light—not as the future Yankee utility man but as the future Yankee first baseman. Still, as the season opened, it was Gehrig at first and Dahlgren on the bench. By the first of May, however, Gehrig was hitting only .143 with no extra base hits. After 2,130 consecutive games, the time had come for the Iron Horse to sit down.

Before the game of May 2, in Detroit, Gehrig approached manager Joe McCarthy. "While the team isn't going so good and while I'm not going so good, I think it would be in the best interests of the club that I be taken out of the lineup," Gehrig said. McCarthy responded, "I'm sorry it has to be this way, Lou. We'll see how it goes and maybe you'll be back in there later." The crowd was abuzz when the lineups were put up on the scoreboard and the Yankees were without a number "4" for the first time in over fourteen years. Gehrig brought out the lineup card, and as he returned to the dugout, the Detroit crowd of 11,379 gave him a rousing standing ovation. "When Lou returned to our bench, he headed to the water fountain for a drink," Dahlgren told Milt Richman of the *Newark Star Ledger* in 1979. "It was a very long drink. Tears began streaming down his face and he put one hand up to his eyes. Johnny Murphy tossed a towel from the bench so Lou could wipe his eyes."

Then the Yankees, and Dahlgren especially, went out and won one for Lou. The score was 22-2, and Dahlgren chipped in a double and a home run. "I almost hit four home runs the day I took his place," said Dahlgren. "I hit one homer, a double off the fence, and two more balls were caught at the fence." After the game, though, the Yankee clubhouse was glum. "This is the saddest day of my career as manager of the Yankees," said McCarthy. Bill Dickey was more philosophical. "Certainly I am far from happy over Lou's going to the bench, but the day comes to all of us. I never before saw a big man lose his power the way Gehrig did. He'd hit the ball pretty well, but it did not go anywhere." Only Lefty Gomez was able to add some comic relief. "It took you fifteen years to get out of the game," Gomez told a disconsolate Gehrig. "Very often it takes me only fifteen minutes."

The next day, veteran baseball writer Dan Daniel tried to put Dahlgren's replacement of Gehrig in historical perspective. "Dahlgren experienced a delight mingled with weighty responsibility such as welled in George Selkirk when Joe McCarthy told him he had fallen heir to the right field post and the celebrated number three lineup position of the one and only Babe Ruth." Daniel was especially impressed with the way Dahlgren rose to the occasion. "Dahlgren got a double and a homer and fielded the position with a dash and elan it had not been favored with in at least a couple of seasons."

A week later, Gehrig had not returned to the lineup. No one as yet knew that he was suffering from the disease that would bear his name, medically known as amyotrophic lateral sclerosis. Eerily, Gehrig told reporters on May 10, "Please omit flowers. And don't write my obituary." He would be dead little more than two years later.

Dahlgren was still making the best of this ill-fated opportunity. In June he shared his feelings about taking over for the great Lou Gehrig. "I'll never forget the thrill I got when, before the game, Arthur Fletcher came to me and said 'You're playing first base today.' I felt sorry for Lou, but since a change was being made and I was picked to take his place, I had myself to consider. I knew my chance had come, and it was up to me to take over, with the hope I would make a satisfactory successor for Lou." He added, "As a kid, Babe Ruth and Lou Gehrig were my heroes, and I drew their pictures on the inside cover of my high school binder. It never occurred to me that I would someday be the man who would replace Gehrig."

Dahlgren replaced him well that first season. He hit a low .234, but he knocked in 89 runs and led American League first basemen in double plays with 140. It was in the World Series sweep of the Cincinnati Reds, though, that Dahlgren really shined. With the Yankees down 1-0 in game one, Dahlgren doubled in the tying run, and the Yanks went on to win 2-1. In the second game, Dahlgren doubled and scored the first Yankee run in the third, and then followed that with a home run in the fourth to pace the Yankees to a 4-0 victory. The Reds never rebounded.

Little did Dahlgren know that 1939 would be his one season in the sun. The following year would be his last as a Yankee. Joe McCarthy initially seemed to be Dahlgren's greatest supporter. "Why don't you fellows give Babe some credit?" McCarthy asked a group of reporters in January 1940. "Don't forget he had a hard man to follow. He stepped in right behind Lou Gehrig, one of the greatest first basemen that ever lived, and he played a whale of a game." The pressure of replacing Gehrig continued to haunt Dahlgren. "I never expect to be a Gehrig or anything close to him," Dahlgren said in spring training of 1940.

He went on to have an adequate season by his standards, but by the end of 1940, Dahlgren had plummeted in McCarthy's regard. The Yankees had stormed back into the pennant race from nine games behind in mid-August only to fall short of the Tigers by two games. In August, Dan Daniel wrote, "Having succeeded the top-ranking first baseman of all-time, it has been Dahlgren's unpleasant experience to continue to be a victim of odious and unfair comparisons. However, only those who watch the Yankees day in and day out appreciate Babe for the defensive marvel he is, and know that he is far from the offensive weakling he is painted in the popular imagination." Just after Daniel wrote this, Dahlgren committed costly errors that "lost" games in both Cleveland and Detroit, and he lost McCarthy's support as well. Sportswriter Joe Williams wrote, "The 'greatest fielding first baseman since Hal Chase' had picked a swell time to be Humpty Dumpty."

In Feburary he was banished to the Boston Braves. McCarthy lashed out at Dahlgren, saying, "I know that Dahlgren is rated a fielding marvel. But did you ever ask yourself why he makes so many sensational plays? His arms are too short for the position, and he is forced to compensate for this handicap with maneuvers which give you the impression that he is another Hal Chase." Just to show it was nothing personal, McCarthy added, "He is a splendid fellow, but he is not the pennant-winning type of first baseman either on defense or attack." This time Joe Williams came to Babe's defense. Writing at the time of the trade, he said, "Dahlgren had drawn no easy assignment and it didn't become any less demanding when the Yankees blew the pennant in 1940. Conceivably, Dahlgren became one of the scapegoats."

From then on, Dahlgren's career was marked by a series of trades that earned him the name of the "Wandering Jew" of baseball, as one writer put it. He played for eight different ball clubs in his final six seasons. Because of a sinus condition, he was rejected by the United States Army, but he travelled as much as any GI. The Braves sold him to the Chicago Cubs after a mere forty-four games in 1941. In 1942 he played a total of 36 games with three clubs: the Cubs, the St. Louis Browns, and the Brooklyn Dodgers. The Philadelphia Phillies landed him in spring training of 1943 only to unload him to the Pittsburgh Pirates that December. Dahlgren had possibly the finest season of his career with the Pirates in 1944, reaching personal bests in games played (158), batting average (.289), and RBI (101). He declined considerably the following season, was traded back to the Browns again in 1946, and was sent to the Baltimore Orioles of the International League for 1947. Finally, he hung up his spikes when he was not brought up to St. Louis in September when the rosters expanded.

"It has been a peculiar and somewhat mystifying career," summed up Joe Williams when Dahlgren was first sent to Baltimore in 1946. And so it was. In particular, Dahlgren never was able to get out of two massive shadows. The first was an unfair label placed upon him, which defined him as having only defensive value. True, he was not a great hitter, but he was not nearly as bad as his reputation. When he did perform well offensively, as in the 1939 World Series, he was treated as the "surprise batter of big series," as a *Herald Tribune* headline quaint-ly stated. Even his defense, which was surely superlative, was called into question unjustly. Joe Williams stated both sides of the case succinctly. "It turned out he was a confirmed Fancy Dan who had a way, consciously or otherwise, of making easy plays look difficult. Well, I'll say this for the fellow. If he was a Fancy Dan, he was the best I ever saw."

But the second and far larger shadow, the one cast by Lou Gehrig, a baseball immortal and an American folk hero, was even more difficult to escape. Dahlgren once said, "I tried so hard to make good I made a botch of things generally." Under the most trying of circumstances, the record shows the Babe did all right.

# 8

# FALL FROM GRACE

ERNIE LOMBARDI PLAYED for seventeen years as a catcher with four teams in the major leagues. His career was marked by many highlights. He caught Johnny Vander Meer's consecutive no-hitters in 1938. He hit four doubles once in a game—in four consecutive innings off four different pitchers. He won the batting title twice, in 1938 and 1942, though the 1942 title would not be accepted under today's standards for required number of at bats. Still, he was only the second catcher in the history of the game to win a batting title, and the only one to win it twice. He won an MVP award and played in five All-Star Games and two World Series. Despite these accomplishments, one play alone stood out as the mark of Lombardi's career. The play occurred in the final inning of the final game of the 1939 World Series and became known as "Ernie's Snooze." Its impact and reverberations would plague Lombardi to his dying day, making him an isolated and embittered man.

Crucial moments in World Series play usually occur in the final innings of the final game in a closely fought contest. If a player drops a fly ball (like Fred Snodgrass in 1912) or surrenders a home run (like Ralph Terry in 1960) or supposedly hesitates for a moment (like Johnny Pesky in 1946), his failure will never be forgotten. But Ernie Lombardi suffered the same infamy for a far less critical offense, committed after the winning runs were scored in the finale of a runaway World Series.

It happened in the tenth inning of the fourth game of the

1939 World Series between Cincinnati and New York. The Yankees held a three-games-to-none lead and were looking for their second consecutive sweep and fourth straight World Championship when Joe DiMaggio stepped to the plate in the tenth inning with runners on first and third. DiMaggio stroked a single to right. Frank Crosetti scored from third to put the Yankees up 5-4, but then the Reds right fielder juggled the ball.

Charlie "King Kong" Keller, running from first, kept churning for home. On the play at the plate, Lombardi, the Cincinnati catcher, was knocked down and out. DiMaggio, seeing Lombardi stretched out past the plate with the ball lying two feet from his hand, rounded third and came in to score. Three runs scored on the single, and the Yankees closed the Series with their 7-4 victory.

Even though the Reds were already down three games to none and DiMaggio's run was meaningless, Lombardi took the fall. The play became immortalized as "Ernie's Snooze." Perhaps Ernie's greatest misfortune was that Grantland Rice was on hand to witness the event. His report ensured its position in the Bonehead Hall of Fame: "You won't believe what I'm telling you—and I don't blame you. But it happened this way—the greatest World Series anticlimax I've ever seen in 35 years of close inspection. . . . Señor Lombardi fell squarely on his broad back. . . . At this point, DiMaggio was just rounding third. Joe kept travelling over the intervening 90 feet as Lombardi still lay at rest, a stricken being."

Lombardi became from that moment a being stricken by the injustice of others' perceptions of him. Even the so-called snooze was an unjust stab at Lombardi. His teammates came to his defense, and Lombardi himself attributed his collapse to heat exhaustion: "It was an awful hot day in Cincinnati and I was feeling dizzy. . . . When Keller came in, he spun me around at the plate and I couldn't get up."

These circumstances did little to vindicate Lombardi. He was too easy a mark. Big, ugly, ridiculously slow, with a queer interlocking batting grip, the "Snooze" fit the caricature of this sad-sack player. It even went well with his nickname: "The Schnozz." These traits simply invited ridicule; even today, Lombardi seems to bring out the comedian or at least the caricaturist in all writers.

Bill James described him as "a huge man, with huge, oak-trunk legs and huge feet and huge hands and a promontory with nostrils that protruded from a lumpy face." Lombardi's short biography in *Total Baseball* begins by saying he "was the slowest runner in the Hall of Fame, including executives, pioneers, and exhibits." Even Arthur Daley took his shot in 1947, saying that "Lumbering Lom did all his running in the same spot. He ran on a treadmill and couldn't outrace a snail, even with a head start."

Yet these pronounced drawbacks also made his accomplishments doubly impressive. The same people who poked fun at his foot speed recognized that it made his batting average even more significant. As Arthur Daley said, "You almost come to the conclusion that he was the greatest hitter of all time. Every hit he made . . . was an honest one." His teammate Harry Craft called him "the best righthanded hitter I ever saw." Another teammate, Kirby Higbe, echoed these statements calling Lombardi "the greatest hitter I ever saw, including everybody," despite the fact that he said he could outrun Lombardi with a mule on his back. And Carl Hubbell once confessed that he feared Lombardi might hurt him or even kill him with one of his screaming line drives. Hubbell's fears were well-founded as Lombardi did hit a line drive which broke three fingers on Cubs pitcher Larry French's right hand.

Pitchers unfortunately did not have the luxury of backing up when Lombardi stepped to the plate. Infielders on the other hand regularly played twenty to thirty feet back on the outfield grass. Since it took Ernie as much as seven seconds to reach first base (by contrast, Ray Chapman, the Cleveland shortstop of the teens, could round all four bases in fourteen seconds), the infielders could still throw him out easily even with the added distance. Lombardi himself maintained his sense of humor about the situation. He once remarked to Pee Wee Reese, the Dodger shortstop, that "it was five years before I learned you weren't an outfielder."

With his batting averages, he could afford to retain his humor. In 1935, he achieved his highest batting average with a .343 mark. Over the next three years, he batted .333, .334, and .342, which earned him the batting title in 1938.

He was a big man—6 feet 3 inches, 230 pounds—and he

swung the biggest bat of his day—46 ounces—but he twirled it like a toothpick in his hands. Early in his career, he developed an unusual golf-style grip with his right pinky interlocked between the first two fingers of his left hand. He did it originally to relieve a blister on his right pinky but never abandoned it. It became another of his distinguishing features and ultimately another object of derision.

After he retired, the derisions piled up on Ernie until it was all he saw or that others saw of him. His failure to receive what he considered fair consideration for the Hall of Fame gnawed at him year after year until it finally left him a desperate and bitter man. Part of the reason for keeping him out of the Hall of Fame at that time was that he was seen, somewhat justifiably, as a single-skill ballplayer (hitting) with pronounced liabilities (speed and defense). There's no argument about his speed. His defensive abilities are more difficult to evaluate. *The Biographical Dictionary of American Sports* terms Lombardi "an excellent receiver." His teammate Harry Craft called him an "exceptionally fine receiver." Nearly everyone concurs that he had a first-rate throwing arm and good hands. Johnny Vander Meer even said that Lombardi would "reach out and catch wild pitches barehanded."

Yet those traits did not make him into a great defensive catcher. He regularly led the league in passed balls, often by comfortable margins even when he was nowhere near the leader in games caught. His complete lack of mobility crippled him and his team on bunts, foul pops, and advancing runners on passed balls.

When it was all added up, there was no denying that Lombardi possessed some remarkable talents. But he just didn't look or move like a ballplayer. In fact, this became one of the public rationalizations for keeping him out of the Hall. It was said that he "hardly resembled a Hall of Famer, that he was more often an object of satire than greatness." Bob Broeg, a Veterans' Committee member during the years when Lombardi was consistently denied entrance, explained: "One of the things that hurt so much was that he was sort of a caricature. He wore big, baggy pants and used a funny grip." Lest his capital offense be forgotten, Broeg added that the Snooze "did make him look ungainly."

As his hopes for the Hall of Fame faded through the years, Lombardi's life took a downturn. In 1953, only six years after his retirement, Lombardi suffered a severe bout of depression. He was on his way to a sanitarium for treatment when he stopped with his wife to spend a night with friends. While there, Ernie retired early saying he was not feeling well. When his wife entered the bedroom sometime later, she found him lying on the bed with his throat cut by a razor. Ernie survived the attempt on his life, but not through his own effort. At the hospital, he fought with the attendants and said he wanted to die.

He lived for another twenty-four years, but they weren't pleasant ones as he brooded on his misfortunes. From 1957 to 1963, he served concessions in the press box at Candlestick Park, but that was his last connection with baseball. He disappeared from public sight for many years until an Oakland sportswriter, Ed Leavitt, noticed him (he recognized the nose) working at an Oakland gas station in the early seventies. Lombardi was still bitter, perhaps even more bitter, about not getting into the Hall of Fame. "Even if they elected me, I wouldn't show up for the ceremony," Lombardi told Leavitt. "All they want to remember is that I couldn't run."

Yet even as his bitterness and reclusiveness were increasing, the support for Lombardi's entrance into the Hall was building. When a poll was taken to determine the best athletes not in the Hall of Fame, Ernie Lombardi was the leading vote-getter. It was also rumored that Warren Giles might have had something to do with keeping Ernie out. Back in his playing days in Cincinnati, Lombardi called Giles, the Reds general manager, "cheap" over a contract dispute. Apparently, Giles never forgot this, as Lombardi was consistently denied entrance during the years Giles served on the Veterans' Committee.

Lombardi finally did make it into the Hall of Fame in 1986, but by that point it hardly mattered. He had died, a bitter man, nearly a decade before. That bitterness became in the end his legacy. As he promised, he didn't show up for the induction ceremony. Renee Lenhart, his oldest living sister, went in his place. It was at best a bittersweet experience for her. "All these people wanted to do was run Ernie down," she said. It was Ernie's curse that it was just too easy to do.

# 9

# THE ONE THAT GOT AWAY

THE BROOKLYN DODGERS WON the National league pennant in 1920, led by their immensely popular manager, "Uncle" Wilbert Robinson. But then they fell under a twenty-year spell of frustration. Throughout the rest of the twenties, the "Robins," as they were also called, could not get the hang of the new-fangled game of the Ruth era, and they contended only once, missing the pennant in 1924 by one-and-a-half games to the arch enemy Giants. For five straight seasons Brooklyn finished an unenviable sixth in the eight team league. By 1932 the team had become so God-awful that first-year Giant manager Bill Terry quipped his famous retort, "Is Brooklyn still in the league?" The late thirties were not much better, even though they were now under the tutelage of a guy named Stengel. Leo Durocher took over the reins in 1939 and brought the Dodgers into immediate respectability by finishing third. They inched closer in 1940, being the bridesmaids to the eventual world champion Cincinnati Redlegs. And in 1941, the twenty-one-year drought was finally over. There was joy once more in Flatbush as the "Bums" won the NL flag. It was on to face the fearsome New York Yankees in the 1941 World Series, the first time the two teams had ever fought for the title.

As good as the Yankees were, that Dodger team was pretty solid as well. Future Hall of Famer Pee Wee Reese anchored the defense at short and sparked the offense at leadoff. First baseman Dolph Camilli led the league in home runs and runs batted

in, and center fielder Pete Reiser's .343 batting average led the
NL in that category, giving the Dodgers a triple crown of sorts.
These three were backed up by a sterling group of supporting
players: Billy Herman, Dixie Walker, Cookie Lavagetto, and Joe
"Ducky" Medwick, who was in the twilight of his brilliant career. On the mound were a pair of 22-game winners, Kirby Higbe
and Whitlow Wyatt. And behind the plate was first-year Dodger
Arnold Malcolm Owen, who incidentally led NL catchers in putouts that season. He had been given the nickname "Mickey" by
minor league manager Burt Shotton, who felt Owen resembled
the great Mickey Cochrane. Owen had a few years experience
under his belt by 1941, having played several seasons as a backup
catcher for the St. Louis Cardinals. His value was perceived primarily as a great defensive backstop, and he had in fact set a record for consecutive error-free chances by a catcher, 507, which
stood for thirty years. In 128 games in 1941, he had committed
only three errors and had been charged with two passed balls.

However, Owen's 1941 season was almost over as early as
June, when he was hurt by a beaning. As he was recuperating in
the hospital, he was notified of his selection for the National
League All-Star team. "The doctors were afraid I would get hurt,"
Owen recalled, "but there was no way I was going to miss that.
One of the doctors said, 'Well, you won't hurt your brains.' "
In his only All-Star at bat, Owen had the misfortune of facing
Bob Feller. "Feller was pitching when I got up, and he was
throwing aspirin," Owen said. "I thought to myself 'Why didn't
I stay in bed?' "

Owen recovered and helped the Dodgers fight off the St.
Louis Cardinals, who were the only serious contender for the
1941 pennant. The Dodgers held on to win by two-and-a-half
games, and the World Series was slated to begin on Wednesday,
October 1, in Yankee Stadium.

The 1941 Yankees were, of course, one of the greatest offensive units of all time. Their lineup had no weak lines: Rizzuto, Gordon, DiMaggio, Keller, Henrich, Dickey. But the pitching was thin, and the Dodger strategy was clear: keep the games
low scoring, and the "Bums" would have a fighting chance.

The first game should have gone exactly according to this
Brooklyn plan. But the Yankees pulled out a 3-2 win behind a
six-hitter from their ace, Red Ruffing. The Dodgers rebounded

to knot the Series the next day, winning by the identical score and getting a gutsy complete-game performance from Whitlow Wyatt. Game three moved across town to legendary Ebbets Field. Little known Yankee starter Marius "Lefty" Russo pitched the game of his life, holding the Dodgers to a single run on four hits and two walks. The 3-1 victory gave the Yanks a two-games-to-one advantage.

But the Dodgers had to like their chances. They had held the formidable Bombers' offense to a measly eight runs in three games. The pitching staff now believed it could keep Brooklyn in the game. And game four seemed to be a mismatch of epic proportions, with one of Brooklyn's 22-game winners, Kirby Higbe, facing Atley Donald, winner of only nine regular season games.

Game four began auspiciously for the Yanks, who scored a quick run in the opening inning via a Charlie "King Kong" Keller RBI single. Keller started another rally in the fourth by doubling with none out. Bill Dickey followed with a base on balls, and after Joe Gordon added a single the Yanks had the bases filled and still no one out. But Higbe got Phil Rizzuto to bounce into a force play at home, and after striking out opposing pitcher Donald, Higbe looked like he might escape the jam unscathed. Unfortunatley for Brooklyn, unsung first baseman Johnny Sturm, playing in his only major league season, smashed a clutch two-run single to knock Higbe out of the box.

Leo Durocher replaced Hibge with Larry French, who on the first pitch uncorked what looked to be a sure wild pitch. Mickey Owen made a spectacular stop, however, and he subsequently trapped Rizzuto between second and third for the final out of the inning. But the damage had been done—after three-and-a-half, the Yankees held a 3-0 lead. In this low scoring Series, a three run lead had proven to be insurmountable.

But the Dodgers were a plucky and resilient bunch, and they came back immediately. Donald began the bottom of the fourth by walking Owen and followed that by walking number eight hitter Pete Coscaret as well. Durocher went to his bench and sent up Jimmy Wasdell, who promptly doubled in both runners to cut the Yankee lead to a run. Then, the Dodgers struck again in the fifth. Dixie Walker doubled, and when Pete Reiser followed with a home run, the Dodgers had their first lead of the day. Durocher left it up to reliever Hugh Casey to protect the slim one-run margin.

And protect it he did. Casey was brilliant in relief, keeping the Yankees off stride with an assortment of breaking pitches, and the Dodgers clung to their precarious lead entering the top of the ninth. That frame opened uneventfully with Casey setting down Sturm on a grounder to second and retiring Red Rolfe on a comebacker. The Dodgers were one out away from evening the Series at two games, with only Tommy "Ol' Reliable" Henrich standing in the way. Casey and Henrich battled to a 3-2 count. The Ebbets Field 33,813 faithful fans braced themselves for a celebration as Casey hurled a roundhouse curve, obviously out of the strike zone. But Henrich lunged and swung wildly at ball four, and umpire Larry Goetz screamed, "Strike three!" The Dodges were leaping in jubilation in the home dugout, and police had taken their positions to prevent fans from coming onto the field.

But to the horror of an observant few, the game was not yet over. The third strike had eluded not only Henrich but catcher Mickey Owen as well. Owen had stopped the ball an inch or two off the ground with the heel of his mitt, but it caromed off his leg and bounced toward the Brooklyn dugout along the first base stands. The alert Henrich streaked toward first, and by the time Owen had retrieved the ball there was no play. It was scored a passed ball.

Mickey Owen recalled being fooled by the pitch which he expected to be the hard, sharp curve Casey had been throwing all along. His big curve wasn't breaking that day, so he had stopped throwing it. But then Casey turned over "the biggest curve I ever saw," according to Owen—the last thing he expected on a 3-2 pitch.

In the Yankee dugout, said Phil Rizzuto, "When Tommy Henrich swung and missed, we all got up and started toward the runway that led out of the dugout. Some of us were already in it. I know I was.

"Then," he continued, "we heard all that yelling, and we jumped back. There was Tommy running down to first. There wasn't any play."

Still, at that point the Dodgers had the lead and were only

an out away from victory. But Joe DiMaggio followed with a line drive single over Reese's head at short, and Charlie Keller doubled off the wall in right on an 0-2 count. Both Henrich and DiMaggio scored giving the Yanks a 5-4 lead. The Dodgers walked Bill Dickey intentionally, but Joe Gordon thwarted the strategy by also doubling, and two more runs came across. Casey finally recorded the last out, but the Yankees held a commanding 7-4 lead. The Dodger crowd, so tantalizingly close to euphoria, was silent in despair. Yankee reliever Johnny Murphy set the Dodgers down 1-2-3 in the bottom of the ninth, and the Yankees held a commanding three-games-to-one lead.

New York Times sportswriter John Drebinger's article of the next day opened with this lead: "It couldn't, perhaps, have happened anywhere else on earth. But it did happen yesterday in Brooklyn, where in the short span of 23 minutes a dazed gathering of 33,813 at Ebbets Field saw a World Series game miraculously flash two finishes before their eyes." Catcher Mickey Owen, to his credit, never made any excuses and took full responsibility for the debacle from the start. "It was my fault and I took the blame then and I will now," Owen said in 1973. He added, "The Yankees still had to get the hits, though, and they sure did." The immediate reaction to the rally, while it was still going on, was shock. Owen recalled, "It was like a punch on the chin. You're stunned. You don't react. I should have gone out to the mound and stalled a little. It was more my fault than Leo's." Durocher was quoted over the winter of 1941-42, "It was the only time in my life I couldn't think." And Drebinger wrote, "The Dodger Board of Strategy appeared paralyzed by the cataclysm."

However, the Series was not over yet—at least not for one more game. The loss in game four forced Durocher to use ace Whitlow Wyatt on only three days rest. The Yankees took advantage and got to Wyatt early for two runs and then held on to clinch the Series, 3-1. But for all intents and purposes, the Series had ended for Brooklyn the day before in that nightmarish ninth inning.

In a 1988 interview with New York sportswriter Phil Pepe, Mickey Owen revealed that he suspected the Dodgers might have won that 1941 Series if they had won game four. A victory in that game would have tied the contest and enabled the Dodgers to rest Wyatt, whom Owen called "practically unhittable" that year, for game six.

But despite the pain of what might have been, Owen has always treated his moment of infamy with a certain amount of humor. "Henrich missed it by more than I did," he once said. "He's the one who ought to be famous. At least I touched the ball."

The missed third strike was not, according to Owen, the biggest mistake of his career. His ability was not seriously affected by his gaffe—he played an additional eight seasons, finally hanging them up in 1954. But Owen was involved in a controversy of a totally different ilk in 1946. In that year he and pitcher Max Lanier of the St. Louis Cardinals jumped to the Mexican League. Because of this, Owen was banned from major league baseball for two full seasons, 1947 and 1948. When reinstated in 1949, he was picked up by the Chicago Cubs. It seems clear that the jump to Mexico was far more detrimental to Owen's career than the 1941 Series.

But in the end, Owen's lasting fame rests on that game-ending third strike that slipped through his fingers. "I wasn't a great ballplayer," he once said while assessing his abilities. "But I had some good qualities. I was good on pop flies, I could throw out base-runners, and I was a good low-ball catcher. I guess I'm the only guy in America who remembers what catcher holds the National League record for consecutive chances without an error.

"But people always remember me for a dumb play." As long as baseball is played, Mickey Owen will be remembered not for the innumerable pitches he caught but only for that one pitch on an October afternoon in 1941 that got away.

# 10

# HE WHO HESITATES

REMARKABLY, OVER ONE-THIRD of all World Series have gone the full seven games. Of the thirty-one Series that went the limit, the seventh game was decided by one run ten times. And of those ten games, five were decided in the winning team's final at bat. The first instance was when the Boston Red Sox defeated the New York Giants in 1912 by scoring two runs in the bottom of the tenth, aided by "Snodgrass's Muff." The Giants were again the victims in 1924 when a bad hop grounder bounded over Freddie Lindstrom's head in the bottom of the twelfth to give the Washington Senators a world championship. Yankee Ralph Terry's fastball was turned around in a hurry by Pittsburgh's Bill Mazeroski in 1960. In 1975, Joe Morgan's soft liner into center in the top of the ninth defeated the Red Sox and erased the magic of Carlton Fisk's dramatic home run of the night before. And in 1946, Enos Slaughter's "reckless run" or "mad dash" in the bottom of the eighth was the margin of victory for the St. Louis Cardinals over the Red Sox. Slaughter earned the laurels and an eventual trip to Cooperstown. But Johnny Pesky, the Red Sox shortstop who may or may not have "hesitated" in his throw to the plate, has had to wear the goat's horns and earned a one-way ticket to Palookaville.

Before that eighth inning, 1946 looked like it would finally be the year the Red Sox would end a twenty-eight-year championship drought. Many of the stars of the team had returned that spring from the service, including their two great outfielders

Dom DiMaggio and Ted Williams, two infielders, Bobby Doerr and Rudy York, and pitcher Tex Hughson. Under the guidance of Joe Cronin the Red Sox won the American League pennant with ease, finishing a full twelve games ahead of Detroit.

There was one other Beantown regular who began his postwar career that season. He was Johnny Pesky, starting his second year at short for Boston. His rookie performance in 1942 was more than impressive. The lefty hitting Pesky hit .331, second in the AL only to teammate Ted Williams, and he led the league with 205 hits, becoming only the sixteenth player to amass at least 200 hits in his rookie year. Pitchers soon learned he was aptly named. Possessing practically no power (he would never hit more than three home runs in any one season—and he played in Fenway!), Pesky's sharp line drives and spray hitting would drive pitchers to distraction. Even great hurlers like Bob Feller had problems with Pesky. "Johnny is the type of hitter that would give me trouble," Feller said in *The Sporting News* in July 1947. "He has a slight crouch at the plate with his bat held high and ready, not leaving you much strike territory. He guards the plate pretty well. And he has good eyes."

But back in 1942 America, there were more pressing matters than baseball. Pesky, like the majority of able-bodied major leaguers, enlisted in the armed forces. Pesky joined the navy and before long he was promoted to ensign. He sacrificed three prime baseball years, ages 23-25, helping to stop the Axis powers.

When he returned, he picked right up where he left off. Pesky's finest season was 1946. He hit .335 (to finish third in the AL), he scored 115 runs (second in the league), and he led the league both in at bats (621) and hits (208). When Pesky collected 207 hits in the following season, he became the first and only American Leaguer to ever string three consecutive 200-hit seasons in his first three years.

He was an unselfish player as well. During the 1946 season, Pesky had a string of 11 hits in a row. At the time the major league record was 12 consecutive hits. But in his next at bat, he came up with runners on first and second with one out in a close game and Ted Williams on deck. He got the sign to bunt, sacrificed himself to get the runners over, and lost his chance at the record. When sportswriters questioned Manager Joe Cronin after the game, he responded, "I'd never have given him the bunt sign if I had realized the situation. The little guy didn't even peep." Pesky's response was even more telling. "What record?" he said.

Pesky and the Red Sox headed into the fall classic to face the St. Louis Cardinals, who did not have an easy time of it winning the NL flag. In fact, the pennant of 1946 was the first one in history to be decided by a playoff. The Cardinals defeated the Brooklyn Dodgers two games to none after tying at the finish of the regular 154-game season. This Cardinal team was solid, led offensively and defensively by Stan Musial, Red Schoendienst, Terry Moore, and Enos Slaughter, and on the mound by Harry "The Cat" Brecheen.

Boston may have been a slight favorite as the Series opened in St. Louis's Sportsman's Park on October 16. The Red Sox had to feel good about their chances after the first game, a terrific ball game, had ended. Rudy York's dramatic tenth-inning home run broke a 2-2 tie, and reliever Earl "Lefty" Johnson shut the Cardinals down for a 3-2 win. But the Cards rebounded to knot the Series behind a four-hit shutout by Brecheen the following day. After a travel day, Boston got a shutout of its own from "Boo" Ferris, who had won 25 and lost only 6 during the regular season. The Cards came back with a vengeance pummelling six Bosox pitchers for 12 runs and 20 hits, and after four games the see-saw battle was dead even. The pattern held the next day as Boston's win pushed the Cardinals' backs to the wall. The Cards would have to take both games in St. Louis to win the championship.

Johnny Pesky was not having a great Series, especially in the field. Sportswriter Dan Daniel wrote on October 12, en route to St. Louis, that "Pesky alone has committed four misplays and thus far has looked like anything but what Boston says he is—the No. 1 shortstop of the American League." In the first five games of the Series the Red Sox had committed ten errors.

So, with no tomorrow, St. Louis handed the ball to their ace, "The Cat." Brecheen responded brilliantly, holding the Red Sox to only one run on seven hits. With the 4-1 win the Cardinals had forced a seventh and deciding game.

There might have been better seventh games. But only maybe. This one was a dogfight. Boston drew first blood by scoring a run in the first on a Dom DiMaggio sacrifice fly. The lead held only until the bottom of the second when St. Louis tied the game on a sacrifice fly of its own provided by Harry "The Hat" Walker. It remained 1-1 until the home fifth when the Cards pushed across what looked like two huge runs. Pitcher Murry Dickson doubled in one run and then scored the second on a single to center by Schoendienst. After five innings it was 3-1, St. Louis.

But the Red Sox weren't dead yet. In the top of the eighth, pinch hitter Glenn Russell led off with a single, and when another pinch hitter, George Metrovich, doubled, the Sox had the tying runs in scoring position with no one out. At this point St. Louis manager Eddie Dyer decided to replace Dickson with none other than Brecheen. The strategy looked like it would pay off beautifully. Brecheen struck out Wally Moses looking and got Pesky to hit a short fly to Slaughter in left. Still two on, but now two out.

It was up to Dominic DiMaggio. Brecheen fell behind in the count to DiMaggio 3-1 and he was forced to groove a fast ball to avoid walking the bases full and facing Ted Williams with the Series on the line. But DiMaggio came through, smacking a double off the right center field wall to tie the score.

And here the first piece of the strange puzzle that would occur in the bottom of the eighth was about to fall into place. "When I knew the ball was between the outfielders," DiMaggio told John Holway in 1981, "I figured if I could get to third it would make it a hell of a lot more difficult for Brecheen to pitch to Ted Williams. Brecheen might have made a wild pitch and I could score from third. So I tried to dig for a little extra. And that's when the muscle went." The "muscle" was in his right leg, and it was pulled so badly that DiMaggio had to leave the game. He reached second, limping noticeably for the last sixty feet. He was replaced by pinch runner Leon Culberson who went in for DiMaggio in center as well. Up stepped Williams with a chance to put Boston on top, but he could manage only a pop fly to Schoendienst at second and the Red Sox threat was over.

And then came the Cardinal eighth, one of those innings that will be retold as long as there are baseball fans. Bob Klinger was on the mound for the Red Sox and Roy Partee was catching. Leadoff hitter Enos Slaughter singled to center. Whitey Kurowski attempted to bunt him over but only popped it up back to Klinger. Then back-up catcher Del Rice smashed a long liner to left that looked like a sure double, if not more. But Ted Williams came from nowhere to track it down, and Slaughter had to return to first.

Harry "The Hat" Walker was next. With the count at 2-0, Cardinal manager Dyer decided to put Slaughter in motion, but Walker only fouled it off. Now with the count 2-1, Slaughter was once again off with the pitch. This time Walker delivered a sharp line drive over short heading for the left-field alley. The dash had begun.

What happened next is still open to debate. Slaughter was near second when he saw Culberson going toward the ball, and he made up his mind to attempt to score. "You know, DiMaggio had a great arm," he said in 1981. "He was a great center fielder. I don't think I would have even tried. But Culberson didn't have too good an arm, and he wasn't as quick as DiMaggio."

Culberson did eventually run the ball down, and he quickly hurled it in to the cutoff man, Johnny Pesky, stationed in short left field. As Pesky turned around, some say he "hesitated" for a fraction of a second, and in that momentary lapse he lost all chance to nail Slaughter at the plate. He "finally" did throw it in to Partee, but Slaughter's hook slide was clearly ahead of the tag. The Cardinals led, 4-3.

Boston still had three outs, and they almost made the most of them. Rudy York opened the ninth with a single and was replaced by pinch runner Paul Campbell. Bobby Doerr followed with a single to put runners on first and second. Pinky Higgins forced Doerr at second for the first out, and Boston had runners on the corners with only one out. But Partee fouled out to Musial at first and the Bosox were down to their final chance. Pinch hitter Tommy McBride worked the count to 1-1, and then he grounded to Schoendienst who flipped to shortstop Marty Marion at second for the force out to end the Series and send 36,143 Cardinal rooters into euphoria. Behind Slaughter, the Hat, and the Cat, the Cards were world champs.

Pesky was branded as the goat of the game as early as the next morning's papers. *The World-Telegram* wrote, "Ultimately the Boston shortstop came out of the ether and heaved the leather to catcher Roy Partee. But Johnny just had handed the world championship to the Cardinals." A different article in the same paper attempted to distinguish the heroes and goats of the Series. The unnamed writer believed Ted Williams was the worst of the Boston goats because of his lack of power and his "ignominious" pop-up to Schoendienst in the top of the eighth. Then the writer said, "immediately behind Williams in the listing of Boston's goats [is] Johnny Pesky, who lost yesterday's game." Dan Daniel's article of October 16 was an apologetic for Williams which ended with this opprobrium: "Johnny Pesky, in this corner's opinion, was the goat of the Series. He handed the Cardinals the winning run when he delayed his throw to home plate in the eighth inning yesterday. The play is described elsewhere in these pages," he continued. "When you see it in the newsreel, you'll think your eyes are performing tricks."

The blame has never let up. Pesky heroically took responsibility from the start. "It was entirely my fault," he said. But exactly what was his fault? According to Pesky, an overlooked key to the play was that Slaughter was running on the pitch. "I was going to cover second," he said. "I was starting toward second and Walker hit the ball to left center." After Culberson threw the ball in, two things happened simultaneously to prevent Pesky's immediate reaction. Teammates say they were screaming for Pesky to peg it home, but Johnny could not hear them over the din of the delerious crowd. And perhaps most importantly, Pesky never dreamed Slaughter would attempt to score. Because of his surprise, Pesky said, "There was a little hitch and maybe that's what people saw. I don't know. I just know when I turned around, Slaughter was about 22 feet away from the plate and the only way I could have stopped him was with a rifle."

The remainder of Pesky's career shows that being labeled the goat of the 1946 Series had little if any effect on his play. The following season Pesky led the AL in hits yet again and batted .324. In 1948 he was asked to switch to third base to make room for a young shortstop named Vern Stephens, and Pesky did so unselfishly and without complaint. In 1950, when teammate Billy Goodman needed at bats to qualify for a possible batting title, Pesky offered to ride the pines and let Goodman play in his stead. Manager Steve O'Neill said, "Johnny was going good, but he had no chance of winning the batting title. Billy had a good chance. In baseball, it's hard to give up your position. Not many people would do it. That's why I think it's a great gesture."

But most fans do not remember or have never heard about Pesky's unselfishness or his 200-hit seasons. What is infamous is his "hesitation." Even eyewitnesses dispute the charge and exonerate Pesky. His counterpart at shortstop in that Series was the slick-fielding Marty Marion. "John got a bad rap," Marion has always said. But it's a rap nonetheless, and one Pesky has had to shoulder for over forty years. In 1979, when Pesky was a first-base coach for the Red Sox, Pesky said, "People still say things once in a while. I'll be coaching and I'll hear some guy yelling 'Throw home Pesky! There goes Slaughter!' " In his usual self-effacing manner, Pesky has come to terms with his fate. "If you're a palooka," he told Leigh Montville of the *Boston Globe*, "you've got to live with it." Unfortunately for Johnny Pesky, a fine career has been boiled down to an easy handle and a cliche: he who hesitated, lost.

# 11

# EIGHTY-SIXED

IT IS A FRANCHISE designed for masochists. Other teams peter out, or don't quite make the grade, or are never in the running in the first place. The Boston Red Sox, on the other hand, test their fans in a uniquely painful way—by coming oh so close only to self-destruct. It has been this way since one month before Armistice Day, when a moon-faced left-hander named Ruth and a submarine-hurling right-hander named Mays won two games apiece to give Beantown its last World Series victory. Boston writer Dan Shaugnessey calls the seventy-three-year championship drought "the curse of the Bambino," or Boston's just desserts for trading away the single greatest phenomenon the game has known.

Nearly three decades passed from the moment of that trade until the Red Sox appeared in the fall classic again. In the Series of 1946, they were the victims of Enos Slaughter and the Cardinals, losing the seventh game by a single run. Two years later, they were beaten by the Cleveland Indians in the first playoff in American League history. The next year, they came up a single game short to the Joe DiMaggio-led Yankees.

Mercifully, they gave their rabid fans a breather by falling out of contention for almost twenty years. When they won their next pennant, in "The Impossible Dream" year of 1967, they once again lost to the Cardinals, once again in seven games. In 1975, they nearly beat the "Big Red Machine" in what has been called the greatest World Series of the television era. Underline nearly. Once more the Series went the limit, and once more they dropped the final game by a run. The 1978 season was only the second in AL history that ended in a tie, necessitating a one-game playoff, and it was the second one lost by the Red Sox. Of course, the margin was a single run.

So one would think that Boston Red Sox players and fans would have learned to expect and accept anything. But even for a team so steeped in misery, the year 1986 will have its own and lasting niche. Never were the Red Sox so close to tasting the champagne, never was New England so near an explosion of euphoria, as they were in the bottom of the tenth inning in game six of the 1986 Series. And then, just like that, it vanished, they all said, through the legs of Bill Buckner. As we shall see, and as we have seen, one play does not a World Series defeat make. Buckner has had to wear the horns, but the blame can be spread around rather liberally.

Bill Buckner had a long and fruitful career before the 1986 World Series. It was a career marked by three distinct characteristics—great, often brilliant hitting; chronic and crippling injuries; and an indomitable sense of self, which sometimes expressed itself as arrogance, sometimes as hot-headedness, and sometimes as courage.

Like most youngsters growing up in Southern California, Buckner dreamed of the day he would don a Dodger uniform. He caught the eye of major league scouts during his years at Napa High School, where he hit .667 one season and was a high school All-American in football as well. The Dodgers drafted him second (Bobby Valentine was their No. 1 choice), and they assigned him to Ogden, Utah, in the Pioneer League. His .344 average in sixty-four games in 1969 earned him a trip to the spring training camp at "Dodgertown" in Vero Beach in 1970.

Ted Williams, who was managing the Washington Senators at the time, caught a glimpse of Buckner that spring. "There is a boy who can become a batting champion," said Williams. Jim Gilliam, ex-third baseman of the Dodgers, said, "I didn't strike out much, but this boy never strikes out." Buckner was named the top rookie in spring camp that year, but he only appeared in twenty-eight games in the early part of the year. He was hitting a mere .191 in May and so he was sent to Spokane for more seasoning. He ripped up minor league pitching at a .355 clip that summer.

At spring training the next year, the cockiness that would become one of his trademarks showed itself for the first time. "I'll hit .300 in the bigs if the Dodgers play me," he said.

Well, not quite. But Buckner did hit .277 in 108 games in 1971, playing mostly in the outfield. And in 1972, he made good on his boast—he hit .319 and impressed manager Walter Alston with his style of play. "Bill is a little hot-tempered," said Alston, referring to the fact that Buckner was known, among other things, for hurling his helmet in anger whenever he made an out. "But he's aggressive and a competitor, and I like that," said Alston. It wasn't long before veteran teammates nicknamed Buckner "Mad Dog."

Although 1973 was a bit of a setback, as his batting average fell to .275, Buckner played on his most regular basis to date, appearing in 140 games. The Dodgers of the early seventies were a solid ball club, but for three straight seasons they had been bridesmaids. That would change in 1974.

Before the season began, Buckner made what sounded to be a brash prediction. "I can steal 30 bases," he said, even though his career total over his first three seasons was only twenty-six. He then went on to have his best season to date and played an integral role in the Dodgers' division-winning season. He hit .314, smacked 30 doubles, struck out only twenty-four times in 580 at bats, and yes, he stole 31 bases. After the Dodgers disposed of the Pittsburgh Pirates in four games in the National League Championship Series, Buckner was headed to the first of his two World Series.

It has been forgotten in the mists of time, but Bill Buckner was involved in the most controversial play of that World Series as well. Although the Oakland A's held a commanding three-games-to-one lead over the Dodgers, the A's were hardly blowing the Dodgers out of the water. The A's had only outscored the Dodgers by a total of four runs heading into game five in Oakland. After a Joe Rudi home run in the bottom of the seventh, the A's had a 3-2 lead. Bill Buckner led off the Dodgers' eighth with a clean single. With no one out, Buckner attempted to go from first to third on a single to right field. Reggie Jackson fielded the ball, hit cutoff man Dick Green, and Green fired the ball to Sal Bando to nail Buckner at third. The play killed the Dodgers' rally, and they lost the game and the Series by one run. Davey Lopes stated after the game that the play was stupid and had cost the Dodgers any chance at a comeback. Writers across the nation agreed with Lopes, and they brought up the old cliche about never making the first out at third base. Buckner rode out the criticism and hoped all would be forgiven in 1975.

In April of 1975 Buckner injured his left ankle for the first time, and for the remainder of his career his ankles would be a source of misery. As he was coming back from the ankle sprain in July, he was involved in a freak injury that he could blame on no one but himself. John Montefusco had just retired him on a pop-up for the last out of a 1-0 shutout, and Buckner slammed his helmet onto the ground in disgust. The helmet bounced straight up into his forehead with such force that the subsequent cut required four stitches. He then injured his thigh in August, and his ankle, which had never fully healed, was operated on in September. All in all, 1975 was a washout.

He rebounded well the next year, but nagging injuries kept plaguing him throughout the season. In May he re-injured the left ankle, and he jammed his wrist in July. Still, he was able to appear in 154 games, and he hit .301 after batting only .243 the previous year. During the off-season he had his second operation on the ankle. And in February he was traded to the Chicago Cubs for Rick Monday. "I don't want to get into a big argument about who's better, me or Rick Monday," he said to Chicago writer Jerome Holtzman. Then he added in his typical self-confident manner, "But I think the Cubs got the better of the deal."

The friendly confines of Wrigley Field could not save Buckner from another disappointing, injury-riddled season. In spring training he fractured his left index finger, and in late April he was placed on the disabled list because his ankle had not yet fully recovered from the surgery performed the previous October. As soon as he came off the DL, on May 4, he re-injured the ankle going from first to third. He was back in action when the Dodgers came to Chicago for a series in June. Buckner, like so many traded ballplayers who wish to show their old team they made a mistake by letting them go, had a tremendous series against the Dodgers. After one game in which Buckner beat up on L.A., Tommy Lasorda said, "When he's on the field playing against us, he's just another guy in an enemy uniform. But after the game, he's my son." Cubs' manager Herman Franks was clearly sickened by Lasorda's sentimentality. "Yeah, I know all about that son stuff," Franks said, "but all I can say is that Buckner was Lasorda's son when he was healthy. As soon as he hurt his leg, Lasorda kicked him out of the house."

There were flashes of brilliance throughout the summer for Buckner. He was named player of the week for the period ending August 21, and *The Sporting News* wrote that "Bill Buckner is one of the guttiest players around today. He plays with a bad ankle, takes an aspirin, and steals a base." When the Dodgers returned to Wrigley in September, Buckner drove in five runs with two homers in one game. Franks chuckled, "Buckner was pretty tough on his daddy, wasn't he?"

Buckner's ankle was still not fully healed, however, and in early 1978 it especially hurt him when turning around first on doubles. Throughout June and July a series of minor ailments relegated Buckner to pinch hitting duty as he tried to get back into shape. In September, the injury-prone Buckner was on the disabled list yet again after pulling a hamstring. Although he hit .317, he started a disappointing 105 games. Over the off-season, he tried a new form of rehabilitation—ballet. "The ankle's never going to be 100 percent again," he said. "I've already faced up to that."

But ballet certainly helped. The next year, 1979, was Buckner's first injury-free year since 1975. That is not to say that he played without pain. "I've had pain for so long now that I'm used to it," he said. He hit only .284, but he played in 149 games. Towards the end of the season, however, Buckner found himself the subject of some rather serious criticism. Herman Franks decided to quit managing the Cubs, and he cited Buckner's behavior as the major reason. "I thought he was the All-American boy. I thought he was the kind of guy who'd dive in the dirt to save ball games for you," Franks said. "What I found out after being around him for a while, is that he's nuts. He doesn't care about anything except getting a hit. He goes berserk if he goes through a game without getting a hit. He doesn't care about the team. All he cares about is Bill Buckner." Buckner bitterly denied the charges. "I've been busting my tail for three years here, and I've played when I was hurt and shouldn't have been playing. Herman had no right accusing me of anything other than I got upset when I made an out. I'll admit that."

The following season, Buckner made his critics eat their words. He finally fulfilled Ted Williams' prediction of a decade earlier by leading the National League in batting with a .324 average. During one stretch of the season, Buckner went 114 consecutive plate appearances without striking out. In September, when it looked as if he would have a shot at the batting title, Buckner said, "It's tough to compete with guys who have speed. I can't beat out any infield hits." But he edged out Keith Hernandez and Garry Templeton for his one and only batting crown. Ken Reitz of the Cardinals said of Buckner's achievement, "Bill did it without the benefit of Astroturf and with his legs hurting."

In the strike-shortened season of 1981, Buckner ironically knocked in more runs than in any previous season. He came in third in the NL with 75 RBI in only 105 games, and he also hit a career high 35 doubles to pace the league in that department. In 1982 he improved again, playing in 161 games, hitting .306 and topping the 100 RBI mark for the first time in his career. But Chicago, under the leadership of new general manager Dallas Green, was beginning a youth movement, and by early 1984 Buckner had lost the first base job to Leon Durham. Buckner resented his part-time status and demanded a trade. Green obliged him by sending him to Boston on May 25 for a washed up starter named Dennis Eckersley. "You don't realize how good you have it until you're not playing," Buckner said at the time of the trade.

Boston and Buckner agreed with each other from the start. "I couldn't have picked a better place to go," Buckner said. "I love the city, I love the ballpark, and I like everybody on the team. It's something to motivate me to do as well as I can so I can play as long as I can." In June of 1984 Buckner collected his 2,000th hit, but manager Ralph Houk praised him instead for his defensive ability. "He's been directly responsible for saving at least three games with his glove," Houk said.

Buckner's best was yet to come. In 1985 he knocked in 110 runs, scored 89, hit .299, and played in all 162 games. He followed that up with 102 RBI in Boston's pennant winning

1986 season. Toward the end of the regular season, Buckner's ankles began to bother him yet again, but this was his first shot at post-season play in twelve years, and he was not to be denied. During the Sox pennant drive in September, he hit eight home runs and drove in 20 runs over a two-week stretch. The media lavished praise on Buckner, intimating that his courage to play in pain on his hobbling ankles was a throwback to players of a less pampered era.

After the Red Sox defeated the California Angels in the American League Championship Series, employing a miracle comeback of the sort of which they were normally the victims, it was on to face the New York Mets in the Series. The Mets won 108 games that season, but they narrowly escaped defeat at the hands of the Houston Astros in the National League Championship Series. Fans had been treated to two of the finest playoffs in history, and it was difficult to expect the Series to be anything but anticlimactic.

Boston jumped out to a two-games-to-none lead, sweeping the Mets in New York. Only one team had ever come back from so ominous a beginning, and New York had to win two of three in Fenway Park to stay alive. They did just that, forcing the Series back to Shea Stadium with the Red Sox holding a 3-2 Series advantage. Then came the sixth game, one of the most improbable games in World Series history.

The teams were deadlocked at three entering the top of the tenth. Dave Henderson, whose home run had staved off elimination for the Red Sox in the American League Championship Series, hit his second dramatic home run on the post season to put the Sox up by a run. Base hits by Wade Boggs and Marty Barrett added an insurance run, and the Bosox were three outs away from their first World Championship since 1918.

The first two Mets went down quietly in the last of the tenth, and the final hope of the New Yorkers rested in the hands of Gary Carter. But Carter came through with a sharp single to left, and when rookie Kevin Mitchell followed with a soft liner to center, the Mets suddenly had the tying runs aboard. Ray Knight battled reliever Calvin Schiraldi, fouling off four 3-2 pitches, before singling to right center to score Carter and send Mitchell to third. Boston manager John McNamara brought in Bob Stanley.

Then Mookie Wilson came to the plate for possibly the most event-filled at bat in World Series history. Stanley ran the count to 2-2, unleashed a wild pitch that glanced off catcher Rich Gedman's glove, and Mitchell romped home with the tying run. "I tried to throw an inside fastball that was supposed to tail back out over the plate," said Stanley.

Mookie then dribbled the next pitch down the first base line. It would have been a close play had first baseman Bill Buckner fielded it cleanly. But the ball trickled under Buckner's glove and through his legs as Knight scored the winning run. The look on Buckner's face at that moment is beyond disappointment or even self-disgust. It was a look of resignation, as if he had already come to terms with his fate. Seven times in the inning the Red Sox were within one strike of winning. They would never get as close in the final game, as the Mets won the game, 8-5, and the Series.

Bill Buckner was immediately branded as the scapegoat of the Series. Although he has had to bear the largest burden of responsibility, many others on that Red Sox team were as, if not more, responsible for the disaster. Clearly the largest portion of the blame should be laid at manager John McNamara's feet, for he should have replaced Buckner with Dave Stapleton as he had at other times during the regular season. He was roundly second-guessed for staying with Buckner, and his reasoning for doing so is commendable but patently stupid. He said the following night that after all Buckner had done for the team, he felt he deserved to be on the field at the end of the game. After McNamara, Bob Stanley and Rich Gedman deserve smaller portions of blame. Although the pitch that scored Mitchell was ruled a wild pitch, replays show it could just as easily have been scored a passed ball; Gedman gets plenty of glove on the ball and should have caught it. Then, the following night in game seven, Bruce Hurst, who had been prematurely named the Series MVP in the tenth inning of the sixth game, blew a three-run lead as the Mets rallied to win. There is no excuse for Buckner missing that slow roller, but he hardly lost the World Series.

He did not do much to win it either. If one could get by all the media hype about Buckner's courage, it was apparent that his presence in the lineup and on the field was a detriment to the Red Sox. Obviously hampered by his ankles, Buckner hit a

woeful .188 and had absolutely no range at first base. In this
Series he would have helped the team more by sitting down and
letting Don Baylor play in his stead.

On opening day at Fenway Park the following year, Bill
Buckner was soundly booed during pre-game festivities. "I don't
think I deserve to be booed at all," said a disturbed Buckner after the game. "The fans have an awful short memory; they don't
remember September when I carried this team. Without that,
we might have never gotten into the playoffs in the first place."
Buckner resolved to silence the boo birds. "I'm going to have
the best year of my career, for this team. And I don't care what
anybody else in the crowd thinks about it."

Halfway through the 1987 season, Buckner no longer had
to worry what the Fenway faithful were thinking. He was released by the Red Sox and picked up as a designated hitter by
the California Angels. "At this point in a career," he said in
1987, "when you're making good money, you have to have a
decent year to stay around. My No. 1 goal is to play in a World
Series again, but I also have this thing about 3,000 hits. I mean
for a guy who was supposed to be finished eleven years ago and
has had to play most of his career on one leg, it would mark my
career as a pretty good one." Buckner did a solid job as a designated hitter for the Angels over the next two seasons, but he
never regained his old form and he was released after the 1989
campaign. The Kansas City Royals took a gamble and signed
him for the 1989 season, but he hit a disappointing .216 in
part-time play. It seemed he had finally reached the end of the
line.

Remarkably, one team was interested in the forty-year-old
Buckner for the 1990 season: The Boston Red Sox. Even more
remarkably, Buckner made the club, primarily as an insurance
policy for the Red Sox if rookie Carlos Quintana was not able
to make the grade. On Opening Day this time, Buckner received
a moving standing ovation. It had taken four years and two other
teams, but Boston fans had forgiven all. Buckner was noticeably
touched. "The fans have always been great to me in Boston," he
told *Sports Illustrated.* "The media made more of the error than
the fans did."

But by early June, Buckner no longer had a place on the
squad. The Quintana experiment was working even better than

the Red Sox could have hoped, and Buckner was released. At the time, his 2,715 hits led all active players. It does not seem he will have the chance to pick up the remaining 285.

There is the possibility that posterity will treat Buckner more kindly than it has treated fellow scapegoats Merkle, Snodgrass, Owen, et. al. What seems more likely is that as time passes, and careers are reduced to simplistic handles, Buckner's impressive batting averages and respectable RBI totals will be forgotten. What will remain is the replay of a Mookie Wilson ground ball going through Bill Buckner's unsturdy legs, a painful conclusion to the most recent installment of baseball's ongoing epic tragedy called the Boston Red Sox.

# Shadows Overhead: Wrong Side of the Pitch

# 12

# ACE OF THE BUMS

DON NEWCOMBE'S PLACE in baseball history seems safe. He entered the National League in 1949, becoming the third black to play in the NL. In addition, he was the first black starting pitcher in major league history. Most of all, he is known as the leader and workhorse for the Brooklyn Dodgers during their greatest epoch, immortalized in Roger Kahn's *The Boys of Summer*. Against this impressive background, it is easy to see why Newcombe has never been held responsible for serving up one of the most important gopher balls in the post-war era, the home run that cost the Dodgers the 1950 pennant.

This is not to say that Newcombe's experience in baseball was trouble-free. He began his career for the Newark Eagles in the Negro National League. Those were the waning days of the NNL, but Newcombe cut his teeth facing the likes of Josh Gibson, Buck Leonard, Larry Doby, and Cool Papa Bell. After Jackie Robinson's historic entry into the major leagues, Branch Rickey attempted to sign many of the younger blacks in those leagues. He picked up catcher Roy Campanella from the Baltimore Stars and Newcombe from Newark in quick succession in 1947. After a little minor league seasoning, Newcombe made it to the big club in 1949.

Perhaps Newcombe was not the dominant pitcher in the league in 1949, but he was close. He was third in the NL in winning percentage, fifth in wins, second in strikeouts, third in complete games, tied for first in shutouts, and first in strikeouts per nine innings. Every one of his 17 wins was needed; the Dodgers won the pennant by only one game over the Cardinals. Just as Jackie Robinson rose to the occasion two years earlier, Newcombe earned Rookie of the Year honors, in spite of the difficulties confronting blacks in the first few years of acceptance in the "big" leagues.

The NL champions were poised to defend their title in 1950. The season opened in Philadelphia, and Newcombe got the start. The 1949 Phillies had finished third, sixteen games behind Brooklyn, but that was still good enough for their best season in thirty-two years. In fact, the Phillies were so terrible that for the twenty-five years preceding 1949, they finished last twelve times, and next to last an additional eight times. The 1950 season opened auspiciously for the Phils, as they beat Newcombe and the defending NL champs.

For the next two months, the Phillies, Dodgers, and Braves shared first through third place in a variety of combinations. The 1950 pennant races were even a point of discussion in Ernest Hemingway's novel, *The Old Man and the Sea*. A young boy asks the main character, Santiago, who he thinks will win the pennant. "In the other league between Brooklyn and Philadelphia, I must take Brooklyn. But then I think of Dick Sisler and those great drives in the old park." How prescient Santiago would be.

Towards the end of July, the Phillies launched themselves into the rarefied air of first place. By September 20, they had built a seven-and-a-half-game lead over the Boston Braves. The third-place Dodgers seemed hopelessly out of contention, trailing by nine games with less than two weeks to play.

But then the Dodgers staged one of the great homestretch pennant drives of all time. Like all miracle drives, the Dodgers needed help, and the Phillies were giving them plenty. Manager Eddie Sawyer said, "We lost Curt Simmons to the service [with three weeks remaining in the season], Bob Miller and Bubba Church were injured, so our pitching was thin. Our hitters weren't hitting, and we couldn't score runs. We kept saying, 'All we need is one win.' We just couldn't get it."

Meanwhile, the Dodgers were playing brilliant baseball, with Newcombe as the workhorse of the staff. In fact, in early September, Newcombe went so far as to emulate the likes of "Iron

Man" Joe McGinnity, a pitcher for the New York Giants at the turn of the century who was renowned for pitching both ends of a doubleheader. In Philadelphia, Newk pitched a shutout for a 2-0 win in the opener of the twin bill and then pitched seven strong innings in the nightcap, which Brooklyn eventually won, 3-2.

The Dodgers kept the pressure on. Brooklyn ended the Phillies' home season on a sour note by beating them two days in a row at Shibe Park. Afterwards, the Phillies embarked on a nine-game road trip which would conclude the season, now holding a precarious five-game lead. That road trip indicates how much has changed in the expansion era, for not one of the teams the Phillies faced remain where they were. It was on to Boston to play three against the fading Braves, and then four in New York against the Giants and the final two in Brooklyn.

While the Phillies took two out of three in Boston, the Dodgers kept pace. Now the Phillies held what looked to be an insurmountable five-game lead with six to play. But Brooklyn's arch-rival Giants did them the greatest favor in their long and bitter history—they swept the Phils in back to back doubleheaders. As the "Whiz Kids" entered Ebbets Field on September 30, they were up by two games with two to play. The Dodgers held destiny in their own hands.

When the Dodgers won the first game of that series, 7-3, New York sportswriters had a field day, renaming the Phillies the "Fizz Kids" and the "Was Kids." In the final game of the year, the Phillies sent twenty-four-year-old right-hander Robin Roberts to the mound. Roberts was trying to win his elusive twentieth game—it would be his seventh attempt and his fourth start in nine days for the pitching depleted Phils. The Dodgers countered with a nineteen-game winner of their own, Don Newcombe.

Both Roberts and Newcombe were brilliant on that "perfectly mild" October first afternoon. The game remained scoreless until the top of the fifth, when the Phillies drew first blood. After Newcombe had retired both Eddie Waitkus and Richie Ashburn on ground balls to first, Dick Sisler started a rally by singling sharply to right, the second of three singles that he would hit that day. Del Ennis followed with a high fly to short right-center that appeared catchable, but Dodger center fielder Duke

Snider was shading Ennis toward left-center, and second baseman Jackie Robinson could not quite reach the blooper. Now
there were runners on the corners, but still two were out. Willie
"Puddin' Head" Jones followed with a clutch single just out of
the reach of Pee Wee Reese through the hole at short. Sisler
scored to give the Phillies a 1-0 lead.

The way Roberts was pitching, one run just may have been
enough. Through the first five, the only hard hit ball was Reese's
fourth inning ground rule double. But the diminutive Reese
would be a thorn in Roberts' paw all day. With two down in
the sixth, Reese sliced a liner towards the right field fence, a
mere 294 feet from home plate. The ball hit off the screen just
above the fence, and it appeared to be bouncing back onto the
field of play. But the ball remained wedged on a piece of coping
between the scoreboard and the fence. Phillies center fielder
Richie Ashburn told writer Ray Didiger: "I would have needed
a ladder to go get it." Reese, hustling all the way, was almost to
third when the umpire signaled that the ball was out of play for
a home run. The bizarre round tripper had knotted the score.

And tied it would remain, with Roberts and Newcombe
exchanging goose eggs over the next three frames. When the
Dodgers came up in the bottom of the ninth, they needed only
one run to force a three-game playoff. They could not have come
closer to scoring one. The Dodgers had still not figured Roberts
out. To that point, Roberts had recorded sixteen ground ball
outs, including six hit right back to the box. But he showed
signs of tiring when he walked speedy lead-off man Cal Abrams
for the second time in the game. Reese tried unsuccessfully to
sacrifice, bunting foul twice, so with two strikes he swung away
and delivered yet another hit, a clean single to left to push
Abrams to second. That brought up Duke Snider, and the Phillies expected him to be bunting. But Snider crossed them up by
jumping on Roberts' first pitch for a sharp single to center.

The home crowd of 35,073 cheered the streaking Abrams
toward home with the winning run. But Phillies' center fielder
Richie Ashburn charged the ball all the way and fielded it on its
first hop. Ashburn then rifled a strike to catcher Stan Lopata to
cut Abrams down by twenty feet. With Snider and Reese moving up to second and third and only one out, the Dodgers still
had a golden opportunity to win the game.

Eddie Sawyer ordered Jackie Robinson walked intentionally, bringing Carl Furillo to the plate. He swung at Roberts' first pitch and lifted an infield pop in foul territory near first base that Waitkus caught for the second out. Still, the Dodgers had to like their chances, for the next batter was Gil Hodges, their leading home run hitter. Hodges barely missed his thirty-third of the season, but Del Ennis tracked down the opposite field shot in front of the scoreboard in right center. At that point, Ashburn remembered thinking, "I felt the game was ours. The Dodgers had their chance and blew it." Miraculously, the Phillies had averted disaster.

Then came one of those innings that only seem to happen to Brooklyn. Unlike Roberts, who had had an easy time of it, Newcombe had pitched in trouble all day. Going into the tenth, Newcombe had surrendered only eight hits, but as Roscoe McGowen of the *New York Times* wrote on the following day, "Newcombe . . . was rather soundly smacked, even when he got his man out." He was obviously tired as he faced leadoff batter Robin Roberts, who had talked Sawyer into letting him stay in the game. Roberts, a lifetime .167 hitter, lined a clean single to center. Eddie Waitkus followed with a single to put runners on first and second with no one out. With Ashburn, a brilliant bunter, at the plate, the Dodgers were poised for an attempted sacrifice. Ashburn did indeed bunt, but he hit it too hard and Roberts was forced at third. Up stepped Dick Sisler, who had pulled three inside fastballs into right field for singles off of Newcombe already. "Just a single," thought Ashburn. "That's all we need."

Newcombe got two strikes on Sisler, both on the outside part of the plate. "My wrist was bothering me," Sisler said. "If Newcombe had come inside with his fastball, he probably would've knocked the bat out of my hands." The next pitch "was a fastball, but outside a little," said Sisler. At this point, Sisler was convinced that Newcombe would not come into him, so he readied himself for another outside pitch. The pitch was high and on the outside part of the plate, and Sisler went with it, lifting a high fly to deep left-center. "As I ran toward first," Sisler told Arthur Daley in 1965, "I could see Abrams backing up toward the fence. I knew I'd hit the ball good but I didn't think I'd hit it hard enough to carry all the way. When I turned first, I saw it land in the seats for a three-run homer." It just cleared the fence, directly above the Disoway and Fisher, Inc. sign, only 348 feet from home plate. Roberts added, "We were all kind of surprised Sisler's ball carried into the seats. The ball was hit on a low trajectory, but it made it." This was more a pop fly than a tape measure homer, but as Sisler once said, "You still needed a ticket to catch it."

Roberts set the dazed Dodgers down in order in the bottom of the tenth, and the Phillies had won the pennant for the first time in thirty-five years. Ashburn said, "If there's such a thing as heaven, I'm sure that's what it will feel like to walk through the pearly gates. That moment, circling those bases, was my heaven on earth."

And the Dodgers once again found themselves in hell. It was the second time in three years that the Dodgers had lost the pennant on the last day of the season. Newcombe's valiant performance, as well as the Dodgers' nearly miraculous pennant drive, had gone for naught. Of his eleven losses, Newcombe had dropped the first and last games of the season to the Phillies. In the end, they were the only two that mattered.

Newcombe's performance in the regular season of 1951 showed no sign of being affected by Sisler's dramatic blast. He won twenty, lost only nine and tied for the league lead in strike-outs. When the Dodgers and Giants faced each other in the final game of the 1951 playoff, it was Don Newcombe who once again was trusted with the start. But Newcombe could not hold a 4-1 lead in the ninth, and although the name "Branca" is the one remembered, Newcombe must shoulder some of the blame as well.

In subsequent regular season play, Newcombe was as effective as ever, including 20-win seasons in 1955 and 1956. This was not the case, however, when Newcombe pitched in post-season play. Perhaps it is only coincidence, but Sisler's homer set into motion a series of failures in "big games" for Newcombe. Besides his failure in the ninth inning of the third game of the 1951 playoff, Newcombe was awful in World Series play. In three World Series, he never won a game and lost four with an ERA of over eight-and-a-half runs.

Unlike most of baseball's victims, nostalgia has been kind to Don Newcombe. But the truth is that Sisler's three-run homer was, ostensibly, as disastrous to the Dodgers as another three-run blast would be a year later. Posterity has forgotten all of that, and all of Newcombe's individual failure. Instead, Newcombe is fondly remembered as the greatest pitcher on that beloved Brooklyn team, perhaps the only team in history that was embraced and immortalized more in defeat than in victory. In reality, Newcombe threw the first dramatic gopher ball in the post-war era. But in that more important game played out in our memory, Don Newcombe will always be the ace of the Bums.

# 13

# THAT PITCH

AT 4:06 PM ON WEDNESDAY, October 3, 1951, Ralph Branca's life became forever frozen in time. It only took one-half of a second. Forevermore, the names Branca and Thomson would be wed. Branca's name became synonymous with "goat" as Bobby Thomson became destiny's darling with his pennant-winning home run. The homer is often referred to as the most dramatic home run ever hit, the climax of "The Miracle of Coogan's Bluff," and "The Shot Heard 'Round the World." But to Ralph Branca it is simply called "that pitch."

That Wednesday was not only the beginning of Branca's lifelong prison sentence, it was also the birth of the pitcher as scapegoat. Try to think of the most dramatic home runs hit before October 1951. Perhaps a few of Frank "Home Run" Baker's clouts in the World Series of 1911 come to mind. Or maybe Babe Ruth's record setting thirtieth home run in 1920. Certainly one thinks of Ruth's sixtieth in 1927. Then there was Gabby Hartnett's "Homer in the Gloamin' " in 1935 that clinched the pennant for the Chicago Cubs. Yet one is hard pressed to remember who threw those gopher balls. The names Rube Marquard (Baker), Christy Mathewson (Baker again), Tom Zachary (Ruth's sixtieth), and Mace Brown (Hartnett) do not leap immediately to mind. In fact, only one year before Branca's pitch, the Dodgers' ace Don Newcombe also surrendered a three-run homer on the final day of the season, but he is never remembered for it. Since Branca, however, the names of such pitchers evoke immediate recall. There is no question that the Branca gopher ball was the first, but hardly the last, in which the pitcher was labeled the goat.

There are many reasons why this home run has captured our imagination. Probably the most important was the fierce rivalry that had existed for over fifty years between the New York Giants and the Brooklyn Dodgers. No rivalry today can be called comparable. Add in the New York Yankees, and a second factor becomes clear: the three best teams in baseball played within three boroughs. Between 1947 and 1966, a twenty-season span, there was only one World Series that did not feature either the Yankees, the Giants, or the Dodgers (albeit, three times they were the Los Angeles Dodgers). During that span there were no less than seven subway series. Never will there again be a climate so conducive to baseball fever in any one city.

The 1951 season was perhaps the most exciting season New York baseball had ever known. The defending world champion Yankees, winners of two World Series in a row, were in the thick of a pennant race with Cleveland. In the National League, Brooklyn seemed sure to return to the Series after just barely missing an opportunity in their nearly miraculous pennant drive of 1950. The Dodgers had built up a thirteen-and-a-half game lead over the Giants by August 13. No one had ever overcome a lead of that size in baseball history.

But then the impossible began to happen, and of course, it was at the expense of the Brooklyn Dodgers. "Nobody mentioned winning the pennant in 1951," said Monte Irvin, who was the left fielder on the Giants that season. "Leo (Durocher) just said, 'Let's see how close we can come.' " Thanks in great measure to Irvin, who paced the NL with 121 runs batted in, the rejuvenated Giants won 37 of their last 44 games. By the final ten games of the season, the Dodgers still commanded their own destiny. They only had to win five to take the pennant no matter what the Giants did. But they won just four, and the two teams ended the season in a dead heat.

National League rules prescribed a best of three playoff, and this was the second playoff in NL history. (The first was five years earlier, with the loser being—who else?—the Brooklyn Dodgers.). Game one was played in the Polo Grounds on October 1. Ralph Branca, a 13-game winner that season, got the start for Chuck Dressen's Dodgers. But the Giants won a closely fought match, 4-2. The key hit in the game was a two-run homer off Branca by New York's third baseman, Bobby Thomson. The Dodgers came right back and shellacked the Giants 11-0 at Ebbets Field the following day. After 156 games, these two closest of teams geographically had the identical record: 97-59.

And after seven innings of the 157th and deciding game, they were tied, 1-1. A season can hardly be closer. Then Brooklyn scored three big runs in the top of the eighth, to take what looked to be a commanding 4-1 lead. With ace Don Newcombe on the mound, the pennant seemed as good as won.

But Newcombe was clearly tiring as he entered the bottom of the ninth. Perhaps he even recalled the pitch he threw one year earlier to Dick Sisler, which cost the Dodgers the pennant. For whatever reason, the Giants quickly mounted a rally. Shortstop Alvin Dark led off with a single, and right fielder Don Mueller followed with another single putting runners on first and second. After Clint Hartung replaced Mueller as a pinch runner, Monte Irvin uncharacteristically fouled out for the first out of the inning. But Whitey Lockman came through in the clutch by serving an outside pitch down the left field line for a double, scoring Dark and sending Hartung to third. The Giants now only needed one base hit to tie the game.

Dressen had seen enough of Newcombe. The previous year, Dressen's predecessor, Burt Shotton, stayed with Newcombe in the tenth inning against Sisler and the Phillies and lost the pennant. Dressen had a choice between two starting pitchers, Ralph Branca and Carl Erskine. Clem Labine was not available, having pitched nine innings the previous day, and Preacher Roe was hurt. "I had relieved on Saturday, and pitched the first playoff game on Monday," Branca said much later. "But Charlie Dressen had lost confidence in Clyde King, and I was in the bullpen with Carl Erskine." On his way to the mound, Dressen noticed that Erskine had bounced a wild curveball, so he decided to take his chances with Branca.

The batter was Bobby Thomson, who had won game one with that two-run homer off Branca. The Dodgers had first base open, but walking Thomson would have violated two unwritten rules of baseball: never put the potential winning run on base, and never walk a man if the on-deck batter is named Willie Mays. So the Dodger brain trust decided to go after Thomson.

The first pitch was a fastball, right down the heart of the plate, that Thomson took for strike one. About the next pitch, Dressen said later, "I used to whistle to Branca to tell him not to 'aim' the ball. He was all right as long as he threw. But when he aimed, it was curtains. He threw the first one down the middle for a strike. On the next pitch, I saw he was getting ready to aim it inside. I went to the fingers, but couldn't get them up there in time. The ball had left his hand."

Thomson swung at the pitch and sent a drive toward deep left field. Branca shouted at the ball frantically: "Sink, sink, sink!" Instead, it landed in about the third row of the bleachers. Branca stood silently gazing at Thomson's delerious jaunt around the bases. "Really, I was only wasting a fastball," Branca said much later. "High. Inside. He kind of guessed me on it. I was trying to set him up for a curve." That curve was never thrown.

Much was made of the fact that as Branca walked glumly toward the clubhouse, his uniform number, 13, "looked huge." But Branca says, "If I knew then what I know now, I might have worn number 77. But maybe then I would have been hit in the head with a line drive." The home run was a fitting and dramatic climax to the Giants' remarkable month-and-a-half-long comeback.

The reverberations of Thomson's blast were profound for Ralph Branca, and they echo to this very day. Before "that pitch" his record was a more than respectable 76-56. He was the starting pitcher in the first playoff game in NL history in 1946. In 1947, at the tender age of twenty-one, he had won 21 games.

But his pitching woes began as early as the following spring. Branca has always insisted that his career's decline was not connected to the Thomson home run, but this is true only to a point. During spring training of 1952, Branca was involved in a freak accident. He and two teammates were playing Monopoly when Branca's folding metal chair suddenly collapsed. Although he thought nothing about it at the time, he had actually thrown his pelvis out of line. Toward the end of the camp he had a severe case of asthma which prevented him from making his last two starts. But as the regular season opened he was back in the starting rotation. He even won his first two starts. "I was throwing the ball hard and winning," he told Rick Cerrone of *Baseball Quarterly*, in 1977. "The last thing I was thinking about was that fall in spring training. Remember, I was out to prove I could still pitch after the homer. I had a lot of pride."

Then, in his fourth start, Branca's effectiveness mysteriously disappeared. "I was a fast ball pitcher," he said, "and here I was throwing hard with my back out of line." In his eagerness to prove that the Thomson home run had had no effect on him, it cost him the 1952 season. "My only regret is that I couldn't pitch well in 1952," he said. "People said it was because of the home run." But, he added, "The only pressure was the pressure I put on myself."

If 1952 was a washout, 1953 was an unmitigated disaster for Branca. After only seven games and an 0-0 record, the Dodgers packed Branca off to the Detroit Tigers. The Tigers were a weak sister in the AL, and Branca did little to help them. His final record was 4-7 as the Tigers finished sixth in the eight-team league, forty games behind the first place Yankees.

After 17 games in 1954, sporting a 3-3 record, Branca was traded again, this time to the New York Yankees. But even joining the greatest dynasty of all time could not change Branca's hapless luck. He was 1-0 for the 1954 Yankees, who won 103 games, only to finish second to the Cleveland Indians. Branca must have felt cursed: 1954 was the only year between 1949 and 1959 that the Yankees failed to win the pennant. To add insult to injury, that ball club also has the sad distinction of being the winningest American League team not to appear in post-season play.

Branca's career was clearly winding down. He did not pitch at all in 1955, and after only one game with the Dodgers in 1956 he was released. On the day of his unconditional release, Arthur Daley of the *New York Times* wrote, "It [Thomson's home run] also seemed to knock Branca out of the pitching business. Maybe that blow really did not crush Ralph's spirit beyond repair, but he never again was the top flight performer he'd once been." His career record between 1952 and 1956 was a disappointing 12-12. "I only won 12 games after that, and sports-writers wrote that the home run ruined me," he said. "It wasn't the homer. It was a bad back and asthma."

Once his playing days were over, Branca began to experience a new ordeal, one that will more than likely haunt him until the grave. He was the first pitcher to wear goats' horns, and he is the pitcher who has worn them longer and more continuously than any other. He has remarked that not one day has passed without someone bringing up the Thomson home run. In the first few years, the notoriety was a blessing in disguise for Branca. "It never haunted me," he said in the early sixties. "Quite the opposite." His reasoning was that his niche in baseball history was secure and an otherwise forgettable career had been saved from oblivion. "Bobby and I once discussed why so many peo-ple remembered it when so many other big home runs seem to be forgotten," said Branca. "I guess it boils down to the inten-sity of that Brooklyn Dodger—New York Giant rivalry. There was never anything like that." In some cases, the home run has taken on the memorability of other huge historical events. Branca said, "What still amazes me is how guys tell me exactly what they were doing the instant Thomson hit it. It's like Pearl Har-bor and the day Kennedy was shot."

But by the early eighties Branca had become clearly fed up with his place in history. On the thirtieth anniversary of the "shot heard 'round the world" in 1981, Ira Berkow of the *New York Times* interviewed Branca. "I've lived with this thing for thirty years, and, really, I think it's about time it died," he said. By 1987, Branca sounded almost bitter. "For twenty-five years, I'd have to say I tolerated going through that ordeal. I had had it. I was tired of being introduced as being the guy who threw the home run pitch." At another time, he said pointedly, "A guy commits murder, and he gets pardoned after twenty years. I didn't get pardoned." What he had once referred to as a bless-ing in disguise had become a thorn in his side. "If I had my druthers, I'd have gotten him out even it if meant being forgot-ten," he said. "I really wish it never happened."

Perhaps "that pitch" did not affect Branca's subsequent ca-reer, as he insists. But no one can doubt it has profoundly shaped his life. "You know what bothers me more than anything?" he asked a few years ago. "It bothers me that nobody knows how good I was." But how can we remember a past that no longer exists? For Ralph Branca there is no past or future. There's just an eternal present where it will always be Wednesday, October 3, 1951, at 4:06 P.M.

# 14

# A Game
# of Redemption

THIS IS A TALE of two World Series, two pitches, and two moments, all bridged by one pitcher. It is a unique pair of moments in the history of the game. Only eight pitchers have had the opportunity to pitch in more than one seventh game of a World Series. Walter Johnson was the first. The Big Train won the seventh game of the 1924 Series in relief, but was battered in the last game of the 1925 Series. The feat remained unduplicated until the back-to-back Series pitting the New York Yankees and the Milwaukee Braves in 1957 and 1958. Lew Burdette was the hero in 1957, shutting the Yankees out for the title, but the Yankees enjoyed sweet revenge by defeating Burdette and the Braves 6-2 in the final game of the 1958 Series. Don Larsen started both of those games for the Yankees, and lasted two-and-a-third innings each time, taking the loss in 1957 and a no-decision in 1958. Hall-of-Famer Bob Gibson is the only hurler in major league history to pitch in three seventh games, winning in complete game performances for the Cardinals over the Yankees in 1964 and over the Red Sox in 1967 but then losing to the Tigers in 1968. Ken Holtzman appeared in the seventh game of both the 1972 and 1973 Series for Oakland, picking up a no-decision in 1972 and a win in 1973. Rollie Fingers also appeared in both of those games, making Holtzman and Fingers the only teammates to appear in two seventh games. And Joaquin Andujar won the seventh game for the 1982 Cardinals over the Brewers and then contributed mightily to the disintegration of the

Cardinals in the seventh game of the 1985 Series against the Royals.

But the story of Ralph Terry is without precedent and comparison. Terry, a right-handed control specialist for the New York Yankees of the early sixties, had the opportunity to win a seventh game only two years after losing one of the most heartbreaking games in major league history. Both of Terry's seventh game performances have been immortalized to become a part of baseball lore.

Before the 1960 World Series, Terry was a mediocre pitcher at best. He had split his first four seasons with the Yankees and the Kansas City Athletics, a team many referred to as the Yankees major league farm club. Terry wasn't the only ballplayer that the Yankees shipped off to Kansas City for fine-tuning in the late fifties. In any event, Terry's pre-1960 record stood at an inglorious 22-38. But he broke the .500 barrier for the first time in his career in 1960, going 10-8 with a respectable 3.40 ERA. Casey Stengel had enough faith in him to tab him as the starter of game four in what was shaping up as a wild World Series.

The first three games of the 1960 Series clearly showed the superiority of the Yankees' offense. The Pirates pulled out game one behind the fine pitching of Vernon Law and Elroy Face, but then the Yankees got their bats going and outscored the Bucs in the next two games 26-3. Terry faced Law at Yankee Stadium on October 9. He pitched adequately for six-and-a-third innings, but he took the loss in a tough 3-2 decision. "That was the time they made the bad call on Berra," Terry told Steve Jacobson in 1962. "There was bases full and one out in the first inning, and Yogi hit one off the end of the bat to third. Don Hoak stepped on third and the ump called Yogi out at first. He was a step past first."

That was Terry's one and only appearance until the seventh game, certainly one of the three or four greatest World Series games ever played. The Pirates had a 4-0 lead after two, but the Yankees took the lead with a four-run sixth. Heading into the bottom of the eighth, the Yanks held a 7-4 edge. Bill Virdon's double play ball took an unexpected bad hop and smashed Tony Kubek in the throat, knocking Kubek out of the game and keeping a Pirate rally intact. A few moments later, reserve catcher Hal Smith delivered a pinch three-run homer over the distant

Forbes Field wall, and the Pirates had a 9-7 lead. Ralph Terry was called in to put out the fire, and he retired one batter, Don Hoak, on a pop-up to end the Yankee nightmare.

The Bombers were not through. It is a testament to their greatness that they rallied for two runs in the top of the ninth to tie the contest. The central play in the rally was a brilliant base-running maneuver by Mickey Mantle, who with one out had drawn a walk. The Yankees had scored one run already, and Gil McDougald was the tying run at third. Yogi Berra hit a wicked one-hopper to Pirate first baseman Rocky Nelson who immediately stepped on first and then fired to second for the tag play on Mantle. But the Mick alertly realized that first base could be re-occupied, and after a fake toward second to draw the throw, he dove back into first safely, as McDougald crossed the plate with the Yankees ninth run.

Ralph Terry's first batter in the bottom of the ninth was Bill Mazeroski. Although he is now known mostly for this single at bat, Mazeroski was probably the greatest defensive second baseman in history. He was nicknamed "No Touch" because his uncanny ability to transfer the ball from his glove to his hand was too fast to be seen. As he approached the plate on that October afternoon, Mazeroski was telling himself to swing for the fences while thinking deep down that the Pirates were bound to lose.

Terry started Mazeroski off with a high slider, for ball one. "Johnny Blanchard, the Yankee catcher, went out to talk with Terry," said Mazeroski. "I figured he's telling him to get the ball down a little. And that's just what Terry did."

The pitch, a fastball, was just what Mazeroski was expecting. He swung and connected. "The instant the bat cracked against the ball I knew it was hit." Mazeroski said. "When I was going into second I saw the umpire giving the home run signal. I was too happy to think. It was a wonderful feeling." The delirious Pittsburgh crowd flooded the field and almost prevented Mazeroski from reaching home. As he touched the plate he remembered thinking "We've beaten the Yankees. We've beaten the great Yankees." It is still the only time that a World Championship was won by a home run in the home team's final at bat.

A dejected Ralph Terry walked slowly off the mound. The Yankee clubhouse was understandably glum, but no one was more downtrodden than Terry. "I felt terrible," he said later. "I felt like I had let the club down." Although many reports of the time implied that Casey Stengel placed the blame on Terry, nothing could be farther from the truth. "He was great," Terry said. "He sensed I felt guilty as hell and he was enough of a pro not to make it worse."

The pain did not let up for a long time. "I nearly caved in after Mazeroski hit that homer," Terry said in 1962. "I was in a state of shock for weeks." To get away from the negative publicity, Terry and his wife, newly married, took a vacation in Mexico. Even there he could not escape his fate. One morning he was browsing through a Spanish language newspaper. "I turned to the sports page anyway and there it was. The headlines, and they looked about a foot high, had two words I understood. One was Terry and the other was Mazeroski."

Terry's guilt was increased over the off-season. Yankee management used the loss in the seventh game as an excuse to fire Casey Stengel. The Yankee brass had felt Stengel was too old for quite a few seasons, but Casey had outwitted them by continually winning pennants. Casey's retort when he learned of his firing was characteristically brilliant and memorable. "I'll never make the mistake of being 70 again," he said. Terry took more than his share of the blame. "Naturally, I felt pretty bad about it."

For the next season "the name of Mazeroski hung like an albatross around Terry's neck," wrote Leonard Shecter in *Sport Magazine*. He was asked about the pitch so often that he finally blurted, "I'll bet if I live to be 100 somebody will mosey up to me and say 'What kind of pitch did you throw Mazeroski?' "

The fortunate thing for Terry was that he was a member of the New York Yankees in the early 1960s which virtually guaranteed a return trip to the World Series. The 1961 team was one of the greatest ballclubs of all time, and certainly the most power laden. With Roger Maris's record 61 leading the way, the Yankees broke all previous home run records. Maris and Mickey Mantle set the record for home runs by teammates: 115. Four other Yankees topped the 20-home-run mark, and the team total of 240 shattered the previous mark of 221 set by the 1947 New York Giants. The pitching was not too shabby either, led by Whitey Ford's 25-4 record and bolstered by Ralph Terry's

.842 winning percentage. The Detroit Tigers won 101 games that year and still lost the pennant by eight games.

The Cincinnati Reds had the dubious honor of facing this juggernaut in the 1961 Series. The Yankees lost only once in that fall classic, and the losing pitcher was Ralph Terry. He went seven innings in game two and was beaten by Joey Jay, 6-2. Then, with the Yankees leading three games to one, Terry started game five and had a chance to close the Series out. The Yankees staked him to a six-run lead, but Terry couldn't hold it and had to be replaced in the third. The final was 13-5 and the Yankees had reclaimed the title, but Terry was still winless.

Over that off-season, New York sportswriters began questioning Terry's "character" and "guts." He was branded as the guy who couldn't win the big one. Still, there was a distinct possibility that the Yankees could repeat as AL champions and give Terry another chance in 1962. The season went according to plan—the Yankees won the pennant by five games over the Twins. The NL representative was the San Francisco Giants making their first World Series appearance since abandoning New York. The Giants were coming off a grueling pennant battle with the arch rival Los Angeles Dodgers that was decided in a thrilling three-game playoff.

Whitey Ford started game one in Candlestick Park, and as usual, he got the Yankees off to a winning start. Terry, coming off his best season which included a 23-12 record, started game two against Jack Sanford. The two staged a classic pitcher's duel, with Terry allowing only six hits. One of them, however, was a Willie McCovey home run that fell just inside the right field foul pole, and the Giants won, 2-0. About the homer, Terry said after the game, "I thought, 'That's gotta go foul.' But it started to curve away from the line and the wind only blew it back a little. It was like a snake." At that point, Terry's World Series pitching line looked like this: five games, 23 innings pitched, 0-4 record. Asked about his seeming ineffectiveness, Terry angrily responded, "Gosh almighty! It was one of the best games I ever pitched." He then added, "I don't feel so bad about the starts. It was that relief job in Pittsburgh that bugs me."

In game five in New York, Terry got yet another chance to win a World Series game. Once again he would face Jack Sanford, but this time Terry won a closely fought contest, 5-3. That gave the Yankees a 3-2 game edge and sent the Series back to San Francisco. After a five day hiatus due to travelling and rain, the Giants finally beat Whitey Ford to force a seventh game.

To Terry's astonishment and joy, manager Ralph Houk handed him the ball. Before the game, Terry said, "No matter what happens today, I've got no kicks. The fact that I've been trusted with the seventh game after what happened in 1960 is the greatest thing that's happened to me. When Mazeroski hit that homer, I never thought I would get into a seventh game again. Even if I blow it today I won't brood. I'll still feel as though the club had faith in me."

For the third time, Jack Sanford was the opposing pitcher. And for the third time, the two staged a great duel. Terry had the greater command, but Sanford pitched out of jams all day. Terry said later, "We should have won it easy. We had the bases loaded twice with none out." From those two golden opportunities, the Yankees could squeeze only one run, and that was on a Tony Kubek double play grounder in the fifth.

Meanwhile, Terry was flirting with a perfect game. He retired the first seventeen batters to face him. Then with two out in the sixth, he surrendered a single to Sanford. "At the end of the inning," Terry said, "I walked past the plate and umpire Stan Landes said 'That S.O.B. A pitcher.' " But that harmless single and a triple to Willie McCovey would be all the offense the Giants could muster off of Terry until the ninth.

It was one of the most exciting ninth innings in World Series history. It looked like Terry would have an easy out when lead-off pinch hitter Matty Alou lifted a high pop fly in the vicinity of the Giants' dugout. "Just as Elston Howard was about to catch it, he was bumped," Terry said. "Howard told me he wasn't sure if it was Alvin Dark or Bob Nieman." The ball fell safely, giving Alou a new life. He promptly dragged a bunt for a single. The tying run was on.

Terry rebounded brilliantly, striking out both Felipe Alou and Chuck Hiller. But staring at Terry from the batter's box was Willie Mays. Mays slashed an opposite field double down the right field line. Right fielder Roger Maris made a brilliant hustling play to get the ball back to the infield and hold the fleet Alou at third. "That was what kept it from being a tie game,"

Terry said. Runners were on second and third, and Terry was still one out away from the title.

At bat now was Willie McCovey, who had hammered Terry for a home run and a triple already in the Series. Manager Ralph Houk came out to talk it over with Terry and Howard. "Ralph asked me how my control was," Terry said. To that point, Terry had walked no one. "Then he told me I could load 'em up and pitch to the next man," the right-handed hitting Orlando Cepeda. "I said I'd just as soon pitch to McCovey. I reasoned this way. If I walk the bases loaded, I've got to pitch too carefully to Cepeda. Now suppose I get behind on the count. I take two chances then. I might walk home the tying run or I might groove one too good and there would go the ball game. I got Cepeda out by jamming him. I didn't want to walk McCovey and then have to make an inside pitch on Cepeda. What if a pitch ticked his shirt?"

So, the decision was made—Terry vs. McCovey with the world championship on the line. Terry admitted he had a quick flashback of Mazeroski cross his mind. On a 1-1 pitch, Terry fired a fastball, and McCovey laced a torrid line smash in the direction of Bobby Richardson. Terry whipped his head around to follow the flight of the ball, but it was hit so hard that "there was no time to worry," said Terry. "I looked and there it was." If the ball had gone three inches in any other direction, the Giants would have won. But Richardson had caught it. "I couldn't believe it," Terry said. "I thought 'It's over!' "

It was indeed over. Not just the game, nor the World Series, but Terry's three-year ordeal was over. "I'm one for two in World Series' finishes," Terry said after the game. "That isn't bad. They balance out, so I'm even. I imagine no matter what I do I'll always be known for those two games in 1960 and 1962." Terry was fortunate to get the chance, but he made the most of what fortune provided. In doing what no one had done before or since, Terry proved that baseball is indeed a game of redemption.

# 15

# FOOTNOTE TO AN ASTERISK

TRACY STALLARD WAS a less than average pitcher who had the misfortune to play for some of the worst teams in major league history. His career record was a woeful 30-57, or a .345 winning percentage. Of course, he never had much support. He came up with the Boston Red Sox in 1960, and although the Red Sox were not terrible, they were not very good either. In his three years with Boston, Stallard posted a 2-7 mark in 48 games for a team that had a combined three-year winning percentage of .456. Stallard went from this mediocre group to the most beloved losers of recent times. In 1963 to 1964 he had the privilege of hurling for the Amazin' New York Mets, who dropped 220 games over those two seasons. His two-year-record was 16-37, but Stallard at least led the National League in one category during his stint with the Mets. Unfortunately, it was for games lost, 20, in 1964. When he finally got to pitch for a .500 team, the 1965 Cardinals, Stallard not too coincidentally had his best season, finishing 11-8. But he was 1-5 the following year and out of baseball by September. As Furman Bisher wrote, "Tracy Stallard was a widely unheralded pitcher. An established loser."

So it is rather ironic that a pitcher of such astonishing mediocrity has such a solid place in baseball legend. For it was Tracy Stallard who was on the mound when Roger Maris connected for his record sixty-first home run in 1961. It is difficult to decide if Stallard or Maris was more the victim of the record.

Maris was a quiet, unassuming man who happened to find himself in a ballpark that was perfectly suited for his home run swing. Most fans think that 1961 was a fluke year for Maris, but he was the Most Valuable Player in the American League in 1960, and he missed leading the AL in homers by only one. The year after setting the record, he finished fourth in home runs.

Throughout the summer of 1961, Maris and teammate Mickey Mantle were stalking the most famous record of all time: Babe Ruth's single-season home run mark of sixty, set thirty-four years before. Ruth had set his record in a 154-game schedule, while Maris and Mantle, in this first year of AL expansion, had 162 games in which to achieve this mark. Because of this, Commissioner Ford Frick, who was one of Babe Ruth's many ghostwriters, insisted on putting an asterisk next to Maris's or Mantle's record if either reached Ruth after game 154. On July 18, Frick handed down the following ruling. "A player who may have hit more than 60 home runs during his team's first 154 games would be recognized as having established a new record. However, if the player does not hit more than 60 until after his club has played 154 games, there would have to be some distinctive mark in the record book to show that Babe Ruth's record was set under the 154-game schedule, and that the other total was compiled while the 162-game schedule was in effect." However, Frick made no such "distinctive mark" ruling the following year when Maury Wills was threatening Ty Cobb's single-season stolen base record. No, it was the sacredness of the Babe that had to be protected.

Under the microscopic and often vicious eye of the newly born mass media, Maris relentlessly pushed toward the goal. It seemed that not only Frick was against him but the entire press corps, who preferred Mickey Mantle's affable humor to Maris's "surly" reticence. It all took its toll on Maris. Mantle said, "You could see him holding it all inside, see his hair falling out. He had rashes all over the place."

Even with the unbelievable pressure he was able to hit number fifty-nine off Milt Pappas in Baltimore on September 20, the 154th game of the year. "As I went around the bases, I was thinking, that's fifty-nine," Maris said. "I had two, maybe even three more shots at it." But he could not tie Ruth in his supposed last chance. Oliver Kuechle of *The Milwaukee Journal* cruelly wrote, "Maris's failure to break Babe Ruth's record of 60 homers in 154 games evokes no regret here. If the record is to be broken, it should be done by someone of greater baseball stature." Maris had lived with this sort of vituperativeness from reporters all season.

It took an additional six days to reach the goal that only one man had ever reached before. Maris finally hit number sixty off Jack Fisher in Yankee Stadium, in game 158. The Associated Press wrote, "Roger Maris blasted his 60th homer of the season Tuesday night, but it came four official games too late to officially tie Babe Ruth's 34-year-old record in 154 games." He was then held homerless through games 159, 160 and 161. If he was going to do it, Maris would have to break the record on the final day of the season.

It was October 1. The Boston Red Sox sent twenty-four-year-old Tracy Stallard to the mound. A rather small crowd of 23,154 eagerly awaited Maris's first at bat, but Stallard retired him on an easy fly ball to left. Maris wasn't the only one Stallard handled that day. He pitched one of the best games of his career. In seven innings work, he gave up only five hits, walked one, and struck out five. One of the five hits came in the third inning.

Maris was up for the second time in the bottom of the third. Stallard's first pitch was up and out of the strike zone. He fell behind 2-0 when he bounced one in front of the plate. The crowd thought Stallard might be pitching around Maris, so amid thunderous boos, Stallard came in with a fastball over the plate. Maris pulled a line drive into the right field porch, about 360 feet from home plate. Fittingly, it would be the only run the Yankees would score that day. Unfortunately for Stallard, Boston would not score any, and Maris's solo home run was the margin of victory.

In the post-game interview, Stallard at first sounded somewhat indignant toward reporters. "Listen, he hit 60 homers off somebody," he said. "I'm not feeling a bit bad. Listen, he hit a good pitch. It was a fastball on the inside part of the plate. I'm not a control pitcher," Stallard continued. "I just throw the ball. I put my best stuff against his best stuff and he hit my best stuff."

In the other clubhouse, Maris praised Stallard. "He was

man enough to pitch to me and try to get me out," Maris said. In the meantime Stallard had lost a little of his edge. He said humorously, "I don't know. I gave up 14 other home runs and nobody ever asked me about them."

For Tracy Stallard, being the victim eventually became a blessing. But for Roger Maris, being a hero was more like a curse. On his day of glory, he said, "No one knows how tired I am. I'm happy I got past 60, but I'm so tired." Many years later, Maris told Joseph Reichler, "It would have been a helluva lot more fun if I had never hit those sixty-one home runs. Some guys love the life of a celebrity. Some of them would have walked down Fifth Avenue in their Yankee uniform if they could. But all it brought me was headaches."

Tracy Stallard was an eminently forgettable pitcher, who, in a negative sort of way, happened to be in the right place at the right time. He finished out his career showing no sign that Maris's homer had affected him in any way. He was hardly a good pitcher before that home run, and he was not much better afterwards.

Thirteen years later, when Henry Aaron was chasing Babe Ruth's career home run record, a reporter asked Stallard how the pitcher who surrendered the record-breaking blast might be affected. "Times have changed," Stallard began. "It won't be as serious a thing now. I don't think the guy will be reminded about it as much as I have. But the guy had better have a sense of humor or he's going to make it real tough on himself." Then, perhaps thinking of his own fate, he added, "Personally, I think he should consider it an honor."

# 16

# CAMEO APPEARANCE

IT WAS THE MOST PUBLICIZED, scrutinized, and analyzed pursuit of a record in the history of sports. The usually reserved Henry Aaron, who preferred to do his work out of the spotlight, had been thrust into the eye of a media hurricane previously unheard of. Aaron, of course, was stalking the one unbreakable record in baseball, the sacred 714 career home run mark of Babe Ruth. That record was the one that Ruth himself thought safe—and with good reason. When Ruth died in 1948, his closest competitor was Jimmie Foxx, who had been retired for ten years, and Foxx was nearly 200 homers short at 534. Among active players in 1948, only Joe DiMaggio had over 300, and only Johnny Mize and Ted Williams had over 200. It seemed the Bambino could rest easy about that one.

But Aaron did not appear in a major league uniform until six years after Ruth's untimely death. Their styles could not have been more different. Ruth amassed his 714 home runs in a relatively short period of time, averaging a home run every 11.8 at bats. Aaron, on the other hand, was the picture of consistency, averaging a home run every 16.4 at bats. Ruth topped the magic 50 home run barrier a record four times; Aaron never reached it even once. Aaron's methodical attack included a staggering nineteen-year period where his home run total for a season never dipped below twenty-four. Slowly and surely, Aaron inched closer to the coveted 714.

As Aaron approached Ruth, he had to withstand more than

just the unflinching eye of the media. He received bundles of hate mail, very often beginning "Dear Nigger." Some of the letters threatened that if he tied or passed Ruth he would be shot from the stands. Slurs were thrown at him routinely from the crowd such as, "Hey nigger, you're no Babe Ruth," and "How come a nigger sonofabitch like you can make so much money and strike out so much?" Aaron kept the abuse to himself until his daughter Gaile, a student at Nashville's Fisk University, became the subject of threats as well. "I'm tired of it," he told a press conference, referring to the hate mail. "It's ridiculous and it's discouraging. I'm disappointed." From that day forward, letters began pouring in supporting Aaron in his quest. The positive letters from then on outnumbered the hate mail fifteen to one.

Entering the 1973 campaign, Aaron, now at age thirty-nine, was 41 homers shy of the record. Few gave him any chance of breaking the record in that season. Besides the intense pressure, no thirty-nine-year-old had ever reached 40 homers in a season before. Aaron came dramatically close—he became the first thirty-nine-year-old to hit 40 homers, but he still needed one more to tie Ruth.

The Hot Stove League of 1973-74 was abuzz with one primary topic—when would Aaron tie the record? Fans awaited impatiently for season schedules to be published to see where Aaron and the Braves would start the season. Finally it was out. It would be in Cincinnati, against the defending National League West champion Reds.

Early in spring training, Reds' manager Sparky Anderson intimated that if all went well, his opening day pitcher would be Jack Billingham. Billingham was the ace of the starting staff for the "Big Red Machine" in 1973. He won 19 games, which tied him for second in the league, and he led the NL in shutouts with seven. Toward the end of spring camp, Anderson decided it would indeed be Billingham on opening day.

In his personal matches with Henry Aaron, Billingham had surrendered four home runs. In 1969, Aaron hit career number 528 off Billingham when Jack was still pitching with the Houston Astros. Aaron also connected off Billingham for number 636 in September 1971 and number 641 in April 1972. His most recent home run off of Billingham was his 709th in September

1973. Billingham had nothing to be ashamed of; he was not even close to the man who surrendered the most home runs to Aaron. Hall of Famer Don Drysdale was victimized by Aaron seventeen times.

The Braves were slated to play a three-game weekend series in Riverfront Stadium in Cincinnati to open the season. The first game of the year was played on Friday, April 5. Billingham was besieged by reporters on the day of the game. Asked how he planned to pitch to Aaron, Billingham retorted, "Very carefully. I'll try to pitch him away from the plate like everybody else tries to do." He was asked if the media hype and huge opening day crowd would disturb him. "Everybody in the place is going to give him a standing ovation when he comes to bat," Billingham said. "My stomach is probably going to turn over a couple of times and I'll swallow hard. Then I'll have to get down to business." He commented that he had already considered the possibility that Aaron might hit the record-tying home run off of him. "It will just be another home run if he gets it off of me," he said. "It's not something that's going to haunt me the rest of my life." Billingham then made an imprecise prediction. "Nobody will remember it a month later."

Aaron came up for his first attempt to tie the record in the first inning. The crowd rose as one in anticipation and in appreciation as Aaron strode to the plate. After a few curves out of the strike zone and one fast ball called a strike, Billingham tried to sneak a fastball past Aaron. "I threw the ball and it didn't sink," he said after the game. "It came into him over the outside part of the plate." Aaron smashed the ball deep into the left-center field stands for the record-tying home run on his very first at bat of the season.

"I didn't watch him circle the bases," Billingham said to a sea of reporters after the game. "I'm afraid all I did was look at the ground. I said a few words to the ground. When I got to the dugout, I told Clay Carroll, 'Well, I got that over in a hurry.' "

"It was my mistake, and he hits mistakes," Billingham added. "You make a mistake pitching to Aaron and you do what everyone else does in the ballpark. You just turn your head and watch the ball sail over the fence." A little later, Billingham went to the Atlanta clubhouse to personally congratulate Aaron.

"Congratulations," he said to Aaron, "but why did you have to do it against me?"

After returning to the Reds' clubhouse, Billingham was asked if he was embarrassed. "Not at all," he replied immediately. "Aaron's a great hitter. He's going to get his homers. He deserves it. He's the greatest I've ever seen. It's unfortunate he hit it against me."

Giving up such a memorable home run had no apparent effect on Billingham's career. He won 19 games in 1973 and repeated the feat in 1974. In addition, more than half of his 145 career wins came after the home run pitch.

About two weeks after throwing his famous gopher ball, Billingham, maybe in an attempt to avoid notoriety, made another faulty prediction. "Aaron won't be remembered for his 714th homer and neither will I. He'll be remembered for the last homer he hits and that will be around 740 because I think he'll hit about 30 more before the season ends." Of course, Aaron ended his career with 755 while a member of the Milwaukee Brewers. But contrary to Billingham, the name of the pitcher who surrendered that final home run is not remembered for the feat. It was Dick Drago of the California Angels. The 714th, on the other hand, along with the name Jack Billingham, has its permanent niche in baseball immortality.

# 17

# NUMBER 44

HENRY AARON tied Babe Ruth's record of 714 home runs in his very first swing of 1974. Unlikely as it may sound, this presented the Atlanta Braves with a dilemma. The next two games, those of Saturday, April 6, and Sunday, April 7, were in Cincinnati's Riverfront Stadium. If Aaron broke the record in Cincinnati, Atlanta would lose its greatest drawing opportunity in recent memory. But if Aaron sat out those games, the Braves would weaken their chances of winning. The Braves decided to rest Aaron and hope he would break the mark in Atlanta on Monday.

But Commissioner Bowie Kuhn saw Aaron's benching as threatening the integrity of the game, and he had a point. If the object of a team is to win as many games as possible, and not to set personal records, then the Braves were misplacing their priorities. Kuhn therefore ordered Braves' manager Eddie Mathews to play Aaron in at least one of the two games in Cincinnati. Mathews considered ignoring the order, but Kuhn had promised a stiff fine and certain suspension if he did. Mathews acquiesced, and Aaron played in Sunday's game.

To Atlanta's, and possibly even Kuhn's delight, Aaron did not hit a home run in that game. That set the stage for Monday, April 8, 1974, in Fulton County Stadium. The pre-game media hype greatly overshadowed the previous Friday's game. Atlanta's opponent was the Los Angeles Dodgers, and the starting pitcher was Al Downing. The day before, when Aaron first heard that Downing would be pitching, he said, "I think I hit a couple of homers off Al." He was right. Aaron had connected off Downing twice in 1973 for numbers 676 and 693.

Downing tried to shrug off the significance of the game and his possible date with destiny. "This night will be no different from any other," he insisted doggedly. Before the game he said, "I don't want to be the guy to give up the home run. No pitcher likes to give up a home run. It could cost me the game." Then he smiled and added, "Of course, the ideal setting would be to have a six-run lead in the ninth . . ." When asked how he was dealing with the media blitz he responded honestly. "I don't think any pitcher can disregard the surroundings. I'll be aware of it. I'll probably even be thrilled by it," he said.

As game time approached, a reflective Al Downing made one more comment at his locker. "Look. If I throw 715 I'm not going to run and hide. There's no disgrace in that. On the other hand, I'm not going to run to the plate and congratulate him. It's a big home run for him, for the game, for the country. But not for me."

Aaron came to bat in the bottom of the first. Ironically, both he and Downing sported the same number on their backs. It was number 44 vs. number 44. Aaron never took his bat from his shoulders as Downing walked him amid thunderous boos.

Then Aaron came up again in the fourth inning. No one was out, and Darrell Evans was on first base. Fulton County Stadium was jammed with 53,775 fans, and an additional thirty-five million or so were watching on a special NBC prime time broadcast. Downing's first pitch, a low change-up, was taken for ball one. Again the crowd voiced its displeasure. The next pitch left Downing's hand and landed in baseball immortality. It was a fastball, right down the middle of the plate. Instead of its usual sinking motion, this fastball hung up and Aaron connected, sending it over the 385-foot marker in left center field and into the Braves' bullpen into the waiting hands of Braves' reliever Tom House. Henry Aaron, at age forty, at 9:07 p.m., April 8, 1974, had done the impossible.

At that moment, Downing showed no outward emotion whatsoever. He just watched the ball disappear over the fence. The ensuing celebration and ceremonies interrupted the game for eleven minutes, and Downing headed to the dugout to watch the proceedings. After things finally settled down, Downing headed back to the mound. But he was clearly shaken by all of the hoopla, and he could not relocate the strike zone. He walked the next two batters in succession, and manager Walter Alston relieved him.

Contrary to his pre-game comments, Downing did "run and hide," at least on this night. Instead of waiting around for post-game interviews, Downing left a tape recorded message in the Dodger clubhouse. It said, "Like a great hitter, when he picks his pitch he's pretty certain that's the pitch he's looking for and chances are he's going to hit it pretty good."

The following day, the Dodgers were still in Atlanta, and Downing talked freely with reporters about his previous night's infamy. "It was a fastball, down the upper part of the middle of the plate. The ball sailed up, and he hit it good. Any pitcher expects Aaron to hit a bad pitch good and he did." One reporter suggested that perhaps Downing "grooved" the pitch. "Groove it?" Downing responded in disbelief. "No, I didn't lay it in there for him. I was trying to get him to hit the sinker, going for the double play. I didn't get it down where I wanted it." Another interviewer asked if Downing had lost any sleep over the pitch. "I slept fine last night," he said, and laughingly added, "No dreams. No nightmares. No wild visions. No hallucinations." Walter Alston added, "He's a great hitter and a great person. I don't think our club should be ashamed that he hit the home run against us and Downing certainly shouldn't be embarrassed by giving it up. A lot of other pitchers contributed to that 715."

The immediate effects on Downing of surrendering the big pitch were negligible. A week later he insisted little had changed, "and I don't expect it to." By August, it was obvious that Downing was tired of the same questions. When asked for at least the thousandth time about the pitch to Aaron, he said curtly, "That's in the past. Let's talk about the future, the rest of the season."

Unfortunately, the remainder of the season would be disheartening for Downing. Even though the Dodgers won the West Division, Downing was a disappointing 5-6. In the post season, Downing pitched only a total of 7.2 innings and he was saddled with a loss in the World Series. His days as a major league starter were numbered, but he did manage to hang on as a middle reliever for three more seasons. He was released in 1977.

This is not to say that the home run by Aaron had anything to do with Downing's effectiveness as a pitcher. After all, Downing was already in the twilight of a stellar career spent contributing to winning teams including the Yankees in the early sixties and the Dodgers of the mid-seventies. To the end of his career he insisted the pitch to Aaron had never bothered him. "I don't dwell on anything," he once said. "It's part of the game and certainly no disgrace." He's right. All he did was throw a fastball that didn't sink. Henry Aaron supplied the magic.

# 18

# THE BUCKY DENT SYNDROME

THE SUMMER OF 1978 will live long and joyfully in the hearts of New York Yankee fans. It will not be forgotten too quickly by the snakebitten Boston Red Sox fans either. On July 10 of that year, Boston held a 14-game lead over the second-place Yankees, who were the defending world champions. The Red Sox were led by the league's eventual Most Valuable Player, Jim Rice, and it seemed that the American League East title was already theirs. But the Yankees staged one of the most unlikely and dramatic comebacks in baseball history. It ranks with the 1914 Braves and the 1951 Giants as one of the greatest pennant drives of all time. After a four-game sweep of Boston at Fenway Park in September, which both the Boston and New York press dubbed "The Boston Massacre," the Yankees were able to ride out the rest of the season and force a divisional tie with the Red Sox. This was only the second tie in the history of the AL, and Boston was involved in—and lost—the first one, exactly thirty years earlier. The scene was set for a near repeat of the 1951 Giants-Dodgers playoff: again, the pennant was up for grabs between fierce rivals; again, one team seemed blessed with exceedingly good fortune while the other desperately attempted to stave off total collapse. In the end, as in 1951, a three-run home run would decide a season. Because he was the man who threw that home run, the name of Mike Torrez will always be anathema in the city of Boston.

Up until that day, Mike Torrez's career could be viewed as

enormously fortunate. He was a well-travelled right-hander who put up eerily consistent numbers year after year. He began his career with the St. Louis Cardinals in their championship season of 1967, and in his first two seasons he was used mostly as a long reliever. In 1969, he reached a modicum of success as a starter, achieving a 10-4 record for the Cardinals. The following season, Torrez regressed to 8-10, and the Cardinals gave up on him. On the trading deadline of 1971, he was dealt to the Montreal Expos.

In Montreal Torrez began turning in what would become the typical Mike Torrez season—15 or 16 wins, 12 or 13 losses, 100 walks allowed, and an earned run average approaching 4.00. Although these are respectable numbers, they were not enough for Montreal, who sent Torrez and Ken Singleton to the Baltimore Orioles for Dave McNally and two throw-ins in December 1974.

It was one of those astute trades that Baltimore seemed to always make at that time, as Torrez went on to have his finest season in 1975. He won 20 games for the first and only time in his career, he led the AL with a .690 winning percentage, and he lowered his ERA to a career-best 3.06. Then, with the Orioles figuring that Torrez's value would never be higher, he was included with Don Baylor in a package to Oakland that brought Reggie Jackson to Baltimore. Torrez reverted to form in Oakland in 1976 with a record of 16-13, and he was traded to the New York Yankees the following April, his fifth team in eight seasons.

The Yankees took a gamble on Torrez, who was in the option year of his contract and able to declare free agency at year's end. He had his typical season plus one—he won seventeen and lost thirteen in the regular season. But it was in the World Series against the Los Angeles Dodgers that Torrez hit pay dirt. He pitched and won game three with a complete game performance. His second victory came in the Series' clinching game six, when he was the beneficiary of Reggie Jackson's historic three-home-run barrage off of three different Dodger pitchers. He had pitched and won two complete games with an ERA of only 2.50.

Free-agent right-handers who have proven they can win the ''big one'' are always at a premium. Torrez was wooed by most of the big-spending clubs, but Boston won him with a $2.7 million contract. Torrez clearly did not let the big bucks affect him. His totals at season's end were 16-13 with a 3.96 ERA.

At one point, however, Torrez and the Red Sox were on top of the world. By mid-August, Torrez was 15-7, and the Red Sox looked like sure pennant winners. But then the bottom fell out of both Torrez's and Boston's season. In his next six starts, Torrez was anything but Boston's stopper. Throughout September, Torrez dropped six straight decisions, and only a victory in his final start with four games left in the season broke his personal losing streak. Boston withstood a final Yankee surge and the season ended in a tie. Boston manager Don Zimmer named Torrez as the starting pitcher for the one-game playoff to be played in Fenway Park on October 3, 1978.

It would be nearly impossible to top the drama of that playoff game. The Red Sox had the unenviable task of facing Ron Guidry, who was close to unhittable that season. Guidry had already won 24 games while losing only three and was on his way to setting the single-season record for winning percentage. Even so, it was the Red Sox who drew first blood, on the strength of a second-inning home run by Carl Yastrzemski. The Bosox added another run and led 2-0 entering the seventh. Mike Torrez, pitching on only three days' rest, was brilliant to that point. He had allowed only two harmless hits all afternoon in outduelling Guidry.

But with one out in the seventh, the Yanks got a rally started. Both Chris Chambliss and Roy White singled, bringing up reserve second baseman Brian Doyle who was filling in for the injured Willie Randolph. Yankee manager Bob Lemon decided to try for the big inning and sent Jim Spencer up to pinch hit for the weak-hitting Doyle. But the strategy backfired as Spencer popped up on the infield for the second out.

That brought up ninth-place hitter, shortstop Bucky Dent. In his previous two at bats, Dent had been handled easily by Torrez, popping up both times. Lemon would have liked to pinch hit for Dent as well, but he had painted himself into a corner. He had no other lefty hitter to use, and more importantly, he had no middle infielders left with which to replace Dent. Lemon and the Yankees had to take their chances with Dent. As Dent said later, "I knew they wanted to pinch hit. But they couldn't."

The unlikeliest at bat in this unlikeliest of seasons was about to happen.

Torrez started Dent off with a fastball out of the strike zone. Dent then fouled the next pitch off of his left ankle, the same leg he had injured earlier in the season causing him to miss 40 games, and he collapsed at the plate writhing in pain. On-deck hitter Mickey Rivers took the opportunity to change Dent's bat, which the keen-eyed Rivers noticed was chipped. "I told the bat boy he should go switch the bat out of Dent's hand and give him this new bat," Rivers said.

The interruption became the key to the at bat. Up until that moment, Torrez said, "My concentration was great. He must have been down five minutes. They worked on the ankle and iced it and sprayed it, and you know what? My concentration got away from me. While Dent was down I lost my concentration."

Still, a now-injured Bucky Dent seemingly presented even less of a threat than a healthy one. Torrez and catcher Carlton "Pudge" Fisk agreed on a fastball on the inside part of the plate as a set-up pitch. But Torrez got too much of the plate, and Dent got all of the ball. His fly just barely cleared the Green Monster in left field for a three-run homer that gave the Yankees a lead they would not relinquish.

"It was a fastball inside," a dejected Torrez said after the game. "And perhaps I didn't get it in as far as I needed to. But it wasn't that bad a pitch. He hit it and I thought for sure it was a fly ball. Pudge told me the same thing. But the ball kept sailing and went over the wall. I was shocked. But there was nothing I could do about it."

Immediately following the home run, Torrez walked lead-off hitter Mickey Rivers. Manager Don Zimmer had seen enough, and Torrez was taken out of the ball game in favor of reliever Bob Stanley. With one swing, Dent had ended Torrez's and Boston's year.

In the Yankee clubhouse immediately after the game, Graig Nettles gave Torrez a little taste of what his life was to become. "It was a great game," said the gloating Nettles, "and I'm happy the Yankees won. But the thing that makes me happiest is that we did it by beating Torrez. We owed him that. He's been bad-mouthing us all year. We didn't appreciate that. If it wasn't for us, he wouldn't have been in the position to sign a 2.7 million dollar contract. Maybe this will teach him to keep his mouth shut."

That October, Torrez and his wife were watching the World Series on television. His wife burst into tears saying, "We shouldn't be watching it. We should be in it." Torrez responded, "Don't worry, honey. It's only one season. There'll be others. We'll be back in the World Series next year." To add insult to injury, nemesis Bucky Dent hit a torrid .417 and was named the World Series MVP.

But Torrez would never come as close to a World Series as he did on that October afternoon in 1978. To his credit, he tried doggedly to put Dent's home run behind him. In the spring of 1979 he repeated what was becoming a litany. "What happened to me last year was obviously disappointing," he told the incessant questioners. "I haven't forgotten Bucky Dent or the home run that beat us in the playoff. That's disappointing too. But it's one of those things that happen in baseball and it's behind me. You can't look back in this game. You must look ahead."

The question was still being raised in mid-season, by which time Torrez had about had it with the topic. "That's history," he would say. "I'm interested in what happens this year." And what happened in 1979 was nearly a carbon copy of the typical Torrez year: 16 wins, 13 losses. One disquieting note was that his ERA had ballooned to an unhealthy 4.50.

There were whispers, especially in Boston, that Torrez's pitching was affected by the Dent disaster. Throughout the season, it was obvious whom the Fenway faithful held responsible for the debacle of 1978. Having been frustrated yet again when victory seemed so near, the Boston fans unjustly vented their frustration on Mike Torrez.

In 1980, Torrez's record took a precipitous dive. He fell to a pathetic 9-16, and he became possibly the most unpopular player to wear a Boston uniform in any sport in recent times. In the strike-shortened season of 1981, however, he made a considerable comeback, posting a stellar 10-3 record. But it was a last hurrah. After a disappointing 9-9 season in 1982, Torrez was traded to the New York Mets, who in the early eighties were entrenched in the cellar of the NL East.

Haywood Sullivan, part-owner of the Red Sox, said in January 1983 at the time of the trade, "Mike was chastised in Boston as the symbol of the Bucky Dent Syndrome. It got to the point where it had to affect him, as strong as he is." After the trade, Torrez was featured in two articles in *The Sporting News*. One headline read "Stigma of '78 Homer Stays With Torrez," and the other article stated that "Torrez never really lived down throwing the three-run home run to Bucky Dent in the '78 playoff game with the New York Yankees."

Torrez admitted as much when he told Joseph Durso of the *New York Times* in early 1983, "It hangs in your mind. It's there. People don't let you forget it. For the next four years, they wouldn't let me forget it. They said George Steinbrenner must have sent me to Boston just to make them miserable there. But now it's something you have to accept."

The change of teams, towns, and leagues did nothing to help Torrez's fading pitching fortunes. In 1983 Torrez won ten games, but he lost a league-leading seventeen as well. Early in 1984 he achieved more notoriety by beaning and almost blinding the fine young shortstop of the Houston Astros, Dickie Thon. After nine games, the Mets released him, and he ended the season, and with it his career, in a second stint in Oakland. Torrez is remembered today invariably in connection with the names of two shortstops.

If it may be difficult to determine the exact repercussions of Bucky Dent's home run, it is rather evident that Mike Torrez was never the pitcher again that he was before that one pitch. It seems he lost more than a ball game and a pennant on that October afternoon. He was able to last six more seasons, but except for the aberration of 1981, he was not nearly as effective as in his earlier career. His unfair treatment by the fans of Boston, coupled with his own admission that the home run continued to haunt him, was a one-two punch that for all intents and purposes finished Torrez as a major league pitcher. He was never able to overcome the only case on record of the dreaded Bucky Dent Syndrome.

# 19

# THE LONG GOODBYE

TOM NIEDENFUER has been in someone else's shadow for his entire career. At first, it was the shadow of Goose Gossage, to whom he was compared when he first arrived in professional baseball in the Los Angeles Dodgers organization. Then it was the shadow of Steve Howe, who at the time was Los Angeles's bullpen closer. But the one shadow he has had the hardest time escaping is Jack Clark's. Clark hit a Niedenfuer fast ball into Dodger Stadium's left center field pavilion for a three-run homer that powered the St. Louis Cardinals into a World Series and sent home for the winter the Dodger fans who had not left during the usual seventh inning early exit. For five years he tried to come back into his own light, and, for at least one brief moment, he did so.

In the free agent draft of 1977, Tom Niedenfuer, who had just graduated from high school, was the next to last selection, number 761. He chose not to sign and went to Washington State University instead. It was not until 1980 that he signed with the Dodgers' system as a free agent. He was a six-foot five-inch, 225-pound hard throwing right-hander who became known for his ability to completely overpower batters. Ducky LeJohn, his manager at San Antonio in 1981, said, "For a first year player in pro ball, Tom has shown so much stamina and poise it's unbelievable. He'll come into tight situations and just blow hitters away for strikeouts." His record in San Antonio was 13-3 with a 1.80 earned run average and five saves, which earned him a promotion to the big club two days after his twenty-second birthday in August.

Immediately, major league beat writers began comparing him to Goose Gossage, which by that time had become routine for Niedenfuer. "Ever since I signed people have compared me with Gossage. That's certainly a compliment, but I'm sure it's because I look like him, not because I throw like him. If I do half as well as Gossage, I'd certainly be pleased." One day after joining the Dodgers, on August 16, he won his first big league game. Manager Tommy Lasorda gave him the middle reliever job, and Niedenfuer responded with three wins and two saves in 25 innings pitched. In the post-season, he pitched in four games, including five innings without allowing a run in the Dodgers' World Series victory over the Yankees.

Niedenfuer continued to develop in 1982, despite facing serious setbacks. In the early part of the season, Niedenfuer choked on a piece of meat so badly that he needed to be revived. On June 30, he was involved in a controversial bean ball war with the San Diego Padres, including a supposed "order" from manager Tommy Lasorda to hit Joe Lefebvre. Lasorda has always denied the charge, but it was Niedenfuer who was slapped with a $500 fine. Finally, on August 30, he suffered a fainting spell because of an ear infection. Niedenfuer overcame these obstacles to post better numbers than the year before. He lowered his ERA more than a full run to 2.71, and he increased his save total from two to nine.

His role seemed defined as the Dodgers entered the 1983 campaign. With 1980 Rookie-of-the-Year Steve Howe firmly entrenched as the team's closer, Niedenfuer was content as Howe's set-up man. But when Howe began to experience his much publicized substance abuse troubles in May and checked into a rehabilitation center, Niedenfuer and a castoff named Dave Stewart were given the chance to share the closer role. It was Niedenfuer who rose to the challenge. From May until September, he was virtually unhittable, going seventy and two-thirds innings and allowing only 11 earned runs, a 1.40 ERA. Lasorda said, "He's a tremendous relief pitcher and I'd hate to think where we'd be if it wasn't for him. When Howe went out, Tom Niedenfuer saved us. He has a chance to be one of the very best relievers in the game."

Niedenfuer credited his success in 1983 to a number of factors. First of all, it was an injury free year. Second, he was no longer in awe of the major leagues, now that he was in his third season and had even pitched in a World Series. Third, his concentration was much more focused. "I listen to a hypnotic tape about two or three times a week," he told Joe McDonnell. "It's a pitching tape, and it helps me relax and concentrate more when I'm out on the mound." With this new-found consistency, Niedenfuer earned the closer job for the 1984 season.

But then a series of unrelated problems began to sap Niedenfuer's effectiveness. During 1984, his development was curtailed by two separate serious injuries. He landed on the disabled list twice, once for arm and shoulder problems and once for kidney stones. He appeared in only 33 games, exactly half of the number from the year before, and heading into the 1985 season he had lost his role as bullpen ace to Ken Howell.

As the season progressed, however, Lasorda began going to Niedenfuer more and more. In July, Niedenfuer said, "I feel as good as I've ever felt," and then he went out and proved it. In 1985 he set personal bests in wins (7), saves (19), strikeouts (102), and innings pitched (106.1). The Dodgers found themselves in a four-team pennant race with the Reds, Astros, and Padres, but they staved off a run by the Reds to win the division by four-and-a-half games. Their opponents in the National League Championship Series were the St. Louis Cardinals.

In game one at Dodger Stadium, Fernando Valenzuela held the Cardinals to one run in six-and-a-third innings. Niedenfuer had his best game of the series, shutting the Cardinals down over two and two-thirds to gain a save and give the Dodgers a 1-0 series lead. The Dodgers trounced the Cards 8-2 the following day and the series moved to Busch Stadium for three games. Obviously, the Cardinals felt more comfortable in the spacious confines of Busch as they took games three and four by the scores of 4-2 and 12-2, respectively.

The series was knotted at two. When Niedenfuer came to the mound in the bottom of the ninth inning of game five, the score was also knotted at two. With one out, Ozzie Smith came to the plate, batting from the left side. Smith had not homered from that side of the plate in his entire career, but he chose this opportune moment to do so and gave the Cardinals the game with one swing of the bat.

Niedenfuer said he received a call that night from Terry Forster, an ex-Dodger pitcher who surrendered a damaging home run to Joe Morgan of the Giants on the last day of the 1982 season. "After Ozzie's homer, he called and told me not to worry, that his was worse," said Niedenfuer. But the Dodgers had their backs to the walls as the NLCS headed back to Los Angeles, with the Dodgers needing a sweep to head to the World Series.

It looked like they would have no trouble winning the sixth game. They held a 4-1 lead in the seventh, but the Cardinals rallied to tie it in the top of that frame. Lasorda called on Niedenfuer to put out the fire, and he did so by striking out Jack Clark. He pitched a scoreless eighth, and he was given a chance to win the ball game when Mike Marshall hit a dramatic solo homer in the bottom of the eighth to give the Dodgers a slim one-run lead.

Niedenfuer got into trouble quickly, and runners were on second and third with two out. At the plate was the fearsome Jack Clark, who Niedenfuer had handled in the seventh. Lasorda went to the mound and discussed strategy. The Dodgers had the option of walking Clark and pitching to a young Andy Van Slyke, a left-handed batter, but Lasorda decided to take his chances with the righty hitting Clark. Few managerial decisions have been second-guessed more. On the first pitch, Clark deposited the ball some 450 feet from home plate in the left field pavilion to give the Cards a two-run lead. The stunned Dodgers went quietly in their half of the ninth.

It was Niedenfuer's second loss in the series, both by home runs in the ninth inning. His line for the NLCS was woeful—an 0-2 record in 5.2 innings with a 6.35 ERA. "It's not the highlight of my career," he told *The Sporting News* referring to Clark's smash. "I'm sure I'll think about it all winter. Who wouldn't? But it goes with the territory. That's what short relief is all about."

Once the initial shock had passed, Niedenfuer dealt with his infamy humorously. He received a second call from Forster. "This time he said, 'Thanks, you just passed me.' " He told *The Sporting News* in January 1986, "It was tough for the first four or five days, but I think I've handled it pretty well. I know one thing: I'm the star of the highlight film. I'm in the last scene, anyway, that's for sure." Like so many other pitchers who have been in the same position, Niedenfuer tried valiantly to put the home run behind him. "It's over, it's done," he said, echoing the cliches spouted by the likes of Ralph Branca and Mike Torrez. "The only thing I can do now is go out and pitch this season."

But by late May, he had not seemed to be over the pitch. He got off to a poor start but denied his weak performance had anything to do with Clark's home run. "It's been awfully tough," he said in May. "It's been a bad six weeks. I'm on a low." He was quick to add, "That [Clark's homer] has nothing to do with this. I'm throwing hard, but I have no consistency." By midseason some were referring to him as Tom "Why-did-Lasorda-make-me-pitch-to-Jack-Clark" Niedenfuer. Baseball analyst Tim McCarver questioned how much of a "hangover" effect the pitch to Clark was having on him. For whatever reason, his 1986 season was a disappointment. He saved only 11 games, and his ERA jumped a full run. His name was in virtually every trade rumor that concerned the Dodgers.

In early 1987, one rumor proved to be true. After fifteen games with the Dodgers, Niedenfuer was traded to the Baltimore Orioles, where he hoped he could start anew. His save totals in 1987 improved slightly but his ERA jumped yet another run to 4.46. Gordon Verrell wrote, "Some critics suggested that he had lost his velocity; others hinted that he had lost it, period." In 1988 Niedenfuer was in his option year, but he had little chance to put up great numbers on that Oriole team, which set a major league record by dropping its first 21 games. He pitched well considering the circumstances, and the Seattle Mariners signed him as a free agent to a two-year contract for a total of $1.75 million.

Niedenfuer hit the nadir of his career in Seattle. He won none, lost three, saved none, and blew the only three save opportunities he was given. In addition he broke a bone in his left hand and was sent to the minor leagues for rehabilitation, his first visit to the minors since he was twenty-one-years old. For the pitching starved Mariners, he only threw 36.1 innings. "I know some people will think I'm the most overpaid player in baseball," said Niedenfuer, who received $22,222 per inning pitched. "It has been a frustrating year for me. I'm not crying about it and saying I want out of here, but I don't see how I fit in. The way I was used . . . they can get a rookie to do that and they can pay him the minimum."

Niedenfuer insisted toward the end of 1989 that he was not washed up at the age of thirty. "Until this year," he said, "I had six years of double figures (in saves). You don't lose that ability overnight."

Just before the end of the 1990 training camp, the Mariners decided that they were not going to wait for Niedenfuer's ability to return. Although it meant they would have to eat his $900,000 contract, the Mariners still chose to release Niedenfuer unconditionally. A few weeks later he was picked up for the waiver price by the St. Louis Cardinals. Whitey Herzog quipped, "We figured we owed it to him after all he did for us."

The acquisition of Niedenfuer was successful for all concerned. Herzog began using him in the middle relief role, and Niedenfuer responded well. Although his won-lost record was a dismal 0-6, he led the Cardinals in appearances, and his ERA was a sparkling 2.46. He even recorded his first save since 1988.

On November 5, 1990, however, Niedenfuer was declared a free agent. He remained unsigned for the 1991 season. At the age of only thirty-one, Niedenfuer was out of baseball. But his final winless season achieved a victory of a different sort. Although he never fulfilled the promise of the mid-eighties, when Tommy Lasorda touted him as possibly one of the best relievers in the game, he had finally made it all the way back out of the confinement of those shadows.

# 20

# DEMON ON THE MOUND

THE NEEDLESS DEATH of Donnie Moore is one of the most tragic events in recent years in American sports. Although it would be ludicrous to imply that a home run pitch alone was responsible for his suicide, there is quite a bit of evidence that his mental collapse commenced with just such a pitch. The tendency may be to overemphasize the importance of Moore's gopher ball, but the facts seem to point to that October afternoon when the California Angels were oh so close to clinching the American League West title. In the final analysis, however, Moore was a victim not of a Dave Henderson home run, but of inner demons of which we will always remain painfully ignorant.

Donnie Moore was not always in the spotlight. A native of Lubbock, Tex., Moore's major league debut was with the Chicago Cubs in 1975. In the course of four seasons with the Cubs, primarily as a middle reliever, he compiled an undistinguished record of 14-13 with five saves. His yearly earned run average always topped 4.00, and it reached a high of 5.18 in his last season with the Cubs. After being traded to St. Louis, Moore's career seemed on the skids. In 1980 he appeared in only eleven games, and his ERA jumped almost a full run. The Cardinals demoted him to Louisville and then traded him to the Milwaukee Brewers in time for the strike-shortened pennant drive of 1981. His problems did not abate. The Brewers used him in only three games, and packed him back to St. Louis.

Moore's first break came in February 1982, when he was

traded to the Atlanta Braves. He stayed with the big club all season, winning three and losing one in Atlanta's last division winning year. Manager Joe Torre gave Moore additional opportunities to pitch in 1983, and by late 1984 he had become one of
the bullpen closers, finishing with 16 saves.

Yet Atlanta must have lost faith in Moore for they left him
unprotected in the free-agent compensation draft. When the California Angels lost outfielder Fred Lynn to Baltimore, they
claimed Moore from the pool. Angels' manager Gene Mauch
gave Moore every chance to prove himself as the Angels' primary closer, and this time Moore took full advantage of the opportunity. The 1985 season was Moore's finest by a long shot.
He saved 31 games to set an Angels' record, as the Angels fell
short of the West Division title by only one game to the eventual world champion Kansas City Royals.

The Angels' management rewarded Moore with a three-year
contract paying him $875,000 per annum. Moore returned the
favor with interest. Although his 21 saves were down from his
1985 total, he was still an integral member of the division-winning Angel team of 1986, their first title in four seasons.

Which brings us to the 1986 American League Championship Series and what proved to be the pivotal moment in Donnie Moore's career, and ultimately, his life. The Angels, under
the precarious leadership of Gene Mauch, had built a commanding three-games-to-one lead over the Boston Red Sox. Game
five was played on October 12 in Anaheim Stadium. Entering
the ninth inning, the Angels held a 5-2 lead and their ace, Mike
Witt, was on the mound. But then, after two were out, their
season unravelled like a cheap suit. Ex-Angel Don Baylor hit a
home run off Witt with a man on, to close the gap to 5-4.
Mauch replaced Witt with left-handed reliever Gary Lucas to
get the platoon advantage over lefty hitting Rich Gedman. Lucas
promptly hit Gedman and right-handed Dave Henderson came
to the plate.

Mauch brought in the Angels' bullpen ace, Donnie Moore.
On a 2-2 pitch, Moore came in with a fastball. Henderson said,
"That was the pitch I was looking for, but I didn't get ahold of
it." Instead, Henderson just got a piece of it to stay alive. Moore
decided that since he had a pitch to work with, he would not
throw Henderson another fastball. His next delivery was a fork-

ball, low and outside of the strike zone. Henderson was fooled by the pitch, but with two strikes, he took a desperation swing. "When I hit it," Henderson said, "I knew it was gone." Henderson's home run barely cleared the left-center field wall to put the Red Sox ahead, 6-5. For once it was the Red Sox who had been the beneficiaries of a miracle.

That home run only put Boston ahead, however. Somehow, the Angels rebounded from the disaster to tie the game in the bottom of the ninth. California even had the bases filled with one out, but they could not put Boston away in the regulation nine. The Red Sox eventually won in eleven innings, forcing game six to be played at Fenway Park. After victories in games six and seven, the Red Sox headed to an eerily similar destiny in the World Series against the New York Mets.

The effect of losing the pennant when it was only one pitch away was devastating on the California Angels. General manager Mike Port said, "At a time like this you can do two things— quit or go at it again. As an organization maybe we're on the right track. In 1985 we were one game short. This time, we were one strike short." Gene Mauch had presided over his third cataclysmic collapse, the first being the infamous 1964 Philadelphia Phillies and the second in 1982 when the Angels became the first team to lose the pennant when leading two games to none in the ALCS. Mauch described the first few weeks after losing the playoffs to Dave Anderson of the New York Times: "Every morning when I woke up, I felt it in my stomach. Like a hot dagger in my belly button." He could not avert a disastrous 1987 season which saw the Angels become the first team since the 1914-15 Philadelphia Athletics to plummet from first to last place in successive seasons. Mauch retired in disgust near the end of the season and was replaced by Cookie Rojas.

But no one was more devastated than Donnie Moore. He irrationally held himself responsible for the loss of the game and the pennant. Because of this, and also because of a sore shoulder and an injured rib cage that had afflicted him during the second half of 1986, Moore got off to a horrendous start in 1987.

California Angels' fans, however, were ignorant of Moore's troubles, and they chose only to remember the previous October. They booed Moore mercilessly during his struggles in early 1987. Mauch said, "I don't know if they're booing him or booing me for putting him out there." Eventually, Moore's chronic shoulder and rib problems landed him on the disabled list, and he saved just five games all season. The once cheerful Moore had become increasingly pessimistic.

While he was on the disabled list, it was discovered that Moore had been pitching with a bone spur in his lower back for quite some time as well. The painful spur was removed surgically in the off-season of 1987-1988, and Moore's comeback, if he could muster one, included the gargantuan tasks of overcoming back surgery, arm problems, a rib injury, and hostile fans. "I feel pretty good," he was still able to say in spring training of 1988. "I just have to try to get back in the swing of things." But his 1988 season began as terribly as the previous year had. After blowing six save opportunities in a row, he finally recorded his first save on April 27. "Everyone else may have lost confidence in me," he said at the time, "but I haven't and Cookie Rojas hasn't." Rojas stood firmly behind Moore. "Moore is what I've got and that's what I've got to use," said Rojas. "Holding him back would mean I have no confidence in him. He's had his bad days, but he'll have many more good ones." Unfortunately, Rojas's prediction proved false. Moore's chronic injuries placed him on and off the disabled list all year, and the Angels decided to release him unconditionally in September. Less than two years earlier he was the closer on a division-winning team. Now, Moore found himself out of work.

In May of 1989, the Kansas City Royals decided to take a chance on Moore and assigned him to their Triple A farm team in Omaha. At first, Moore responded well, pitching strongly in his first four performances. But then he pitched poorly in three successive appearances. His final game, on June 11, was particularly bad. He lasted only one and one-third innings and gave up three runs on five hits. He was released by Omaha the next day.

While his professional life was dissolving, Moore's personal life was disintegrating as well. In the middle of June his wife, Tonya, moved out of their beautiful ranch home in a wealthy section of Anaheim. Although it is unclear why the estrangement occurred at this time, one bone of contention was that Moore had decided he wanted to leave Los Angeles for the quiet life of his native Lubbock. When his wife returned with their three children for a visit on July 18, the couple became embroiled in an argument which turned increasingly violent. At one point, Tonya went outside and told her children that Moore had hit her.

Then, Moore brought a .45-caliber semi-automatic pistol into the kitchen. He shot his wife three times, critically wounding her, and then he turned the gun on himself, firing one bullet through his brain. His wife was rushed to the hospital and survived. But Donnie Moore, aged thirty-five, was dead.

Over the next few days, friends and teammates attempted to come to grips with the senselessness of Moore's death. His teammate Doug DeCinces and his agent, David Pinter, both stressed Moore's inability to forget about that pitch to Henderson and how it haunted him. His teammate Brian Downing suggested angrily that the haunting was not all self-inflicted. When he was told about Moore's suicide, Downing lashed out at the press and the California Angels' fans. "Everything revolved around one _____ pitch. You destroyed a man's life over one pitch. The guy was not the same after that. You buried the guy. He was never treated fairly. He wasn't given credit for all the good things he did. Nobody was sympathetic. It was always 'He's jaking it, he's fooling around.' He was a very sensitive guy. I never, ever saw the guy be credited for getting us into the playoffs because all you ever read about was one _____ pitch."

Of course, Moore's death cannot be attributed solely to that pitch he surrendered on October 12, 1986. But that home run set in motion circumstances that overwhelmed a confused and befuddled Donnie Moore. Added to his injuries and combined with the unjust insults heaped on him by Angels' fans, Moore, so recently the star reliever, had found his abilities had deserted him. Omaha Royals' broadcaster Frank Adkisson suggested, "Maybe it was sinking in on him that he wasn't able to pitch any more." Brian Downing said, "That has to be a tough job, going from on top of the world to the bottom in a split second. Unfortunately, he never got back to the top."

They say that unlike most of us, athletes must experience death twice. The first time is when their magnificent bodies have betrayed them to the point that they must quit the games they love. Both of Donnie Moore's deaths were much too sudden.

# Shadows Descend:
# Abrupt and Final Endings

# 21

# AN EXCELLENT
# HEAVY BATSMAN

DAVID ORR is not a name known to most followers of baseball today. For one thing, he played in the wrong century—the
nineteenth—to readily come to mind. He also played for most
of his career in the wrong league—the American Association—
which only existed from 1882 to 1891. He even spent the majority of his career on the wrong team—the New York Metropolitans—in a city dominated by the National League New York
Gothams. But one more factor has contributed to David Orr's
obscurity today, a factor probably more important than the other
three: His career was cut short in 1890 after only eight seasons
when at the age of thirty-one he suffered a stroke. It had been a
very impressive career to that point.

Orr's professional career began in earnest late in 1883 when
he was called up to the New York Metropolitans from Hartford
to fill the place in the roster left by the injured outfielder, John
O'Rourke. He was an immediate success. *The New York Clipper*
of June 14, 1884, reported that Orr's "hard hitting against the
Columbus Club September 27 and 28, when he made six safe
hits, including two home runs, two three-basers and a two-bagger,
materially helped to establish his reputation, and secured for
him a permanent place in the Metropolitan team."

Orr played in only thirteen games for the Metropolitans
that season, but batted .320 with two home runs, three triples,
and four doubles in only 53 at bats for a .604 slugging percentage. *The New York Clipper* noted that "there are few instances of

a player attaining such an exceptional batting record in his first season."

The Metropolitans finished in fourth place that year, but that was still better than their hometown rivals, the Gothams, who finished sixth in the National League. In the post-season City Series that year, the Metropolitans beat the Gothams two games to one with one tie. In the only game the Gothams won— the fourth—they bombed out the Metropolitans' starting pitcher, Jack Lynch, with 12 runs in the first three innings. David Orr then came in to stop the flood, and though the Metropolitans lost 15-3, he only gave up three safe hits in six innings. It was a successful finish to a successful year.

The next year proved even more successful for Orr and the Metropolitans. Dave took his place as the everyday starting first baseman and batted .354 to lead the league in his first full season. He also led the league in hits with 162 and total bases with 247, placed third in doubles with thirty-two, third in home runs with nine and third in slugging average with .539. He also placed second at his position in putouts with 1161. (These numbers are according to *Total Baseball*. *The Baseball Encyclopedia*, 8th ed., gives the batting crown to Harry Stovey with a .404 average, but *Total Baseball* places Stovey fourth at .326. *The Baseball Encyclopedia* also gives Stovey the total bases crown.) *The New York Clipper* sized him up as a complete ballplayer and worthy of comparison to the greatest names in the game: "Orr . . . has proved himself—both in fielding and batting—to be a decided acquisition. He is an excellent heavy batsman, and promises in time to equal even Anson and Brouthers in handling the ash."

Led by Orr's bat and Tim Keefe's pitching, the Metropolitans went on to win the league championship with a .701 percentage. In a post-season contest generally accepted as the first World Series, the Metropolitans met the National League champion Providence Grays to crown the "Champions of the World." The Metropolitans carried only two pitchers that year, but that wasn't unusual in that era. Each pitcher, Tim Keefe and Jack Lynch, won 37 games. The Grays carried only two pitchers, that year, too, but not together. One of those pitchers, Charlie Sweeney, set a record on June 7, 1884, that stood for over a hundred years when he struck out nineteen batters in one game. By mid-July, however, Sweeney was kicked off the team and out of the league for his drunk and disorderly behavior. After winning 17 games for the Grays, Sweeney went on to win twenty-four more that year for the St. Louis Club in the Union Association.

The loss of Sweeney left Providence in a precarious and embarrassing position. One week before dismissing Sweeney, the Grays manager, Frank Bancroft, had suspended his other pitcher, Charles Radbourne. With Sweeney (the cause of Radbourne's discontent) gone, Radbourne offered to return and pitch all the remaining games, which he did, winning twenty-six of twenty-eight. In all, Radbourne pitched 679 innings that year, won 60 games, posted a 1.38 ERA and earned the nickname "Old Hoss."

In the World Series, Old Hoss won all three games against the Metropolitans. Tim Keefe pitched against him in the first two games and umpired the third (perhaps to get a better look at what all his teammates were missing). Orr managed only one hit, a single, in ten at-bats against Radbourne, but then Hoss only gave up eleven hits in all and only one extra-base hit, a double. The New York team batted only .143 against him, and Orr batted only .111. It was a rare occasion that Orr not only batted so poorly but also batted so poorly in relation to the rest of his team. In fact, in his eight years of major league baseball, Orr always led his team in batting—often hitting close to 100 points or more above the league average on a team that batted below it.

The performance of Radbourne in 1884 dramatically illustrated the dominance one player could exert on the game in that early era. Orr and the Metropolitans were given another lesson in the difference one player could make when Tim Keefe jumped to the National League Gothams (along with manager Jim Mutrie) in 1885. The Metropolitans tumbled to seventh place where they remained for three years before dropping out of the league completely. Orr found himself surrounded by low .200 hitters, but it did not affect his performance. He also showed that in some circumstances one player might make no difference at all.

In 1885, Orr led the league in triples, with twenty-one, and slugging average, with .543. He also placed second in batting average (.342), fifth in home runs (6), third in doubles (29), and third in total bases (241).

In 1886, he enjoyed perhaps his finest season. He led the

league in five offensive categories: hits (193), triples (31), home runs (7), slugging (.527), and total bases (301). His batting average of .338 placed him third, just .004 points behind league-leading Guy Hecker. He also hit 25 doubles and scored 93 runs. The 31 triples and 301 total bases were marks that had never before been attained in the short history of major league ball.

As with most triples hitters, Orr's preponderance of three-base hits was due to his speed. But unlike most triples hitters, whose speed turned doubles into triples, Orr's lack of speed in this unfenced outfield era turned home runs into triples. His tremendous size—6 foot and up to 250 pounds—gave him the power to blast the ball as far as it had ever been hit, but it also slowed him down a base or two. If he had played with fenced outfields, you might easily switch his home run and triple marks. For unlike Ned Williamson of the NL White Stockings, who benefitted from an extremely short right field porch (less than 200 feet) when he hit 27 home runs in 1884 to set the pre-Ruthian standard, Orr did not hit cheap shots. Reporting on an Orr blast in May 1884, *The New York Clipper* reported that Orr "hit the ball over the left-field fence into the river for a home run, it being the only time up to date that this batting feat has been accomplished on the local grounds." Five years later, he would hit another that became the stuff of legend.

In 1889, St. Louis was going for a fifth straight American Association pennant. It went down to the end of the season before they were beaten out of it by the Brooklyn Bridegrooms—those "damned married fellows" as flamboyant St. Louis owner Chris Van der Ahe called them. (The Bridegrooms received their nickname because so many of their players were married—in an era when most ballplayers were bachelors.) As recounted by Frederick G. Lieb in *The Baseball Story*: "Among old-timers, there is a legend that a terrific tenth-inning home-run blast by Dave Orr of the Columbus team, supposedly the longest homer up to that time, knocked out the Browns in their final 1889 inning."

Orr also posted some impressive defensive statistics during his great offensive years of 1884-1886. He placed second at his position in putouts in 1884 and 1885 and came in second in double plays in 1885. In 1886, he finished first in putouts (1445), total chances per game (11.1), and fielding average (.981).

In 1887, he encountered a series of mishaps that curtailed his playing to 84 games and only 345 at-bats. He still batted .368 and slugged .516. His misfortunes continued in the off-season. Coming to the aid of a woman in distress, Orr tossed her attacker down a flight of stairs. Unfortunately, he tumbled down the steps himself, breaking his elbows, fracturing his hand and spraining his ankle.

By 1890, Orr was a member of John Montgomery Ward's Brooklyn team in the newly formed Players' League, which in the words of historian David Voight, "arose out of the long smoldering hostilities between major league players and owners, dating back to the NL seizure of power in 1876." For Orr, it meant a chance to play once again on a good team. It also stood him against the great National League sluggers like Roger Connor and Dan Brouthers who had also jumped to the Players' League. (Tellingly enough the great sluggers of the 1880s in the National League—Dan Brouthers, Sam Thompson, King Kelly, Roger Connor—are all in the Hall of Fame, while the American Association's three great power hitters—Pete Browning, Harry Stovey, and David Orr—are not.) The Brooklyn team finished second that year to the Boston club, and Orr stood up well against his competition. His .373 average placed him second to Pete Browning's .387 but put him ahead of Connor, Ward, and Brouthers. He also placed second in RBI and third in slugging.

Still, it would prove to be a difficult year for Orr. In July, he suffered two broken ribs when he was hit by a pitched ball. He continued to play until the threat of erysipelas (the word itself would scare a lesser man) forced him to sit down. In October, during an exhibition game in Renova, Pa., he suffered an even more violent attack. A stroke left him paralyzed for a time on his left side and ended his playing career. He was only days past his thirty-first birthday.

As would happen with J. R. Richard ninety years later, there was talk at first of a return to the diamond the next season. But big Dave never made that return, except years later when he became caretaker at Ebbets Field. He died on June 3, 1915, at the age of fifty-five. As the papers reported, "He had been suffering from heart trouble for some time and found great difficulty in walking even a short distance."

Though he's virtually forgotten today, it is through no failing of his own. It is a failing of our memory instead. For it's no less true today than in 1915 when his obituary called David Orr a "famous old baseball player of the eighties, the idol of the fans of his day, and one of the greatest batters who ever sent a ball over the fence."

# 22

# THE RAZOR'S EDGE

THE BOSTON BEANEATERS of the 1890s were blessed with two outstanding catchers. Charlie Bennett, the better of the two, was generally considered the best defensive catcher of his era. He joined the Boston club in 1890, but his career came to an abrupt and tragic end when he lost both legs attempting to hop a moving train in January 1894. In 1896 Boston acquired another backstop standout in Marty Bergen, who was also known for his defensive prowess, particularly his accurate and powerful throws. Though Bergen took a few unexpected and notorious train rides, he never suffered the misfortune of losing his legs under one. He did, however, lose his head on more than one occasion. The final time, in January 1900, ended his career as abruptly as his predecessor's, but with even more shocking and tragic consequences. It was an isolated incident but nonetheless cast a macabre shadow on what had been a bright decade of baseball in Boston.

When Frank Selee came in as manager of Boston in 1890, he revamped the team from top to bottom. Only catcher Charlie Bennett remained as part of the regular everyday lineup. Selee's most significant addition, however, was a twenty-year-old rookie pitcher named Charles "Kid" Nichols who fired fastballs and won 27 games for Boston in that first year. He went on to win 297 games in the decade. By comparison, Cy Young, who also broke in that year for Cleveland, won only 265 games in that time.

With his new team in place, Selee's Beaneaters swept three straight pennants in 1891, 1892, and 1893. After seeing the team slip in 1894 and 1895, Selee changed his team again for the 1896 campaign. He added Fred Tenney at first base, Jimmy Collins at third, and Sliding Billy Hamilton in center field. He also acquired Marty Bergen to play behind the plate and fill the defensive gap left by the retirement of Charlie Bennett. While these moves helped to bring the pennant back to Boston in 1897 and 1898, the acquisition of Bergen came at a higher cost than Selee expected.

A newspaper profile of Bergen from April 1898 illustrated why Boston wanted him and why they lived to regret it: "He [Bergen] handles himself gracefully behind the bat, throws with wonderful speed and accuracy and is a class student of the game. He is of an erratic disposition and at times it requires a diplomat of Selee's ability to handle him."

When Bergen arrived in Boston in 1896, he was not physically sound and his play "was so unsatisfactory, that the Boston papers demanded his release." Frank Selee stuck by him, however, and the next year Boston won the pennant and, in the words of The Sporting News, "Bergen developed into the greatest catcher the game has ever had."

Eighteen ninety-eight proved to be an even greater year for Bergen and Boston, which won 102 games and lost only forty-seven. Bergen played in his most games ever (120) and posted his highest offensive numbers (.280 average, 62 runs, 60 RBI), but it wasn't his offense that mattered. His reputation rested on his defense, although it may have been a reputation that exceeded its worth both in his own time and in ours. An examination of his fielding statistics shows him to be an average or slightly better than average catcher at best. He never led the league in any defensive category, except errors, and trailed far behind John Warner, the New York catcher, who seemed to truly be the outstanding catcher of his time.

Yet contemporary accounts consistently lauded Bergen's defense, even in open contempt for the numbers. After the 1898 season, The Sporting News said: "The worthlessness of fielding average in determining the ability of a player finds fitting illustration in the 1898 record. . . . Bergen ranks [only] third among the catchers." His reputation seemed to rest on his arm and his daring. "Marty Bergen, with nerves of steel and a throwing arm as true as a bullet from the pistol of Ira Paine, is indeed the premier backstop of the major leagues. Bergen's work as a chance-taker eclipses the old-fashioned safety play of those backstops who lack the nerve to whish the ball around the infield at critical points in a game."

Regardless of whether he was truly as great defensively as generally accepted, there is no doubt that he played a pivotal role in Boston's championship of 1898 and its decline in 1899. His antics off the field were as important as his actions on it. One such incident in the summer of 1898 nearly cost Bergen his position on the ball club and Boston its position as league champion.

Through the first half of the 1898 campaign, the Beaneaters found their supremacy in the National League threatened by their old nemesis Baltimore and by Buck Ewing's Cincinnati ball club. In fact, Cincinnati led the race from late April. The tight race of 1897, which was not decided until a late September series between the Orioles and the Beaneaters, was a recent reminder to Boston that first place was no sure thing. In mid-August 1898, Boston finally took the lead for the first time that year. On September 1, the three teams were bunched together with Cincinnati on top (74-43), Boston one game back (71-42), and Baltimore three games back in third (68-41). Baltimore got hot in September winning 21 and losing 8, but Boston got even hotter winning 23 and losing only 4. In fact, Boston won 33 of its last 37 games to end the season 6 games above second-place Baltimore and 11½ above Cincinnati.

But on October 15, *The Sporting News* printed a story that revealed how close the Beaneaters had come to blowing their entire season in mid-summer: "A sensational scene at the Southern Hotel in St. Louis on July 28 came near terminating Catcher Bergen's career and but for the diplomacy of Manager Selee might have destroyed the Champions' chances of winning the pennant in 1898."

The "sensational scene" was an unprovoked face-slapping that Bergen administered at the breakfast table to Boston's outstanding rookie pitcher, Vic Willis. Only the intervention of other players and hotel employees prevented a full-scale fight from erupting. Selee acted immediately to defuse the situation, asking Willis to forget it and warning Bergen that he would be traded if that's what he wanted. Willis restrained himself in deference to the interests of the club and in recognition of the peculiarity of Bergen. Bergen replied that he wanted to stay with Boston but wouldn't back down.

The immediate cause of Bergen's complaint came on the train ride the night before the face-slapping. All the players, including Bergen, were acting up and playing practical jokes when, as *The Sporting News* reported it: "Suddenly Bergen grew morose and refused to join in the horseplay. He growled at Willis, but no one paid any attention to it, as it was nothing unusual for him to relapse into one of his spells when he would not talk with nor be talked to, by any one."

The next morning at the Southern Hotel, the headwaiter made the mistake of seating Willis next to Bergen, who was still in his growling mood. It was then that he slapped Willis' face. Probably the most remarkable part of the whole incident was how Frank Selee convinced the reporter who learned of the incident to hush it up until season's end. "Print that story," Selee told the writer, "and Boston is out of the race." Selee was convinced that if the story came out, Bergen and Willis would be useless to him for the rest of the season. With four regulars already sidelined, Selee felt he could not afford to lose either Willis, who was en route to a 24-win season, or Bergen, who was considered the best catcher in the game. As it turned out, the incident passed by, and Boston went on to win the pennant.

Selee's promise to trade Bergen was no idle threat. The trade rumors surfaced late in the 1898 season and escalated for the next 15 months. The reason was never in doubt. On September 17, 1898, *The Sporting News* reported that "Bergen of Boston is on the market for personal rather than professional reasons." But no trade ensued, so Bergen started the 1899 season with Boston once again. It was a year during which his situation became increasingly worse.

For Boston, the first half of the 1899 season followed the pattern of 1898. By late July, they trailed first-place Baltimore, but based on their second-half performance of the year before, that position instilled confidence. One possible stumbling block, however, was a western road trip in early August in which they were scheduled to play 13 games in two weeks, including five games in three days at Louisville. As he had done in mid-season the year before, Bergen added an extra difficulty at this crucial time. As *The Sporting News* reported it: "The team has but one catcher. Bill Clarke will have the opportunity to go in and catch every day for some time to come if Martin Bergen don't [sic] change his mind. The 'king of catchers' and the greatest thrower that the game has ever produced has an attack of illness which makes him feel blue and unwilling to work."

Bergen's complaint this time was over a $25 fine that Selee levied against him the previous season. He was also brooding over money that he alleged the Boston club promised him if he behaved for the remainder of the 1898 season. On August 5, *The Sporting News* reported that "a friend pretty close to the catcher says Bergen will positively refuse to catch any more games this season for the Boston Club, unless the manager shows a disposition to meet him halfway."

Along with his imagined troubles, Bergen suffered a real tragedy early in 1899 that compounded his problem. His five-year-old son died in the spring when Martin was away on a baseball trip. Despite his antisocial nature, Bergen was to all appearances a devoted husband and father. The loss of his son only heightened his morose and brooding disposition and made his road trips away from home even more unbearable for him.

Nonetheless, Boston survived its western road trip without Bergen, winning six out of ten. When they returned home, Bergen returned to the team. It was a strangely triumphant return. In the first home game for Boston after their trip, they entered the ninth inning down one run to Washington. Boston loaded the bases on two hit batters and a walk. Bergen then delivered a single to score the tying and winning runs. The newspapers called him "the star feature of the opening melee." He not only drove in the game winner, but also stopped three runners on attempted steals of second.

Perhaps most surprising of all was the fan reception. As reported in *The Sporting News*: "When Bergen came to bat the crowds rose with one accord and gave him an ovation the like of which the oldest fan could not recall since old John Burdock got back on earth, or the days when 'King' Kelly was in his glory." After his game-winning hit: "If Bergen had not fled before the oncoming tide of cheering fans, he would have been given a ride around the lot on the shoulders of his enthusiastic admirers."

But there would be no late season rally for Boston in 1899. Bergen's name is absent from the box scores of most of the final games of the year. The Beaneaters ended up in second place, eight games behind Brooklyn. Poor hitting and disappointing pitching were blamed, but not exclusively: "The trouble between Bergen and his teammates and the complications which ensued are ascribed as the cause of the Champions' failure to play to form this year." He almost cost them the pennant in 1898 and certainly cost it in 1899. The trade talk intensified in the off-season.

On December 23, 1899, *The Sporting News* reported: "There is a prospect of the Cincinnati Club securing catcher Marty Bergen from Boston. The Boston management wants to get rid of Bergen and is casting covetous glances at several of the Reds' twirlers."

But in mid-January 1900, Bergen would remove his name from the trading block in a horrifying way. It happened on January 19, 1900. Michael Bergen, Marty's father, walked about a half mile to his son's house in North Brookfield, Mass. at eight o'clock in the morning to get some milk. It was quiet inside and the curtains were drawn, so he went away. He returned a short while later and finding things unchanged, he entered the house on his own and discovered a grisly sight.

Marty Bergen had butchered his wife, Harriet, his daughter, Florence, and his son, Joe, with an axe. Then he nearly severed his own head from his body by cutting his neck with a razor. *Sporting Life* dubbed it "An Awful Tragedy" in its January 27, 1900, edition. Its description was gruesome:

"Martin Bergen's body and that of the little girl, Florence, 6½ years old, were lying on the kitchen floor, while in the adjoining bedroom were the bodies of Mrs. Bergen and her 3-year-old son Joseph. Mrs. Bergen was lying on the bed with her feet over the side, while her hands were raised as though in supplication or trying to ward off a blow. The little boy was lying on the floor with his brain oozing from a large wound in the head. Mrs. Bergen's skull was terribly crushed, having evidently been struck more than one blow by the infuriated husband. The appearance of the little girl also showed that a number of blows had been scored upon the top and side of her head."

In the days that followed, there was much speculation, conjecture and rumination on the cause of the heinous crime. It was rumored that Bergen's $1650 mortgage worried him as did the near certainty that he would be traded from Boston, the only team he cared to play for. The lingering effects of anesthesia from an operation nearly a year ago seemed to turn him for the worse. The death of his five-year-old the previous March weighed heavily upon him. And though his family life always seemed beyond reproach, a neighbor did suggest that Mrs. Bergen feared her husband would someday kill her.

Whatever the precipitating cause, Martin's insanity had been growing noticeably worse in the preceding months. The signs of increasing insanity were so obvious that even Bergen himself could not help but notice them. He told his doctor that he was afraid he was not in his right mind and confided in his pastor, the Rev. Humphrey J. Wrenn, that "he thought he was insane, and he feared that someday he would so far lose his mind that he would do something that he would not be responsible for. He wanted the help of the church to keep him from it."

But Bergen was tragically beyond help. The remembrance of a teammate, Ted Lewis, ironically revealed the depth of the tragedy: "He [Bergen] had a pretty little wife and was always talking about her and his children. For hours he would talk about his family and say that he loved to be home on Sunday afternoons and set on the bank of the brook and watch his children wade in the water."

It was in the end another delusion. There was no safe haven for Marty Bergen, not in the green fields of his profession nor in the comfort of home. Perhaps in the quiet memory of a Sunday afternoon, it seemed like the tracing of sunlight passing through trees, but it was in fact a more sinister and terrible darkness descending. The shadow cast across his mind was the shadow of death.

# 23

# OVER THE EDGE

JAMES DELAHANTY HAD A RIGHT to be a proud father. Not one, not two, but six of his sons played professional baseball, five of them on the major league level. Of the five, easily the greatest and most famous was the eldest brother, Edward James. Writers have been running out of adjectives attempting to describe Big Ed Delahanty for about a century. Except for Rogers Hornsby, Delahanty is often considered the greatest right-handed hitter of all time. Many believe him to be either the best or the second-best player of the pre-1900 era. His lifetime batting average of .345 places him fourth on the all-time list, and he hit with awesome power, even though his entire career was spent during the "dead ball" era. Many years after his untimely death, he was renamed the "19th-century Babe Ruth."

Not only was Delahanty the greatest player of his day; he was also the most controversial. He jumped from the National League twice: once, in 1890, when he joined the Players' League; and a second time, in 1902, when he joined the newly formed American League. His reputation as a drinker, in an era of heavy-drinking ballplayers, was almost as legendary as his reputation at the plate. It is said about many, but in Delahanty's case the cliche seems true: He was larger than life. As bizarre an ending as his life had, it seemed only natural.

The first clue about Ed Delahanty was his birth date, October 30, 1867. The day before Halloween goes by various names in different parts of the country, such as Hell Night or Mischief

Night, but never was a human being born on a more prescient day. "Del," as almost everyone close to him called him, began playing ball as most young boys of his time did—on the vacant sandlots of his hometown. By his mid-teens he was already the talk of Cleveland's West Side, where his hitting was matched by his versatility in the field. At the age of nineteen, the 6 foot 1 inch, 175-pound Delahanty ran away from home to play for Mansfield in the Ohio State League, and he moved to Wheeling the next season. In May 1888, Delahanty was signed by Philadelphia of the National League for a then record bonus of $1,900. He became their second baseman, with additional playing time in the outfield, for the next two seasons.

When Delahanty jumped to his hometown Cleveland of the Players' League, he still was developing as a ballplayer. In 1891 he rejoined the Philadelphia club when the abortive PL folded, and the following season he broke the .300 barrier for the first time. From then on, Ed Delahanty's career was nothing less than stunning.

Individual season honors came easily to Delahanty in his prime years. He led the NL in doubles five times, including a peak of fifty-six in 1899, and led the AL in doubles in his only full season in the junior circuit. In 1893 his nineteen home runs paced the NL and the year before he led the league in triples with twenty-one. He topped the 100 runs batted in mark seven times, with a high of 146 in 1893, and he led in slugging four times. Most distinctive of all, no one before or since Ed Delahanty has ever led each major league in batting average. His .408 mark led the NL in 1899, and his .376 average won the AL title in 1902. Delahanty broke the .400 barrier twice, and he failed to reach it in 1896 by the margin of three hits and in 1895 by only one hit. Only Ty Cobb, Rogers Hornsby, and Shoeless Joe Jackson have higher career batting averages.

The Philadelphia outfield of 1894, including Ed Delahanty, Sam Thompson, "Sliding" Billy Hamilton, and "part-time" player Tuck Turner hit a combined .404. Turner led the quartet with a .416 average, second in the league only to Hugh Duffy's all-time record of .438. Thompson hit .404, Delahanty .400, and Hamilton .399. It is the only time in history that two, let alone three, teammates hit .400.

Delahanty was also the architect of some of the most extraordinary single-game performances in baseball history. Once he smacked four doubles in a game, twice he went six for six, and he hit safely in ten straight at-bats over a two-game stretch of July 13-14, 1897. There must have been something about the 13th of July, because on that same date in 1896, Delahanty had possibly the finest offensive game of all time. Philadelphia was playing Chicago, and Delahanty had an almost unbelievable 17 total bases in five at-bats, a record that stood for fifty-eight years. He smacked four home runs and a single off Chicago pitcher William "Adonis" Terry. When Delahanty came to bat for the final time that day, Chicago's center fielder Bill Lange ran back to the clubhouse steps in the deepest reaches of dead center field. "Now let's see you hit one over my head, Del," shouted Lange. Sure enough, Delahanty blasted his fourth homer of the day, not only over Lange's head but onto the roof of the clubhouse. In the quaint gentlemanliness of the time, Terry left the mound and congratulated Delahanty at home plate.

Yet these eye-popping statistics tell only a tiny part of the story. Sportswriter and contemporary John H. Gruber wrote, "Edward J. Delahanty was one of the grandest ballplayers that ever shed lustre on the game." From Gruber we have a glimpse of Delahanty at the plate. "Del often used a full swing, hands going back from ear to ear in a true golf stroke. This was, indeed, his natural stroke. It was the most beautiful, full swing I have ever seen on a baseball field." Another sportswriter of the day, Sam Crane, tells us that Delahanty's talents were not limited to the bat. "He was a strong thrower," writes Crane, "and while he looked to be a bit cumbersome on his feet, he covered lots of ground and was a sterling base runner." Still, it was in the batter's box that Delahanty had no peer. "He was a natural hitter to all fields," writes Gruber. "He always swung easily, yet he was liable to take a leg off any man in the infield at any time."

After thirteen seasons with Philadelphia in the NL, Delahanty, like many other top-notch players of his day, made the jump to the fledgling American League. Delahanty joined the Washington Senators in their second season, 1902, who awarded him a $15,000-a-year contract, making Delahanty the highest paid player of all time. He more than earned his pay. In 1902,

Delahanty led the AL in batting, doubles, and slugging. He was third in total bases, triples, and home runs, and fifth in runs batted in. With all of that, however, Washington finished sixth in the eight-team league, a dismal 21 games behind the pennant-winning Athletics of Philadelphia.

Delahanty never took a liking to the city of Washington. It was much too quiet a town for a man whose "idea of life included drinking and gambling." During the 1902-1903 off-season, a deal was struck between the Senators and the New York Giants, sending Delahanty to New York. Besides getting his wish to play in the cosmopolitan capital of America, Delahanty was also promised an increase in his base salary. The Giants forwarded him $4,000 of his 1903 salary just as spring training was about to open, and Delahanty promptly frittered it away in a wild spree in New Orleans.

However, there was no love lost between the two leagues, and the sorest point of contention was player raiding. After the AL successfully lured away many NL stars in 1901, the NL began returning the favor, and the so-called "baseball wars" were on. Both leagues realized their existences were threatened as long as contracts were not binding, so a "peace conference" was called in March 1903. While Delahanty was blowing his wad in New Orleans, the leagues decided to bury the hatchet, and the central provision of the fragile peace was that all player deals since the end of 1902 were declared null and void. The Giants contacted Delahanty, told him the bad news, and understandably asked for their money back. Of course, Delahanty no longer had it, and he began the season in debt.

In debt and banished. That was how Delahanty, in essence, viewed his 1903 season in the wasteland of Washington. He began to break spring training, which did not sit well with manager Tom Loftus. The two fueded frequently, and Delahanty was particularly upset when Loftus insisted he move from his normal position in left field to right. His drinking, which was always legendary, became harder and even more frequent, and Delahanty was entrapped in a vicious cycle of self-destruction. By early June he was hitting .333, but the team was hapless and mired in the cellar of the AL, increasing Delahanty's depression. As the club headed on the road for a late June trip, Delahanty found himself riding the pines for the first time in over a decade. The once "jolly, good-hearted and happy hearted" Delahanty had reached his nadir.

The last straw came while the Senators were in Cleveland. During the game of June 25, Delahanty found out that George Davis, another player whose contract with the Giants had been voided in the spring, had been allowed to join New York. As one sportswriter put it, "Davis was playing for the Giants while Delahanty was sentenced to Washington." Delahanty left the game before it ended and spent the rest of the afternoon and evening in Cleveland's bars. Loftus caught up with him and suspended him both for going AWOL and excessive drinking. *The Boston Globe* was putting it mildly when it wrote, "Del proceeded to stray from the path that a discreet ballplayer usually follows."

A distraught and despondent Delahanty took out an accident insurance policy on himself, naming his young daughter as beneficiary. He began to threaten suicide, and in a letter to his wife he wrote he hoped the train that was bringing him to Detroit ahead of the team would jump the track. His carousing did not abate, even though his mother and one brother were now accompanying him. Once again, his behavior made the papers, and Washington rescinded his suspension in hopes he would regain normalcy. On July 2, the final game of the series against Detroit, Delahanty was back with the club, but was once again on the bench. He left the team in disgust, and without telling his family, he started for New York by himself.

He boarded Michigan Central's train number six, heading for Buffalo, at about five or six P.M. on July 2. John Cole, a conductor on the train, said Delahanty consumed five shots of alcohol, and he very quickly became "despondent and anxious to make mischief." By about 10:30, Delahanty was disrupting the train—he insisted on smoking in non-smoking areas, he smashed a wall, and he pulled a razor on a conductor. Next he began pulling sleeping passengers bodily from their Pullman compartments by the ankles. The conductors tried to calm him, but he only became more rabid, and he went so far as to pull the emergency cord. Just after midnight, at Fort Erie, Ontario, on the Niagara River about fifteen miles above the Falls, Delahanty was put off the train without his bags or equipment.

Delahanty was beyond reason. He resolutely decided to follow the train in the hope of catching up to it on foot. At about 1:00 A.M. on July 3, he reached the Niagara River railroad bridge. The only eye-witness of the subsequent events was the bridge watchman, Sam Kingston. As Delahanty started to cross the bridge, Kingston attempted to dissuade him, telling him that the bridge was up and he was heading for certain death over the Falls. Instead of heeding this advice, Delahanty knocked Kingston out. The last thing the dazed Kingston could recall was Delahanty's shadowy figure walking onto the dark bridge. By the time Kingston was able to gather his faculties, Delahanty was nowhere to be seen.

The search for Delahanty did not produce results until a week later. A mangled body, missing its left leg, washed up at the dock of a large propeller boat, "The Maid of the Mist," on July 9. Eighteen-year-old brother Frank Delahanty, playing with Syracuse of the New York State League at the time, positively identified the remains. Delahanty had not yet reached his thirty-sixth birthday.

Veteran baseball writer Dan Daniel wrote in 1928 that "Delahanty was one of the grandest hitters baseball has ever seen." At the time of his death, Delahanty was at "the zenith of his reputation," according to John Gruber. It is hard to argue with either statement. For twelve of his sixteen seasons, "Del" hit over .300, and had he lived he unquestionably would have collected 3,000 hits. The previous season he led his league in batting and slugging, so it is obvious his powers were not waning. Although his disappointments of 1903 help to explain some of the mystery, the psychological maladies that brought Delahanty plummeting from the pinnacle of baseball stardom to his watery grave in Niagara Falls will most likely remain cloudy. But the record is crystal clear. He may very well have been the most dominant player of the 19th century. Unfortunately, living so close to the edge for so long, Ed Delahanty could not stop himself from going over.

# 24

# PAST PERFECT

THE ALL-STAR GAME, as every fan knows, began in 1933. On July 6 of that year the midsummer classic pitting the best of each league was held for the first time in Chicago. The American League won in a fitting manner: Babe Ruth's home run was the margin of victory. However, few followers of baseball know that some twenty-two years earlier, the shining stars of the American League, including Ty Cobb, Walter Johnson, Tris Speaker, and Eddie Collins, interrupted their season, formed a team, and played an exhibition game. The opponent was the 1911 Cleveland ball club, which at the time was known as the "Naps" because of their star, Napoleon Lajoie. The purpose was to raise money for the widow and children of one of the greatest pitchers of the first decade of this century. His name was Addie Joss.

Adrian Joss was born in the small town of Juneau, Wis., on April 12, 1880. His pitching career began as the star pitcher for Juneau High School and continued at Sacred Heart College in Wisconsin. In his spare time he also pitched with Sheboygan's semi-pro team. It was here in 1898 that Joss was spotted by Bob Gillis, manager of Toledo's fine minor league team. Addie signed with Toledo and the town became his adopted home for the remainder of his life.

Cleveland signed Joss to his first major league contract in 1902. Joss's big league debut was auspicious, to say the least. The right-hander faced the St. Louis Browns in Cleveland on April 26. The first fifteen Browns were set down consecutively, but Jesse Burkett led off the sixth with a pop fly to shallow right. Right fielder Erwin Harvey raced in to make a brilliant shoestring catch, but umpire Robert Carruthers ruled he had trapped it. Harvey argued vociferously but to no avail. The contested single was the only baserunner the Browns would get that day. Joss followed that start with a second one-hitter on May 4, this time losing the no-hit bid with one out in the ninth.

Some of Joss's success can be attributed to his unorthodox yet highly effective delivery. Sources say he "pitched out of his hip pocket. Joss had not only great speed and a fast breaking curve, but a very effective pitching motion, bringing the ball from behind him with a complete body swing." In addition to the two pitches already mentioned, Joss threw a "false rise," which would come straight at a batter for "55 feet and then, defying gravity and its initial impulse, suddenly break into a horizontal course for eight feet more!"

This array of pitches and deceptive motion quickly brought stardom to Joss. By 1905 Joss was acknowledged as one of the best pitchers in the league, and for the next four years he was arguably *the* best. From 1905 until 1908 Joss averaged 23 wins and a .680 winning percentage for a team that barely won as many games as it lost. He set a then major league record of seventeen strikeouts in one game, and he had a ten-game winning streak in 1907. In a time when pitchers completed what they started, Joss completed games at a higher ratio than anyone. His 90 percent completion rate was a full 8 percent more than even "Iron Man" Joe McGinnity.

Nineteen hundred and eight was clearly Joss's best season, perhaps one of the five best seasons any pitcher has ever had. Addie's 24 wins were a distant second to Big Ed Walsh's league leading forty, but that was about the only category in which Joss came in second. He led the AL with a 1.16 earned run average, a league record. Most remarkably, in 325 innings pitched Joss walked only thirty batters, far fewer than one per game. He hurled eleven shutouts and allowed only 7.25 base runners per nine innings, a mark second only to Walter Johnson's all-time record of 6.97 per nine innings in 1913. With Joss as their workhorse, the Naps were in the thick of the pennant race along with the Detroit Tigers and the Chicago White Sox.

It seemed only just that the pennant should be decided, in

part, by the two best pitchers in the league in a face-to-face duel. That duel, between Joss and Ed Walsh, occurred on October 2, 1908. Both pitchers were on top of their game that day. In the third inning Cleveland eked out a run. After a lead-off single, Walsh attempted a pick-off throw which hit the head of the runner and caromed down the right field line, allowing the runner to reach third. Walsh then unleashed a wild spitter and the only run of the game came across. Big Ed allowed only three other hits, walked one, and struck out fifteen.

And Addie Joss? With the pennant on the line, Addie Joss decided to throw a perfect game. The White Sox only managed to hit four balls to the outfield. Joss later related the game this way. "About the seventh inning I realized that not one of the Sox had reached first base. No one on the bench had said a word. When I thought about it I touched wood. I guess it helped. I did not try for the record. I was seeking to beat the Sox, and Ed Walsh had the same purpose in view. Ed was pitching the game of his life. I never saw him when he had so much stuff."

In his typical modest way, Joss added, "In giving me credit for the feat, the writer should not forget the boys behind me. Lajoie in particular went great and killed three balls that ordinarily would have been base hits."

Joss's feat was only the second perfect game in major league history up to that time, and only Don Larsen's World Series perfect game in 1956 can compare with it in terms of importance. To this day no single game has produced two such outstanding pitching performances under so much pressure. As Red Smith wrote, "Big Ed was great but Addie was perfect."

Oddly enough, Joss's physical problems presented themselves for the first time on the night after that perfect game. While boarding the train for the next game, Joss inexplicably fainted. No explanation or reason has ever been found for this brief spell. In any event, Joss's supherhuman effort of October 2 eventually went for naught. The Naps lost the pennant by one-half game, the slimmest margin in history. Both Cleveland and the AL pennant winning Detroit Tigers had won ninety games at the close of the season, but the Naps had played one more game and had lost it. The Tigers were not forced to make up a rainout and were handed the title. American League officials realized the inherent injustice of this situation during the subsequent off-season and decreed that a pennant could never again be decided by less than a full game. Needless to say, this edict came too late for Joss and the 1908 Naps.

Joss was never able to duplicate his season of 1908. In the following season he won only 14 games despite his 1.71 ERA, the fifth best mark in the league. Nineteen ten began more auspiciously as Joss hurled the second and last no-hitter of his career. Again the poor White Sox were his victims. Although not a perfect game, Joss's April 20th performance was damn close. He gave up only two walks, one error was committed behind him, and only two balls were hit to the outfield. It seemed 1910 would be another banner year.

But halfway through the season, in a game against the eventual world champion Philadelphia Athletics, something "snapped" in the elbow of his pitching arm. The injury sidelined Joss for the remainder of the season with his record at a disappointing 5-5. Joss himself, writing for *Baseball* magazine over the off-season, described what he believed happened. "The mere physical exertion required of a pitcher is little compared to the strain on his nerves. In order to do his best, in any contest, he must be keyed up to ninety-nine percent of his energy. When one is forced to do this more than once every three days, something is bound to give."

The following spring, Joss reported to the Cleveland spring training camp at New Orleans in "the best of health," and he assured everyone that the arm troubles were a thing of the past. However, Joss was not at all well. He had lost his appetite in February and had dropped quite a few pounds. At the start of the season he remained behind in New Orleans for "one more hard session." He confidently added, "I'll be ready in May."

In fact, he felt so much better that he rushed to join his teammates at Chattanooga where they were playing one final exhibition game on April 3. As he disembarked at the Chattanooga station, he mysteriously fainted and was rushed to the hospital. He regained consciousness rather quickly and seemed well enough to join the team in Cleveland. But the fainting spells returned and Joss was sent home to Toledo. He still believed he would be pitching within a matter of weeks.

This would not be the case. Joss's condition quickly worsened, and his physicians, Dr. M. H. Castle and Dr. George L.

Chapman, who were baffled up until now, were finally able to diagnose him. He was suffering from tubercular meningitis, a rarely contracted incurable illness. Chapman said that Joss must have contracted the disease "some time ago," but it did not present itself until the fainting spell of April 3.

Joss's last days were racked with pain primarily from a "violent and perpetual headache." He was in a semi-conscious condition described as a "deep stupor shaken by paroxysms and convulsions." But he did not suffer long. A mere eleven days after the Chattanooga incident, at 1:45 A.M. of Friday morning, April 14, 1911, Addie Joss was dead. He was thirty-years, two-days-old.

The baseball world and most of the rest of America were shocked and saddened. Cy Young, who had once been Joss's roommate, said, "You can't say anything too good for Addie Joss." Napoleon Lajoie added, "I am feeling very glum that my friend and teammate is no more." George Stovall said, "No better man ever lived than Addie."

Addie Joss's funeral was the biggest Toledo had ever known. The unabashedly maudlin eulogy was said by none other than ballplayer-turned-evangelist Billy Sunday. Young and Lajoie wept unashamedly and openly. A minor controversy arose when the American League president, Ban Johnson, refused to postpone the Cleveland-Detroit game on the Monday of the funeral. An adamant Cleveland team stood its ground and refused to back down to Johnson's threats of forfeiture. It was Johnson who eventually backed down and postponed the game.

Obituaries lionizing Joss poured in from all over the country. The Boston Globe wrote, "He was at the zenith of a superlative career. He was the Christy Mathewson of the American League." The local Toledo News-Bee editorialized that "he seemed the personification of health. He belonged to that younger generation of ballplayers who have brought honesty, native culture, dignity, poise, temperance, and sterling manhood to raise the sport to the high plane it now occupies."

Only a few hours after Joss's death, Charles W. Somers, the president of the Cleveland ball club, announced that a tribute to Addie Joss, "Joss Day," would be held at Cleveland's League Park on July 24. The proceeds of an exhibition game would go to Joss's widow, Lilian, and their two children, Norman, eight, and Ruth, four. Cleveland, of course, would be one of the teams involved. The opposing team was the original American League all-star team, and it was a sight to behold. The Yankees' "Prince Hal" Chase played first; the immortal Eddie Collins of the Philadelphia A's was at second; at short, the Browns' stellar Bobby Wallace; and Frank "Home Run" Baker was at third. Ty Cobb (who, incidentally, went two for twenty-eight against Joss over his career, a paltry .071) was in left, with fellow Tiger "Wahoo" Sam Crawford in center and Boston's inimitable Tris Speaker in right. Smoky Joe Wood of the Red Sox got the start with Walter Johnson, among others, seeing action from the bullpen. Their battery mate was Senator catcher Gabby Street.

The Naps started two future Hall of Famers as well—Cy Young was on the mound and Napoleon Lajoie was at second. In all, nine participants would eventually head to Cooperstown. The game was tightly contested with the stars coming out on top 5-3. More important, the day was a financial success. Fifteen thousand two hundred eighty-one paying customers brought Joss's family $12,914 in proceeds. In addition, the Philadelphia, Boston, St. Louis, and Detroit clubs each contributed $1600, bringing the after-expenses total to $14,572.

Addie Joss is, justifiably, a member of the National Baseball Hall of Fame. He was not an original inductee in 1936. He was not elected, in fact, until 1978, and only after relentless pressure from veteran baseball writers Red Smith, Fred Lieb, and Bob Broeg convinced the Veterans Committee to waive the ten-year minimum requirement by a special resolution. He reached the Hall a full sixty-seven years after his death; that span was well more than twice his lifespan. Perhaps it was an unduly long wait. But the career of the great Addie Joss is enshrined with the careers of many of those men who played on a July day in 1911, for his family and in his honor. Joss is, today and forever, exactly where he belongs.

# 25

# THROWN OUT STEALING

PLAYERS HAVE BEEN BANNED from baseball for fixing games, for allegedly fixing games, for offering to fix games, and for knowing about fixed games. They have been banned for jumping contracts, for playing in "outlaw" leagues, for playing against outlaw teams, and for associating with outlaws. In recent years, alcohol and drug abuse have been the favored motive for banning. But in 1921, Benny Kauff was banned from baseball for life because of a stolen car. It seemed to be a draconian response, but harsh measures were the rule of the day in 1921. Baseball was just beginning to come out of an era of bitter contract fights between owners and players, rival leagues, and suspicious behavior on the field. Money was the main player; if it could not be gotten in one way, it would be pursued in another. Benny Kauff personified that era as well as anyone.

Benny Kauff grew up in the coal mining country of Middleton, Ohio. As a teenager he worked in the mines alongside his father. The work was difficult, dangerous, and dreary. Like others before him and after, Kauff looked for a way out. "Seven years I worked in the dust and grime," Kauff told *Baseball* magazine in 1914, "and baseball proved my way of escape from a lifetime spent in the same monotonous way."

His "escape" took a typical route for ballplayers of that era: weekend town ball to a minor league contract to a big league tryout and then more years on minor league teams. He spent four years in the minors from 1910 to 1913, never batting below

.300. He was given two brief tastes of major league ball with the Yankees in 1911 and 1912, but never stayed. In fact, his only appearances in the major leagues to this time was in five games with the Yankees early in 1912. When he batted .345 at Hartford in 1913 to lead the Connecticut League, Kauff felt his real chance would finally come. Instead, he was dealt to Indianapolis of the American Association.

But this was 1914, and Kauff was about to see baseball offer him his second escape. A rival league to the National and American was being organized. It was called the Federal League, and to players it offered money, opportunity, and a release from the stranglehold of organized ball. The Indianapolis Club of the Federal League offered Kauff twice the salary promised him by the minor league team. He was not only a major leaguer but a rich one.

The Federal League lasted for only two years, but Kauff was its unrivaled offensive star. He led the league in batting average and stolen bases both years. In his first year, 1914, he nearly led it in everything. He was first in batting average (.370), hits (211), doubles (44), total bases (305), stolen bases (75), runs scored (120), and on-base percentage (.440). He was second in slugging average (.534) and third in RBI (95) and walks (72). His team also won the Federal League pennant. The next year the Indianapolis team switched to Newark, and Kauff was sent to Brooklyn in moves designed to bolster the stability of the league. Though his team was far less impressive, finishing one position out of the cellar, Kauff was still the offensive standout of the league. His batting average (.342), slugging average (.509) and stolen bases (55) led the league, and he was among the leaders in several other categories including home runs (third with 12), total bases (fourth with 246) and walks (second with 85).

Partially through the 1915 season, John McGraw tried to steal Kauff away for the Giants. On April 30, Kauff took his position in center field at the Polo Grounds in a game against the Boston Braves, who immediately left the field in protest. The National Commission which ruled organized baseball had an edict in effect that prohibited signing Federal Leaguers under contract. Its goal was to avoid a bidding war and to intimidate players to remain in the National and American Leagues under fear of never returning. The Giants signing of Kauff threatened that strategy.

When the Braves left the field, umpire Mel Eason called league president Tener on the phone. Tener said that Kauff was ineligible to play for the Giants. In the meantime, the other umpire declared the game a forfeit to the Giants (perhaps under the gentle persuasion of McGraw and fear of the Polo Grounds faithful). At that point, the Giants and Braves agreed to play an "exhibition" game which the Braves won 13-6. The next day, President Tener upheld his own ruling and also declared the exhibition would count as a regular season game in the standings. For the time being at least, the Giants lost all the way around.

Kauff made an extra $2,000 on the transaction. He returned to the Brooklyn Federals for the rest of the 1915 season at $6,000 per year. When the Federal League collapsed at the end of that year, the Giants purchased his contract legitimately. However, as they had already learned, getting Kauff into uniform would not be that easy. Benny, who originally jumped to the Federal League in 1914 and then tried to jump out of it in 1915 over salary disputes, was by now well-accomplished in contract negotiation. Even though the Giants signed him at a salary of $6,000 per year, Kauff held out for a piece of his purchase price. He made an extra $5,000 on that before finally reporting to the Giants spring camp in Marlin, Tex.

His belated arrival in the National League was accompanied by much fanfare, anticipation, and controversy. A year earlier, during his contract squabble with Indianapolis and Brooklyn, Benny told a newspaper reporter about his frustration at the shabby treatment he was getting from the Federal League. He was also frustrated at not being able to play for the Giants. He then made a remark that would haunt him, saying that if he got a chance out there in a Giants' uniform, "the fans [would] see a player in action that [would] make Ty Cobb look like a bush leaguer."

The comparisons to Cobb were prevalent. *Baseball* magazine entitled a November 1914 article on Benny Kauff, "The Ty Cobb of the Federal League." Newspapers commonly referred to him as the "the Federals' Ty Cobb" or "the second Ty Cobb." Kauff himself added to the boastful rhetoric by his accessibility to the

press and quotability. Yet as early as June 1915, Kauff was denying that he made the Cobb claim.

By the end of the 1916 season, his first with the Giants, he
would prove that the comparison did not fit. Nineteen sixteen
was an off year for Cobb. He stroked over 200 hits (201) and
led the league in runs (113) and stolen bases (68), but his .371
average placed him second to Tris Speaker—the first time in ten
years that Cobb did not win that title. Benny Kauff still could
not come close. His forty stolen bases placed him second in the
league, but that was still twenty-three behind Max Carey. His
.264 batting average was barely above the Giants' team average
of .253. In the two prior years, the Federal League was accused
of being less competitive than the American and National. Its
hefty batting averages were attributed to deader arms and a live-
lier ball. Kauff's performance in 1916 seemed to bear out these
allegations.

But Benny endured other trials that year—all due to the
pressure of being the Federal League's biggest star and now having to prove his standing with Cobb. As reported in the newspapers of the time, Kauff "was a mark for fans and pitchers
alike." With everyone so intent on knocking him down, it was
tough for Kauff to concentrate on his game. "No major league
player, with the possible exception of Fred Merkle," sportswriter
W. J. Macbeth wrote in 1917, "suffered so hard a 'riding' from
the fans of other cities." The pressures finally wore Kauff down.
"It made him anxious. He continually swung at bad balls. He
wound up the season a sadder but wiser young man, with a batting average of .264."

The effects were not lasting. The next year, Kauff bounced
back to bat .308 for the pennant-winning Giants and was batting .315 midway into the 1918 season when he went off to
war. He was never to be the great star he was in the Federal
League, but he was a more than capable starting outfielder for
John McGraw's Giants—not another Ty Cobb, but at least a second Fred Snodgrass, whom he replaced.

And Kauff never let his somewhat disappointing show on
the field affect his always entertaining display off it. In an era
when money and greed were hallmarks of the game, Benny Kauff
took center stage. As sportswriter James P. Sinott said, "Kauff

not only acted the part of baseball's prima donna, but dressed it, too.'' He wore loudly colored, expensively tailored suits, shirts, and ties. He sported diamond rings and pins that cost thousands of dollars and drove ''a big ninety horse power car.'' He was said to carry as much as $6,000 on his person—a sum equal to his annual salary with the Giants. Damon Runyon tagged him ''a sort of Diamond Jim Brady reduced down to a baseball salary size,'' but it must have been Cobb's salary he was thinking of.

How Kauff was able to support his ostentatious life style is open to conjecture, and by 1920 it became wide open. After returning from World War I, Kauff joined the Giants again for the 1919 season in which he batted .277 with 21 stolen bases. He also opened an automobile sales business with his half-brother. There's no record of his sales average there, but he did get credit for at least one steal. In February 1920, he was arrested and indicted for stealing an automobile and receiving stolen automobiles in December 1919. He played the 1920 season while released on bail with his case still pending. He batted only .274 in 55 games and spent part of the year on a minor-league team in Toronto.

The Chicago grand jury was investigating gambling in baseball throughout the 1920 season, most notably in regard to the fixing of the 1919 World Series by eight Chicago White Sox players—a story which finally broke open in September 1920. Benny Kauff's name came up repeatedly in the proceedings, usually relating to the shenanigans of his teammates Hal Chase and Heinie Zimmerman in 1919. Zimmerman accused Kauff of being in on fixes. John McGraw defended him and nothing was ever proven.

Kauff's car-stealing case was still up in the air as the 1921 spring training season was about to begin. He found himself officially banned from playing with the Giants until the matter was resolved. Finally in May 1921, Kauff was acquitted. The Giants prodded Kauff to apply to the commissioner's office for reinstatement. Judge Landis flatly refused. After reading the papers from the trial, Landis declared, ''The acquittal smells to high heaven.'' Kauff appealed. He got a temporary injunction restraining Landis from preventing his playing. In the end it made no difference. Benny Kauff was thirty years old. He never played in organized baseball again.

Kauff was one of the first players permanently banned by Landis, whose more famous lifetime banning of the eight "Black Sox" players later in the year would follow the precedent set down with Kauff. An acquittal in the courts would not mean mercy from the Judge. His decisions would not always be seen as consistent, but Landis was clear in his reason for banning Kauff and later the Black Sox. They threatened the game, and he was protecting it. In a letter to Kauff of August 25, 1921, Landis stated that "your [Kauff's] mere presence in the lineup would inevitably burden patrons of the game with grave apprehensions as to its integrity."

Several years later, Ban Johnson, the president of the American League in 1919, would state that according to the notorious gambling kingpin Arnold Rothstein, Benny Kauff was the one who first broached the entire scheme of fixing the 1919 World Series. It's an after-the-fact, second-hand story, rife with innuendo and self-aggrandizement, that takes a poke at an easy target like Kauff. It is unsubstantiated, almost certainly inaccurate, and probably totally untrue. But Kauff personified the era as well anyone, so why not blame him? He had already taken the rap.

# 26

# STRIKING HIS STRIDE

WHEN THE INITIAL BALLOTING for entrants into the Baseball Hall of Fame was tabulated in 1936, forty players received votes. From top to bottom, the names were the best known in the game and most eventually received induction. Ross Youngs received ten votes, more than Frank Chance, Johnny Evers, Home Run Baker, Sam Crawford, Three-Finger Brown, and Rube Marquard, among others. Over the next twenty years, Youngs consistently received a strong share of votes. In 1972, he finally received his due when the Veterans Committee voted him into the Hall of Fame. His name is generally forgotten now, but in the twenties when he played for John McGraw's Giants, and for at least several decades afterward, he was considered to be one of the best outfielders and all-around players in the game.

John McGraw for one did not think of it as idle praise. A notorious Ruth-basher to begin with, McGraw clearly showed his preference in right field when he stated that "he would not accept him [Babe Ruth] in a trade for Pep [Ross] Youngs." But then, Youngs was the personification of McGraw's type of player: small, stocky, fast, dedicated, exuberant, and not a home run hitter. Youngs was a high-average hitter who was regularly among the league leaders in hits, doubles, triples, and bases on balls. He was a pesty player who made things happen. And perhaps best of all in the eyes of McGraw he was "not a player who [found] it difficult to sign a contract in the spring." The latter remark was an unveiled stab at Edd Roush, the slick-fielding

Cincinnati outfielder, who won batting titles in 1917 and 1919 and was notorious for his yearly contract holdouts, one of which (1930) lasted an entire year. John McGraw was leaving no doubt as to whom he considered to be the best outfielder in the game.

McGraw first saw Youngs when the Giants were in their Marlin, Tex., training camp in spring 1917. He had already signed him a few months earlier for $2,000 after Ross had finished the 1916 season tearing up the Western Association for the team in Sherman. He led the league in batting average (.362), total bases (249), hits (195), and runs (103). Despite his impressive offensive numbers, Youngs was still barely nineteen years old and still a bit rough, especially defensively, as a ballplayer. But in the eyes of McGraw "he was so fast, so full of life and so ambitious" that McGraw decided "to give him a chance on his general prospects as a player."

Youngs spent 1917 in Rochester of the International League where he batted .356 with 85 runs scored. The Giants meanwhile were running away with the National League pennant by virtue of their slugging third baseman Heinie Zimmerman and the hard-hitting outfield of Dave Robertson, Benny Kauff, and George Burns. Zimmerman led the league in RBI (102), Robertson in home runs (12), Burns in runs (103), and Kauff placed fourth in average (.308).

All three outfielders were only twenty-seven years old and appeared to be set in the Polo Grounds for years to come. It did not look as though Youngs would be able to crack that lineup no matter how well he played in the minor leagues. But his break came sooner than he expected. Dave Robertson, who was not quite as steady in the mind as he was at the plate, quit the Giants for the 1918 season. Youngs stepped into his right field position and in 121 games batted .302. (The Giants played a war-shortened 124-game season that year.) He also had 22 assists to place second among all outfielders in the league. The next year Robertson returned, but was traded to the Cubs. The Giants no longer needed him in right field; Ross Youngs stayed there for the next seven-and-a-half years.

He improved steadily each year. In 1919, he got off to a torrid start and was batting well over .400 near the end of May. He was unable to keep that pace for the entire season, but still finished the year at .311, third in the league. He led the league in doubles (31), outfield assists (23) and double plays (7). Two years previously, there looked to be no place for him in the Giants' lineup. Now with Robertson gone and Kauff's troubles with left-handers and the law mounting, Youngs was quickly becoming the anchor of the team.

By 1920, en route to a .351 batting average with ninety-two runs scored, he was being talked about as one of the premier players in the game. His accomplishments and youth, his natural hitting ability and unnatural speed, his spirited play and dedication all marked him as a player of unlimited promise. *Baseball* magazine said: "In short at twenty-two, 'Pep' Young[s] has already travelled a long way toward the heights of stardom. His life is still before him. What that life will be no one can safely predict. But already he has laid a beginning for a career that should be inferior to very few in baseball."

Those remarks would become hauntingly prophetic and ironic within seven years, but at the time few players' futures looked brighter. "In the big leagues," said John McGraw, "a youngster like Young[s] ought to improve for three or four years before he fairly strikes his stride." Not surprisingly, McGraw was correct. Youngs' stride was about to coincide with one of the brightest periods in Giants history: their four-straight pennant years of 1921-1924.

Youngs' outstanding 1920 season was a harbinger of his performance over the next four years. From 1921 to 1924, he batted .327, .331, .336, and .356. His RBI totals were 102, 86, 87, and 74. Runs were 90, 105, 121, and 112. He hit double figures in doubles and triples every year. These were of course the early days of the dramatic climb in offensive numbers that occurred throughout baseball in the twenties and thirties. But Youngs' figures were still well above the league averages and occasionally placed him with the league leaders. His .356 average in 1924 placed him third; his 121 runs in 1923 was first; his 102 RBI in 1921 was third best.

Now that he had hit his stride, he was being called "the greatest right fielder in the National League" and the "best outfielder in the National League." He was being compared on equal terms with the greatest players of his time. An article by sportswriter Robert Boyd in 1924 stated that Youngs "lack[ed] the color of Speaker, Roush, Eddie Collins, or Ruth, although [he was] just as great a player in the different departments of the game."

The next year something went wrong. The Giants missed first place by eight and a half games. Youngs batting average crashed to .264, a .092 point collapse from the year before, and the first time he had batted below .300 in his professional career. He was only twenty-eight years old. After the season ended, he was diagnosed with Bright's disease, a fatal kidney ailment.

Youngs' reputation as a hustler and fierce competitor was never better displayed than in the next season. The Giants assigned a private nurse to travel with Youngs in 1926. Despite the advance of his illness, he managed to play in 95 games that year and brought his average back above .300 to .306. He also taught a seventeen-year old named Mel Ott a few things about playing right field in the Polo Grounds. Two years later, Ott would take over the position, stay there for eighteen years and establish himself as the greatest outfielder in Giants' history (before Willie Mays). One year later, Youngs would be dead at the age of thirty.

His death followed the death of another Giants' great from a prior generation, Christy Mathewson, by two years. Though Mathewson also died young (at the age of forty-five), he played a full career. Both of them were favorites of John McGraw—his surrogate sons in effect. McGraw hung photographs of each of them in his office at the Polo Grounds. They were the only player photos that hung there. When McGraw himself was nearing his own death in 1936, the photos were transferred to his home in Westchester County.

Christy Mathewson entered the Hall of Fame in 1936 on the balloting for the first inductees. Ross Youngs would have to wait another thirty-six years. But it hardly mattered. He had long ago joined Mathewson in a more hallowed and selective place.

# 27

# Is There a Doctor in the House?

DEL BISSONETTE was twenty-eight years old when he finally made it to the major leagues, after nearly ten years of trying. The long struggle had ended, but a harder struggle was about to begin. From this point on, his career would be marked by a series of accidents, injuries, and disease that would shorten his stay in the majors to only five years and earn him notoriety as the unluckiest man in baseball.

Bissonette began his career as a pitcher with his high school team in Winthrop, Maine, continuing on to Brookton Academy, Kents Hill Seminary, Westbrook Seminary, and New Hampshire State College. He finally made it to Georgetown University where he had some success until injuring his arm in 1921. The injury was serious enough that he had to carry his arm "in a sling or . . . pocket for a year and a half." While it did not end his career, it did force him into beginning it all over again. As Bissonette himself summed it up, "I spent four years trying to cure a sore arm, and then I spent four more years learning to play first base."

In 1922, Del played semipro ball in Montreal as an outfielder. The next year, he managed and played first base for the Star Taxi team in his hometown of Lewiston, Maine. In 1924, he finally entered organized baseball with York in the Pennsylvania League, though he spent much of that season on loan at Binghamton, N.Y. He was back in York in 1925 when he attracted the attention of the Brooklyn Dodgers (affectionately known as

the Robins in that day after their manager, Wilbert Robinson)
who signed him near the end of the season. He spent 1926 in
Jersey City and then in 1927 established himself as a premier hitter with the Buffalo Bisons of the International League.

In leading the Bisons to the pennant, Bissonette led the
league in runs scored with 168; in hits, with 229; in total bases,
with 408; in doubles, with 46; in triples, with 20; in home runs,
with 31; and in RBI, with 167. His marks in runs, total bases,
and RBI set new league records. He also batted .365.

When he broke into the majors the next year with Brooklyn, his numbers did not drop off by much. In 155 games, he
gathered 188 hits, 30 doubles, 13 triples, 25 home runs, 90
runs, 106 RBI, and a .320 average. He was also generally recognized as more than capable defensively. But it had not been easy
for Del to finally reach this level, and he would soon find out
how difficult it would be to stay there.

In 1929, he was hit in the head by a pitch during the first
week of the season. Then in May, he injured his right shoulder
sliding into home. Sinus trouble sidelined him for a month. He
ended up missing nearly forty games that year and his numbers
dropped off dramatically: .281 average, 12 home runs, 68 runs,
and 75 RBI. In December, he underwent an operation for sinus
trouble. On New Year's Eve, he had another operation, this time
for mastoiditis behind his right ear.

In 1930, he bounced back from his troubles to again play a
full season and produce impressive offensive numbers: 192 hits,
33 doubles, 13 triples, 16 home runs, 102 runs, 113 RBI, and a
.336 average. He had a respectable and virtually trouble-free year
in 1931 as well, appearing in 152 games and batting .290 with
90 runs and 87 RBI. But following that 1931 season, his troubles accelerated once again.

Late in 1931, he underwent a shoulder operation to correct
a muscle condition that had bothered him since his college days.
Then in spring training of 1932, he tore an Achilles tendon
while playing volleyball. Again, he underwent an operation, this
time on the Achilles tendon. The operation was successful, but
an infection set in following it, and Bissonette nearly died from
blood poisoning. He missed the entire 1932 season.

He made a brief comeback in 1933, but appeared in only
thirty-five games and was generally ineffective at the plate. That

was how his major league career ended. He retired with a lifetime .305 average but was known more for his appearances at
the doctor's office than for his appearances at the plate. Twelve
sinus operations between 1928 and 1933 prompted one sportswriter to refer to him as the "human hospital ward," but Bissonette never shared in this bleak portrayal. He considered himself "pretty lucky just to play in the majors."

After his major league career ended, he played briefly in
the minors and then went on to a long and successful career as a
manager and coach. In this capacity, luck served him somewhat
better. His ailments disappeared, and he won several pennants
in the minors before serving as a major league manager, coach,
and scout in the late forties and fifties.

However, trouble came back to haunt his last days. In his
seventies, living alone and suffering from emphysema, he decided
it was time to quit. The final out was a bullet fired by his own
hand in his orchard in Winthrop, Maine. True to Bissonette's ill
fortune, even this solution did not deliver the immediate relief
he sought. For one week, he lingered in a hospital bed while
officials tried unsuccessfully to contact relatives. Finally, on June
9, he died. The struggle had ended.

# 28

# THE GAME
# SHOULDN'T END
# THIS WAY

THE BLOW TO THE HEAD was serious. As Mickey "Kid" Cochrane was carried unconscious from the field, few in attendance expected his return that afternoon. But those who knew him knew he would plead his return convincingly if he did revive in time. And revive and return he did—with his team desperately behind and little time left. But time enough for Cochrane to carry his team to their only scores and rescue them from almost certain defeat. When it was over, it seemed the drama had been staged wholly for Cochrane's heroics. It seemed only fitting it should end this way.

But for Mickey Cochrane, this was only the beginning. He was barely twenty years old, a star athlete at Boston University, and had just led his team on a fourth-quarter, 65-yard scoring drive against a superior Holy Cross football team. Cochrane scored the touchdown and kicked the point to gain a 7-7 tie and the moral victory.

Yet despite his ability and accomplishments, there was, even in those early days, an apprehension or nervousness that accompanied his preoccupation with success. And his successes were never without struggle. When Connie Mack brought the twenty-one-year old Cochrane into the Philadelphia Athletics' camp, Cochrane had already proven himself as a hitter, runner, and leader, but had yet to prove he could catch a foul pop. Mr. Mack thought of switching Cochrane back to third, but Cochrane stuck at it behind the plate.

In 1925, his first year of major league ball, Cochrane caught 133 games and batted .331. The Athletics won 88 games that year, good enough for second place in the American League, but more importantly, it was their first winning season since 1914 when they won the pennant. By 1929, Cochrane would help bring that pennant back to Philadelphia once again. He didn't do it alone and he may not even deserve the most credit, for those Athletics teams contained several stars: Al Simmons, Jimmie Foxx, Lefty Grove, Ty Cobb, Tris Speaker, Eddie Collins, and Zack Wheat. But Cochrane's star shone nonetheless bright among these giants. His distinction was that he played great on great teams and made them even greater.

Between 1928 and 1933, the Athletics took all four MVP awards. (In 1929, there was no selection in the American League; in 1930, there was no award.) Cochrane won it in 1928, Grove in 1931, and Foxx in 1932 and 1933. In 1934, Cochrane left Philadelphia for Detroit and took the award with him. In his first year as a player-manager, he caught 129 games and batted .320 while guiding the Tigers to 101 wins and the World Series. It marked Detroit's first winning season since 1927 (except for a 76-75 mark in 1932) and their first appearance in the World Series since 1909 when the team was spirited by Ty Cobb.

But while Cobb played with a fierceness of personality that didn't always transform itself into team success, Cochrane channeled his own desire into the driving force of his ball club. In his thirteen years of major league ball, Cochrane never played on a losing team. He appeared in five World Series and his team won three of them. His role as catcher may have accounted for some of Cochrane's effect. His fiery temperament undoubtedly accounted for the rest. In 1928, his first MVP year, the Athletics made a remarkable run at the Yankees coming from as far back as thirteen games on July 4 to pass the Yankees briefly in September and finally lose by only two games at season's end. Cochrane won the award that year primarily in recognition of his inspirational example during that long stretch drive.

In a pivotal four-game series against the Yankees in September of that year, Cochrane put that spirit on dramatic display. The Athletics had already lost the first three games and entered the ninth inning of game four with a one-run lead and Rube Walberg on the mound. Walberg walked the first batter on four pitches. Cochrane immediately stormed out to the mound, punched Walberg in the stomach, and returned to his position behind the plate. Walberg retired the next three batters and the runner never got past first.

But Cochrane didn't have to punch out his teammates to show his spirit. He could also knock out the opposition as he did in the 1930 World Series against the Cardinals. Waiting on the mound as Cochrane stepped to the plate in the first inning of the first game, the aging spitballer Burleigh Grimes shouted at Cochrane that if he had a pointer dog that looked like him, he'd take him down to the river and shoot him. Cochrane responded with a home run.

In the next game, when Cochrane stepped up to hit in the first inning, he saw the entire Cardinal bench under the leadership of Grimes shouting "Mule Ears! Mule Ears!" and wriggling their hands behind their heads. Cochrane homered again.

In the decisive fifth game, Cochrane faced Grimes one more time. After eight scoreless innings, Cochrane managed a base on balls in the ninth inning. He then stood menacingly off first base facing Grimes and wriggling his ears. Jimmie Foxx followed with a home run to win the game, and the Athletics took the Series on the next day.

When the Athletics won their third consecutive American League pennant with 107 victories in 1931, they appeared to be virtually unbeatable. Lefty Grove had just completed the greatest single season ever recorded by a pitcher—31-4 with a 2.06 ERA. Al Simmons led the league in batting with a .390 average. Jimmie Foxx hit 30 homers and knocked in 120 runs. Cochrane batted .349 with 17 homers, 89 RBI, and 87 runs scored.

But the Athletics and Cochrane were hounded in the Series that year by Pepper Martin, the Cardinals' young center fielder, who batted .500 with 5 runs scored, 5 RBI, and 5 stolen bases to lead his team to victory in 7 games. Cochrane collected only 4 singles in 25 at-bats, committed an error, and saw 3 other bases stolen by Cardinals in addition to Martin's 5. Most observers concurred that he wasn't solely responsible for the stolen bases and the Series, but not all observers were so forgiving. "I believe the thing that hurt the chances of the Athletics most was the illness and consequent 'off-formness' of Mickey Cochrane," noted sportswriter James M. Gould in *Baseball* magazine following the Series. "Mickey . . . wasn't even mediocre in the Series. He batted .160 and dropped several third strikes. His throwing to second was generally wretched."

At the ballpark Cochrane was unable to shrug off the Cardinals' taunting with home runs. His physical ailments and nervous disposition prevented his getting any rest at night. And his stock market investments, which had already suffered in the crash of 1929, were again falling fast. Several urgent margin calls from his brokers were delivered to Cochrane on the Athletics' bench as games were being played. For the first time in his career, the qualities that had previously contributed to his success now seemed to conspire against him.

The effect on Cochrane and the Athletics was devastating. Despite the mitigating reasons, "he [Cochrane] was doubtless the Athletics' goat. Throughout the Series, he showed little of the pep, of the fighting spirit of the greatest of catchers," explained sportswriter F. C. Lane in the same *Baseball* magazine. For Cochrane, it was a time of utter turmoil and collapse as he "played in Philadelphia amid the echoes of crashing banks in a financial hurricane."

That Series marked the end of the Athletics' dynasty. Within three years nearly all the stars of that team, including Cochrane, were playing elsewhere.

When Cochrane went over to Detroit in 1934, he was thirty-one years old and coming off a typical Cochrane season: 137 games behind the plate, .322 average, 104 runs, 60 RBI and 15 round-trippers. The Tigers won the A.L. pennant in Cochrane's first year, beating the Yankees by seven games. Cochrane won his second MVP award. But again the Cardinals plagued him in the Series. This time, it was the Dean brothers assuring the Cardinals' victory in the seven-game Series, but once again Pepper Martin made his presence felt with two stolen bases, a .355 average, and eight runs scored. As in 1931, physical and emotional troubles plagued Cochrane throughout the Series. When the games were played in Detroit, Cochrane spent his nights sleeping fitfully in a hospital and discharged himself to play in the day.

In 1935, Cochrane would gain some revenge with a World Series championship, though over the Cubs not the Cards. With the score tied 3-3 in the final game of the Series, Hack Wilson tripled to lead off the ninth inning. Cochrane immediately walked out to the mound; but instead of punching his pitcher, Tommy Bridges, in the stomach, he instructed him to throw "breaking balls, nothing except breaking stuff." Bridges followed instructions, but almost too well. He threw a ball that hit the dirt two feet in front of home plate. Suddenly, it looked as though the Series would torment Cochrane again. But he managed to block the wild pitch and save the game from that final irony. Bridges got out of the inning without surrendering a run.

In the bottom of the ninth, Cochrane beat out an infield grounder to lead off. Charlie Gehringer then hit a shot down the first base line which looked like it might win the game. Fifty-five years later, Gehringer still had vivid recollections of the play. "I thought I had a double," he recalled, "but the first base-man knocked it down, got the force out and almost got Coch-rane at second." However, the throw hit Mickey's back as he slid safely into the bag. Goose Goslin then singled Cochrane home with the deciding run, and Detroit celebrated its first World Series victory. But instead of crossing home plate, Coch-rane jumped up and down on it in jubilation. He had taken an arduous path back to this feeling and was in no hurry to pass it by.

Those two years would be all the Tigers could get from Cochrane. The years wore him down, physically and emotionally. He missed most of the 1936 season due to nervous exhaustion, appearing in only 44 games that year. He got off slowly again in 1937, but by May things were beginning to come around for him. In one game in mid-May against Washington, Coch-rane connected for three singles and a double. As he stepped to the plate for his last at-bat of the game, Buck Newsom, the Senators' pitcher, shouted from the mound:

"Say why don't you go back to that hospital and stay there."

Cochrane responded with a single to left.

Before a Tuesday afternoon game on May 25 at Yankee Stadium, Cochrane laughingly recounted that story. His game was returning to form, and he was starting to feel more relaxed.

Bump Hadley was scheduled to pitch for the Yankees that day. Hadley was a veteran pitcher who had entered the league around the same time as Cochrane with a great deal of promise and a reputation for wildness. Years before, Cochrane himself

had picked Hadley to be a great pitcher saying he had everything, including "a fastball that buzzes by your chin." Unfortunately, a batter's chin is seldom in the strike zone. In 1932 and
1933, Hadley led the league in walks and he regularly issued
more bases on balls than strikeouts.

On this sunny afternoon, Cochrane tagged Hadley for a
home run in the third inning. When he stepped to the plate in
the fifth inning, the Tiger right fielder, Pete Fox, was on first,
with two out and the score tied. Cochrane worked the count to
3-1 and what happened next is open to some conjecture. In one
account, Cochrane said he crowded the plate to be sure to pull
the ball behind the runner, and in another he said he was relaxed and taking all the way. Some accounts mistakenly put the
count at 3-2. In any case, all accounts agree on one thing—
Hadley's next pitch was a fastball that buzzed Cochrane not by
his chin but about four inches north of it just above his right
temple.

The photograph that appeared in newspapers the next day
shows Mickey hitting the dirt before his bat or the ball touch
the ground. He cowers on his left side, arms coming to cover his
head. The written accounts dramatize the impact: "Then he
[Hadley] threw a fastball, high and inside. Cochrane, a left-
handed batsman, dropped to the ground to get away from it,
but the ball seemed to follow him. There was a sickening whack
and Cochrane lay still."

Cochrane would say later that the sun caused him to lose
sight of the all about six feet in front of the plate. H. G. Salsin-
ger's account of the incident in the next day's newspaper con-
firms this explanation: "His [Cochrane's] action at the plate
showed plainly that he lost it. He threw up his right arm the way
an outfielder does when he loses a fly ball in the sun. The ball
passed over Cochrane's forearm and struck him in the temple."

It was a serious blow, and though Cochrane did not immediately lose consciousness, his life was in immediate danger and
remained so for several days. The pitch fractured his skull in
three places with one break extending around the back of his
head nearly ear-to-ear. He lay unconscious for ten days.

There was little talk of a comeback. Perhaps it was because
he was thirty-four years old and had thirteen impressive years
behind him. Perhaps it was because he had the manager's role to

keep him in the game. But it's hard to believe that Cochrane would have accepted these as consolations. A more plausible explanation is found in a picture that the doctors showed Cochrane in late July 1937. As reported at the time:

"Displaying with a slight shudder, X-ray photographs of his cracked skull, which resembled a road map more than anything else, Gordon Stanley [Mickey] Cochrane said this afternoon that he guessed his playing days were at an end.

"All during the six weeks in the hospital, he had an idea that he'd play ball some more some time. He had been hurt before—broken legs, fractured fingers, a broken nose—and they told him his recovery would be complete. And then the other day, they pulled out that X-ray picture on him. 'Gee,' said Mike. 'Is that my head?' "

But even though Cochrane would never play again, his financial future was secure with his $45,000 salary as manager and vice-president and his office adjoining the office of the owner, Walter O'Briggs, who had initially bankrolled Cochrane's coming to Detroit. It would take little over a year before Cochrane would find that this secure future could shake again. The front page of the *Detroit Free Press* of August 7, 1938, contained a banner headline announcing that Mickey Cochrane had been fired. The article searched for a reason.

"Mickey's transition from playing manager to bench manager probably had more to do with his dismissal than anything else. The fighting type, Cochrane found the inactivity of the bench manager difficult to tolerate." To Cochrane it was like getting beaned a second time: "It all hit me like a sudden pinch between the eyes. When I stopped blinking, I was no longer manager of the Tigers."

When he stopped blinking, it was only to see how quickly and how hard he could fall. But injuries and firings are part of the game. Though his dismissal was a blow, it would not be a catastrophe. As the *Detroit Free Press* saw it on the day after the firing, "One of the most popular figures in baseball, Cochrane should not find much difficulty in making a new connection."

But that new connection never did come through, at least not in the way the paper seemed to envision. Baseball faded from Cochrane's horizon in his final years. He told an interviewer that he even preferred watching football games—the Chicago

Bears and Northwestern University—on television. In 1961, the year before he died, his old friend and mentor, Ty Cobb, passed away in Georgia. Cobb, as is well known, was not well-loved. Still, he was the first player elected to the Hall of Fame, and except for Ruth, the game's greatest figure. When Cobb died, Ruth was gone, Gehrig was gone, Wagner, Mathewson, Johnson—gone. His death marked not only the passing of a man, but the passing of a generation of ball players, of a game no longer played. One would have expected a funeral with crowds of mourners and nostalgic testimonials from the game. But from all of major league baseball, only three men came—Hall of Fame director Sid Keenor, and former players Ray Schalk and Mickey Cochrane— three lone figures to bid farewell to a man and his game.

Cochrane knew the sound of a World Series champion city when it exploded in celebration above the sound of cleats pounding on home. He knew the sound of a stadium shocked into dead silence by a moist, sickening thud. He knew the sound of a door closing behind him, of losing his place in the game he loved. And now as they carried away the casket of Ty Cobb and placed it in the family mausoleum, he knew the sound of footsteps that echoed hollow and dim, that sounded for a moment and were forgotten. It was the sound of something passing and gone. The end should sound better than this.

# 29

# HEADBANGER'S BALL

IN HIS TEN-YEAR MAJOR LEAGUE CAREER, Pete Reiser
played for the Brooklyn Dodgers, Boston Braves, Pittsburgh Pirates, and Cleveland Indians, primarily on an outpatient basis.
He appeared in 137 games in 1941, his first full year in the majors, and generally saw his playing time decline steadily in the
succeeding years until it reached 34 games in his final year, 1952.
The decline was not due to a lack of ability on Reiser's part.
Quite the contrary. He was the most multi-talented player of his
time. It was one of those talents—running into concrete walls—
that kept knocking him out of the lineup. But Reiser always
bounced back, often unconscious, and each time with a little
less of the other talents that made him such a blazing, and fading, star.

Fittingly enough, Pete Reiser's first opportunity in his professional career came as a result of an injury. In 1937, after being bounced around as a benchwarmer on a few teams in the
lower reaches of Branch Rickey's St. Louis Cardinal farm system, Reiser was finally sent to Newport in the Northeast Arkan-
sas League to take over at second base for their player-manager,
Tharp Hamilton, who had been hurt. It was only a temporary
fill-in position, but then luck struck again, as Reiser himself recalled it: "About the time he [Hamilton] was ready to play again,
our shortstop broke his leg, so I filled in for him and had a
steady job for the rest of the season."

The pattern continued when he had his first crack at the

major leagues two years later. By this time he was with the Dodger organization and playing impressively in their minor leagues. In spring of 1939, Reiser played with the major league team, but mainly as a ball shagger. Then on March 17, his twentieth birthday, Reiser got a chance to fill in for Leo Durocher at shortstop, who was feeling a bit ill. Reiser went 4 for 4 and played every day for the rest of the spring. He did not make the major league team that year. He joined them in mid-season the next year. But in 1941 he took over as the full-time center fielder for the Brooklyn Dodgers. In that rookie season, he put all his talents on display and helped lead the Dodgers to their first pennant since 1920.

Pete Reiser led the league in five major offensive categories that year: runs (117), doubles (39), triples (17), slugging (.558), and batting average (.343), making him the first National League rookie to ever win the batting crown. He earned the starting center field position in the All-Star game, ahead of St. Louis's great center fielder, Terry Moore. In the Most Valuable Player award voting, he finished a surprisingly distant second that year to his teammate Dolph Camilli, but that was partly a testimony to Camilli's outstanding year (league-leading 34 home runs and 120 RBI) and Reiser's position as a rookie.

Pete also put his less rewarding talents on display that year— getting beaned twice, crashing into one outfield wall, and missing 17 games. These latter talents would establish the dominant pattern of his already shortening career.

The first beaning came only two weeks into the season. He was carried off the field and into the hospital, conscious but unable to talk. The next day, he checked out of the hospital, though his doctor advised additional confinement. Reiser promised not to play, but Manager Durocher convinced him to at least suit up and sit on the bench. Then, in the eighth inning of a tied game, Durocher suddenly sent Pistol Pete up to pinch hit. He hit a grand slam to give the Dodgers the victory 11-7. He was so dizzy that he could barely circle the bases.

Five days later he ran into the exit gate in center field racing down a fly ball hit by Enos Slaughter of the Cardinals. It was a minor incident compared to his later run-ins with walls.

In 1942, Pistol Pete continued his bravura performance. Late in July, he went on a stretch where he got 19 hits in 21 at bats to bring his batting average near .400—"and just starting to get warm," as Reiser recalled it. The Dodgers had a thirteen and one half game lead as they began a series in Pete's hometown of St. Louis.

In the twelfth inning of the second game of a doubleheader, Reiser found himself chasing down another Enos Slaughter fly ball. As Reiser recalled it, "I caught it going at top speed. I just missed the flagpole in center field, but I hit the wall, hard." The impact caused Pete to drop the ball, but he picked it up and threw it in to Pee Wee Reese on the relay home. Slaughter beat the throw home for a game winning inside-the-park home run. Reiser collapsed and was carried off the field in a stretcher. When he woke up in St. John's Hospital in St. Louis, he found out he had a severe concussion and a fractured skull. This time his doctors advised him to take the rest of the year off. He was back in uniform a few days later.

As he had done a few years earlier, Reiser made his reappearance as an unexpected pinch hitter, this time in the fourteenth inning with two runners on. Pete lined over second base to drive in the winning run but was only strong enough to collapse on first base. He was back in a hospital again.

Reiser missed twenty-nine games that year, and the Dodgers missed first place by two games to the Cardinals. They still had a good year (104 wins) as did Pete (33 doubles, 89 runs, .310 average, and 20 stolen bases to lead the league). Then World War II intervened.

The war was not much easier on Pete. He served in what would always be for him the most dangerous theater—a baseball field. While serving a stint in Fort Riley, Kans., Pete chased a fly ball through a board fence and down a thirty-foot embankment. He broke his right shoulder, but his team still won the war.

In 1946, he returned to the Dodgers and, picking up where he left off, led the league in stolen bases with thirty-four (seven of them steals of home). He also crashed into a wall again. In fact, he crashed into walls four times that season. He also ripped his clavical muscles, pulled a muscle in his left leg, and then broke his left ankle during the final month of the season when the Dodgers and Cardinals were neck and neck in a pennant race.

In the first playoff ever held to decide the National League winner, the Cardinals easily swept the Reiser-less Dodgers in two games. Manager Leo Durocher could not send in a one-legged Reiser to save the day, but he probably considered it. In Durocher's mind, there was never a better player than Pete Reiser, even one with pieces missing. Durocher consistently stated that the Dodgers would have won the pennant with Pistol Pete in the lineup. "Nobody makes more of a difference than Reiser," he said, "Even a one-armed Reiser."

Of course, by that time, Durocher must have realized that a one-armed (or its equivalent) Reiser was the most he could hope for most of the time. Though he was still a force when in the lineup, Reiser's time there was declining and some of his skills, particularly his throwing arm, were deteriorating from the years of abuse. The Dodgers moved him over to left field in 1946 and placed Carl Furillo in center. Reiser appeared in only 122 games that year and went down to 110 in 1947. His batting average went back above .300 that year—recovering from his .277 of 1946—but overall his offensive numbers declined. He also suffered his most serious encounter with an outfield wall.

Chasing down a fly ball in Ebbets Field hit by Culley Rikard of the Pirates with the bases loaded, Reiser caught the ball, smashed into the concrete wall, and held on to the ball. He did not know these details at the time. The collision knocked him unconscious, which was not unusual. But even Pete himself would admit that this one was serious. He was administered last rites of the Roman Catholic Church and lay in a coma, partially paralyzed, for over a week. His skull was fractured; his shoulders were dislocated; and his career was effectively over.

The Dodgers made it into the World Series that year, despite losing the services of Reiser for 44 games. He still managed to make his impact felt in the Series, even after breaking his ankle in the third game. In the fourth game, Yankee pitcher Bill Bevens was working on a no-hitter with two outs and one on in the ninth when Leo Durocher sent Reiser up to pinch hit. The Yankees walked him intentionally and passed up the chance to finish a no-hitter at the expense of a one-legged, dizzy ballplayer. Eddie Miksis ran for Reiser. Cookie Lavagetto came up next and doubled both runners home to take away the no-hitter and give the Dodgers the victory 3-2.

The Dodgers added a new spark plug to their team that

year. Like Reiser, he combined speed with power in a way that presaged a new style of play in a coming generation of ballplayers (Doby, Mays, Mantle, Robinson, Aaron) who posed complete offensive threats at the plate and on the bases. He displayed the same fiery intensity on the ball field as Reiser with none of the penchant for running through concrete walls. Most remarkably, he was the same age as Reiser, twenty-eight, though Pete's body was far more shell-shocked. But then it took Jackie Robinson a little longer to break into the major leagues. He found walls of another order in his way.

Robinson was just entering his remarkable ten-year career; Reiser was entering the end of his. Reiser played for four teams in the next five years—Brooklyn, Boston, Pittsburgh, and Cleveland—never as a regular and never in more than eighty-four games in a season. He was troubled throughout that time by headaches, dizzy spells and a nervous stomach—the legacy of being carried off the field eleven times (nine times unconscious).

Still, his contributions to the game were lasting. After watching Pete play, teams laid down warning tracks made of dirt in front of home run walls and installed outfield fences that "gave" on impact. In 1947, they even padded the walls in Ebbets Field for Pete's sake, which seemed a fitting testimony to a crazy outfielder. But it was really too late to help Pete by that time. He should have been playing inside padded walls years before.

From 1960 to 1973, he coached with several teams. In 1973, when he was serving with the Cubs, he tried to break up a brawl with the San Francisco Giants. He was knocked out and carried off the field on a stretcher. On October 25, 1981, he died in his home in Palm Springs, Calif., after a long history of heart and respiratory trouble.

One feels an almost irresistible temptation to look back on Pete Reiser's career, especially its bright promise, and speculate on what might have been had it not been for the injuries. Red Smith said he "had as much natural talent as Willie Mays, Joe DiMaggio, Stan Musial or Mickey Mantle." Leo Durocher went further when he said, "I think Willie Mays was the best I ever saw, but Pete might have been better." But to think of Reiser without the injuries is to think of someone other than Reiser. For Pete's injuries were part of his talent and cannot be separated from the rest of his game. Reiser himself stated as much:

"It was my style of playing; I didn't know any other way to play ball."

In his own defense, Reiser often pointed out that every time he crashed into a wall it was in pursuit of a game-tying or game-winning fly. So what might have appeared as taking stupid chances to others was a reasoned and selective risk to Pete. It may have cost him in the long run and stopped him from becoming the ballplayer he might have been. But it made him into the ballplayer he was, and he bore that burden himself without complaint.

# 30

# THE RULES
# OF THE GAME

THE GAME CREATES its own time. Infielders taking easy ground balls, outfielders playing catch. Eventually the catcher throws the ball to second, and it's tossed around the infield before arriving back at the mound. A batter steps to the plate, digs into the dirt, steps out, and digs in again. The fielders settle into position. The pitcher stares at his catcher for a sign as the batter takes his habitual swings. A pitch is thrown. There is no sense of urgency here. The game has begun.

The pattern will repeat itself as the innings progress. You begin to notice a marked indifference toward time, as though it didn't exist here, or at least had no dominion. It doesn't. There is no clock in this game. No ticking minutes measure down the action. There is never the hint of a premature ending, of time running out, of "if only we had a few seconds more." The game ends when the last player makes out, however long that takes. It is one of the rules of the game.

There are no such rules outside of the game. The end can come at any time for any reason to anyone. You could be 25 years old, athletically fit, and suffer a bout of pneumonia. You could just die. It happened to Harry Agganis.

In the late 1940s, Harry Agganis was the most celebrated schoolboy athlete in New England history. He probably still holds that distinction today. From 1945 to 1947, he was a three-sport standout in basketball, baseball, and football at Lynn Classical High School in Lynn, Mass., but his greatest accomplishments came on the football field. In his junior year, he took over the quarterback position and led his team to an undefeated season, including a 21-14 victory over Granby High of Norfolk, Va., on Christmas night at the Orange Bowl in Miami. The victory ended Granby's 32-game undefeated streak.

By the end of his senior year, he had passed for over 4,000 yards, thrown 47 touchdowns, scored 24 other touchdowns, and averaged over 40 yards per punt. Lynn's 13,000-seat Manning Bowl would find over 20,000 in attendance when Harry's team played. He was picked as a quarterback and captain on an All-American high school football team and was recruited by major colleges nationwide. Frank Leahy, the Notre Dame coach, saw films of Agganis in action and called him "the finest football prospect I've ever seen." Warren McGuirk, the athletic director at the University of Massachusetts went one step further by saying that Agganis was "ready for the National Football League right now."

With these accolades, it was expected that Agganis would attend a football powerhouse such as Notre Dame or perhaps Holy Cross to stay closer to home. When he chose Boston University, a school not known for its football, it caused some surprise, even among his own family members who thought he was going to Cornell. But Harry's reasons were quite simple and had little to do with the world of football. Al Hirshberg listed them in *Sport Magazine* in November, 1950: "First, he didn't want to leave his widowed mother alone. Second, he didn't want to build up a national reputation elsewhere and then try to find employment around Boston. Third, he didn't want to play football for anyone but the brilliant little Boston University coach, Aldo (Buff) Donelli."

The lack of a major college program did nothing to hinder Harry's performance and little to diminish his fame. In New England, it made him an even greater hero. And he was already a big enough hero to draw an "unprecedented crowd of 20,000 for a meaningless game between the Boston University and Holy Cross freshman teams."

In his sophomore year, he set a school record for touchdown passes (15) and best punting average (46 yards) and led the East in defensive pass interceptions (15). Football had already moved into a two-platoon era, but Agganis never seemed to leave the field. During that season, Boston University defeated several major football schools, including Syracuse and West Virginia, while losing to Maryland by only one point. Harry Agganis had single-handedly transformed Boston University into a respectable football team.

He spent the next year at Camp Lejeune after being called to active duty from the Marine Reserves. Some suspected that his conscription had less to do with national defense than it did with the needs of the Marines' Camp Lejeune football team. With Agganis on the field, the Lejeune team won the championship of the Sixth Naval District, but it was still no match for the Quantico Marines, led by Eddie LeBaron. On September 20, 1951, he received a dependency discharge as his mother's support and returned home to his mother in Lynn and to football in Boston. Two days later he quarterbacked his team in a game against William & Mary. By the end of the 1951 season, Agganis would establish a school record for most yards passing in a season (1402) and be chosen on several All-American offensive and defensive teams.

Paul Brown, the coach of the Cleveland Browns, was impressed enough to make Agganis his first-round draft choice following that 1951 season. Though he still had another year left at Boston U., Harry was available in the draft because his original class had graduated. Brown was looking for a good passing, T-formation quarterback to replace the aging Otto Graham. He was willing to wait a year for Harry Agganis.

Harry would never report to the Cleveland Browns. He culminated his outstanding football career with a remarkable performance in the Senior Bowl of January 3, 1953. He played fifty-nine minutes, threw two touchdown passes, punted, kicked extra points and starred defensively. He was named the Most Valuable Player in the game. Red Grange called him the best football player he had seen that year. It was the last year he would be seen in that role. Harry Agganis played baseball, too.

After graduating from Boston University, Agganis turned down the offer of pro football to sign with the Boston Red Sox. Though his decision surprised many of his fans, it probably pleased his mother who had "never seen her fabulous son play football. She won't even listen for fear she'll hear that her youngest boy has been hurt." Harry explained his choice by saying,

"I'd already proved myself in football, but I haven't proved my-self in baseball." The "whopping baseball bonuses" of the time (Harry reportedly received $40,000) may have also had some ef-fect. Years later, his brother Philip explained that the Red Sox convinced him with the evidence of longer careers (and better long-term earning potential) in baseball. Nonetheless, his mother probably played no small part in his decision. For as he had shown in choosing Boston University four years earlier, the im-portance of staying at home and playing in Boston was always paramount in Harry's mind.

He had, of course, shown some promise as a baseball player during his high school and college years. While only a sopho-more in high school, he was picked as the outstanding high school baseball player in New England and won a place on the East team for the All-American Boys' game at Wrigley Field, Chicago. The next year, he was picked as one of two New En-gland players on the United States All-Star team and appeared in a charity game at the Polo Grounds in New York.

His first season of professional ball promised continued suc-cess. Playing for the Red Sox Triple-A affiliate at Louisville in 1953, he batted .281 with 23 home runs and 108 RBI to tie for the American Association RBI title. By the next year, he was the Red Sox's regular first baseman. Only Mickey Vernon of the Senators played more games at first base that year among Amer-ican Leaguers. Only Vernon was more productive. Still, in his rookie season Agganis batted .251 in 434 at bats with 11 home runs. And he led all American League first basemen with 89 as-sists while tying Vernon for the league lead of 9.8 chances per game at his position.

Agganis seemed destined for an impressive career. Not sur-prisingly, he played particularly well at home, batting .400 in his first five games as a starter at Fenway Park, including a homer, triple, and double. Over the course of the year, he hit eight home runs at home—the only left-handed Red Sox hitter other than Ted Williams to hit that many in thirty-five years.

But in 1955, he got off to a slow start. In May, he was hos-pitalized for ten days. An hour after discharge he was back in uniform working out at Fenway Park. His mother, of course, worried that he went back to playing so soon after his release.

But as Harry explained to his brother Phil: "If I don't go out to play, they (the Red Sox management) will think I'm goofing off."

By June 1, he started a road trip in Chicago with his team. He regained his starting position and raised his average to .313. But on June 4 in Kansas City he complained of chest pain and a fever. The next day he was sent back to Boston on a plane. Joe Cronin met him at the airport and drove him directly to Sancta Maria Hospital. On June 15, a newspaper article mentioned the long road back that lay ahead for Agganis. On June 16, he was placed on the voluntarily retired list to make room for shortstop Milt Bolling.

While he was bedridden in the hospital with a relapse of pneumonia, Harry developed phlebitis in his leg. He feared that an operation might hurt his baseball ability, so the doctor placed his leg in an ice trough to dissolve the clots. The treatment worked. Thirty-five years later his brother Philip could still remember Harry squeezing his leg where the clots used to be and remarking, "It feels good, Phil."

On June 27, Harry Agganis sat up in his hospital bed and died. Blood clots in his lungs were the cause.

"The Agganis death stands out alone," a newspaper mourned, "stark tragedy in an era of triumph for penicillin and other antibiotics." It was incomprehensible. A superb athlete. A young man. Provided the best care and best doctors. Killed by a lung infection. Something as common as pneumonia, as strange as a massive pulmonary embolism.

The Massachusetts House adjourned to pay its respects. The Red Sox players wore mourning bands for thirty days from the date of his funeral. Western Union reported that the telegrams sent to the family constituted the largest one-day volume in memory. The church where his body lay in view remained open around the clock. The young man who had thrilled so many followers with the brilliance of his efforts and filled so many hearts with the innocence of his gifts now stunned those followers with his death and left their hearts empty. His exploits had entered the local mythology and now he too would fade into the mists of time and myth.

He was laid out in his funeral bier "dressed in a blue suit [with] a tiara of apple blossoms . . . placed on his head and a wedding ring on his finger in traditional Greek Orthodox fashion." Ten thousand people filed past in less than four hours. In Pine Grove Cemetery, he was laid in his grave "with the tears of his grieving mother still wet on his cheeks." It wasn't supposed to happen in the game that Harry chose to play, but time took dominion. The clock was running after all.

# 31

# A LIFE UNSPENT

THE LIFE AND DEATH of Lyman Bostock is a tragic, peculiarly American tale. He was a remarkably gifted athlete who, in his own words, was in the right place at the right time—he was one of the very first ballplayers to strike it rich from the windfall contracts of the mid-seventies. But in the end, Bostock's timing proved fatally flawed. His stunning meteoric rise to fame and stardom, followed by his needless, violent death at twenty-seven form stark extremes within which we can attempt to understand a life.

Lyman Wesley Bostock's beginnings could not have been less promising. He was born in November 1950 in a poor section of Birmingham, Ala. Lyman Bostock, Sr. was a baseball player as well, but the racism of his time prevented him from reaching the major leagues. Instead, the senior Bostock spent ten years in the Negro leagues playing for teams with denigrating names such as the Birmingham Black Barons and the Ethiopian Clowns. The birth of his son could not save an already disintegrating marriage, and the elder Bostock separated from Lyman's mother, Annie, in mid-1952. Five years later, Annie Bostock decided to try her luck on the West Coast, and she and her son arrived on a Greyhound in Los Angeles with "7 dollars and a prayer," as Lyman would later put it.

Living in the slums of L.A. taught Lyman two things—how to survive on mean streets and how to have compassion for others. His athletic prowess first came to light at L.A.'s Manual

Arts High School, for which Lyman lettered in three sports. But baseball was clearly his first love, and he was good enough to play for perennial power Cal State Northridge. As a social psychology major, Bostock began working with misguided L.A. youths, an endeavor he would pursue in one way or another for the rest of his life.

Bostock's college career ended abruptly in 1972 when he was selected as the 595th player in the free-agent draft by the Minnesota Twins. After a two-and-one-half-year minor league apprenticeship, Bostock reached the majors where, auspiciously, he homered in his very first game. By the end of the 1975 season *The Sporting News* was calling Bostock an "excellent defensive center fielder" who batted .282 in the leadoff spot. However, 1975 was not adversity-free. Bostock sustained a broken ankle making a diving catch of a Bert Campaneris liner and missed 27 games.

The year Bostock came into his own was 1976. After Lyman hit for the cycle in late May, *Sporting News* writer Bob Fowler wrote, "It appears the Twins will have an excellent center fielder for the next decade. And a possible All-Star performer." There was a slight negativity to this budding stardom, however. Some of the players around the league accused Bostock of being a "hot dog," and ex-teammate Eric Soderholm disparagingly labeled him "the Muhammed Ali of baseball." His own teammates facetiously referred to him as "Abdul Jibber-Jabber" because of his nonstop monologues during pre- and post-game interviews. Bostock dismissed the criticism as peer jealously, saying, "Some guys play baseball because they don't want to work and other guys play because they were born to. I was born to." This contention proved to be beyond doubt by the end of the 1976 season. Bostock finished fourth in the American League in batting with a .323 mark, a mere .010 behind George Brett's circuit-leading pace.

It was only a rehersal for greater achievements. Bostock's 1977 season was substantially greater than anything he had accomplished heretofore. His .336 batting average was second only to teammate Rod Carew's AL leading mark, and his 104 runs scored plus 90 runs batted in were personal bests. He also tied a major-league defensive mark by recording 12 putouts in one game. And he was doing all this in his option year with the

Twins. It became evident early in the season that Twins' owner Calvin Griffith would not come up with the huge amounts of money Bostock would be able to command on the free-agent market. His future as a ballplayer seemed unlimited, but his future with the Twins was doomed.

Many teams tried to woo Bostock in the off-season of 1977-1978. The eventual winner was ex-cowboy star Gene Autry, owner of the California Angels, who signed Bostock to what was then termed the "most lucrative contract in baseball history." By present standards the $3 million over three years seems less than earthshattering, but at the time no one had ever hit the free-agent jackpot for more. Entering the 1978 season, Lyman Bostock was the highest paid player in baseball.

Because of this, Bostock was the target of intense criticism and scrutiny. Many openly stated that Bostock was not worth that kind of money, using the irrational argument that great players of the past, like Mantle or DiMaggio, were paid only a fraction of Bostock's enormous salary. But Bostock responded with grace and a newfound modesty. "Am I a better outfielder than Clemente, Mays, or Mantle?" he asked rhetorically in response to a reporter's question. "I have to say no. But if you ask if I was in the right place at the right time, I have to say yes." As the relentless media attention increased, Bostock's responses became more pointed. "My father played in the Negro leagues for nothing," he said. "He had no choice. I had a choice." He went on, "For me, I had the major leagues as my goal. They knew what they had was the best it could be for them."

So, Bostock was forced to open the 1978 campaign under a media microscope. He did not respond well to the pressure. In fact, he could hardly have been worse. At the end of April his batting average was .049. Every sportswriter in the nation jeeringly pointed to Bostock as an example of today's overpaid, pampered athlete. In his frustration, Bostock went so far as to call his father. "It was the first time I've ever called my dad for help," he said. But above all else, Bostock felt he was letting Gene Autry down. "I've got a man here who shows me all the respect in the world." Bostock commented, "and I can't do a darn thing. That hurts."

To make amends, Bostock offered to let the Angels hold back one month's pay. Of course, the Angels refused this gallant gesture, stating that they would not pay Bostock any extra if he hit .400 some month. But Bostock was determined to make a statement, and he decided to donate his April salary to charity. The $20,000 he gave away was more than he made the entire previous season in Minnesota. At first Bostock was besieged by letters from individuals down on their luck, but he decided to support three local institutions: One was L.A. Teen Challengers, an early drug and alcohol abuse treatment center; a second was an orphanage; and the third was the neighborhood church of his youth, the Vermont Square Methodist Church. "Too many people grow up taking from a community," Bostock said when he presented the church with a check for $10,000, "and it isn't every day when you can go back to that, community when you have fame and fortune." After all this, some cynics accused Bostock of the worst form of grandstanding, but he simply retorted, "I'm not doing this for the publicity, just for the satisfaction I'm going to get. This is what I believe in."

Things started turning around on the playing field almost immediately for Bostock. He hit a torrid .478 in June to bring his average hovering around .300. On a personal level, his reconciliation with his father reached new heights when Lyman, Sr. was invited to play in an Angels' Old Timers game. The elder Bostock promptly lined a single up the middle. Lyman, Jr. was featured in the Angels scorecard with the caption, "Lyman Bostock was and is a million dollar person." Teammate Dave Garcia gave high praise by stating that in three short months "he [Bostock] has become one of our leaders." Finally, Big Brothers of Orange County made Bostock an Honorary Big Brother for life in August.

And the Angels were in a pennant race. When the team got to Chicago for a weekend series in September, Bostock was hitting .290 with 70 RBI. As usual when in Chicago, Bostock made arrangements to stay with his uncle, Edward Turner, of nearby Gary, Ind.

In the day game of Saturday, September 22, Bostock rapped out two hits in an Angel win. That evening he was sitting in his uncle's living room with Thomas Turner, another uncle. Thomas asked Bostock if he remembered a Joan Hawkins, who was a good friend of Bostock's in his youth. Bostock wondered aloud how Joan was doing, and Thomas decided to give her a call. He tracked her down at her sister's home, Mrs. Barbara Smith, also of Gary. After a short visit, Mrs. Smith asked Turner and Bostock if they would give her a ride to another friend's home. The four piled into Turner's 1976 Buick, with Bostock and Mrs. Smith in the back seat.

At 10:44 P.M. while the Buick was stopped at a traffic light, another car pulled alongside. The driver brandished a shotgun, and Turner desperately tried to elude the madman, running two red lights in the process. At the corner of 5th and Jackson Streets the driver of the second vehicle opened fire, blasting the rear window of Turner's car hitting Bostock with full force and spraying Barbara Smith. Bostock was rushed to a nearby hospital where doctors worked frantically for three hours to save his life. But it was to no avail. Lyman Bostock, the twenty-seven-year-old star of the California Angels, was pronounced dead at 1:30 A.M., September 23, 1978.

Police began to piece together the story of Bostock's murder almost immediately. The assailant was Leonard Smith, the estranged ex-husband of Barbara Smith. He confessed to shooting Bostock but he said his intention was to kill his ex-wife. Perhaps he mistook Bostock for Barbara's lover. Whatever the reason, or lack of it, Bostock had been the innocent victim of the madman.

Reaction was immediate and widespread. The baseball world was in shock. Ex-boss Calvin Griffith said, "Ballplayers of his caliber don't come along very often." Angels General Manager Buzzy Bavasi said sadly, "He was the backbone of our club. We were going to build around him." Gene Mauch, who had managed him in Minnesota, said, "I thought the world of that man." Larry Hisle stated, "He was the best friend I had." The Angels wore black armbands for the remainder of the season.

Even the press, who had hounded Bostock so mercilessly earlier in the year, were kind in death. One Gary newspaperman led his piece on Bostock's murder by recalling Bostock's words of only a few months before: "Bostock once said he was in the right place at the right time. Last night, he was in the wrong place at the wrong time." One of the more eloquent editorials was written by Bill Gleason of the *Chicago Sun Times*. "Lyman Bostock," wrote Gleason, "joined the company of many others who have been blown away in the ghettos of our nation."

Bostock's death had some other effects as well. A Lyman Bostock Memorial Game and a Memorial Scholarship were instituted at his alma mater, Cal State Northridge. More importantly, when Bostock's killer, Leonard Smith, was released in June 1980 because of an insanity plea, the outrage was so great that a new law was enacted in Indiana, Illinois, and Michigan. The new legislation declared that a criminal could be both guilty and insane. Jack Crawford, prosecuter of Lake County, Ind., said, "The new law is directly attributable to Bostock." His influence was felt even in death.

Some say Bostock's murder was another instance of a mysterious jinx that has haunted the Angels since their inception in 1961. No fewer than eight Angels have met either violent or untimely deaths. Of them all, none seemed as senseless as Bostock's. His life and death are a painful reminder of the vast differences of lifestyles in this country. From his birth and youth in ghettos, to his success as a millionaire athlete, to his violent end in a ghetto, Lyman Bostock's story is a tragic circle. In this one life we can see both the pinnacle of our American dream and the abyss of our American nightmare.

# Shadows Cast Behind: Triumphs, Comebacks, and New Beginnings

# 32

# UP FROM THE ASHES

JOE WOOD WON 18 games and struck out 224 batters for Hutchinson of the Western Association in 1907, his first year in professional ball. At seventeen years old, he seemed to have sprung fully armed onto the pitcher's mound, his prior experience consisting of assorted positions on town teams in Ouray, Colo., and Ness City, Kans., and a curious eight-week engagement with an all-female outfit known as the Bloomer Girls. In his first game as a pitcher with Hutchinson, Wood struck out seventeen, won 2-0 and beaned the first batter he faced—putting him in the hospital for three days. He could throw the ball hard.

At the end of the season, Wood's contract was sold to Kansas City of the American Association for $300. Addie Joss saw Wood pitch at Kansas City and immediately informed his Cleveland ball club to sign him if they could. "I don't know what Kansas City wants for him," Joss reported, "but whatever it is, it is not enough; he makes my fast ball look like a floater." Cleveland tried, but Boston had already purchased Wood's contract from Kansas City for $3,200. He was still a teen-ager with less than two years of minor league experience behind him when he appeared in his first major league baseball game on August 24, 1908. He would only be twenty-two years old in 1912 when he pitched the season he is still remembered for.

In 1912, the Red Sox set a new standard for American League victories with 105 and won the division by 14 games. Much of the credit goes to their Hall-of-Fame outfield of Duffy

Lewis (LF), Harry Hooper (RF), and Tris Speaker (CF) who had been together for two full years when the season started. Player-manager Jake Stahl, who joined the team for the 1912 campaign, also played a major role. But the most significant contribution came from young Joe Wood who was already a veteran of five years with the team and who was coming off a 23-win season in 1911. In 1912, he would win thirty-four and three more in the World Series.

Joe Wood's 1912 pitching performance proved to be one of the greatest single seasons in the history of the game, but it was just barely the greatest pitching performance of 1912. Rube Marquard of the New York Giants led his team to the World Series that year by posting 19 consecutive victories—a record that still stands today. On July 3, the day that Marquard won his nineteenth, Walter Johnson of the Senators started a streak of 16 consecutive victories, which still stands as the American League record. Not to be outdone, Smoky Joe Wood started his own string of 16 consecutive victories on July 8, the day the Marquard streak ended.

As the summer progressed, the rival fortunes of Johnson and Wood became the feature attraction of the American League. When the Red Sox and Senators met in Boston for a weekend series on September 6, 7, and 8, they seized the opportunity to create some excitement. Johnson's streak had ended less than two weeks earlier on August 26. Wood's streak was still alive at thirteen entering the weekend. Johnson was scheduled to pitch on Friday with Wood going on Saturday, but the newspapers and the fans clamored for a head-to-head match-up to give Johnson a chance to defend his record. The Red Sox management, recognizing the attendance possibilities, willingly obliged. Manager Jake Stahl pushed Wood's assignment up to Friday and thus forced the confrontation.

Though Fenway Park was less than six months old, it held perhaps the greatest crowd in its history on that Friday afternoon. Over 30,000 fans crowded into the ballpark with many standing behind ropes rigged up for the occasion in front of the outfield wall and bleachers. Neither team could use their dugout, but instead had to sit on chairs set up along the foul lines in front of the paying crowd. Wood, himself, warmed up amidst a parted sea of spectators dressed in summer suits and white straw hats. He then went on to win the game 1-0.

It was not an easy victory. There was no score through five-and-a-half innings, though Wood loaded the bases in the third. With two outs in the bottom of the sixth, the overflow crowd did their part for the home team. After Tris Speaker dropped an opposite-field double into the crowd in left, Duffy Lewis did the same in right to score Speaker. If the fans had not been on the field, Lewis' fly ball would have been caught for the final out with no runs scored. As it was, Wood struck out nine, walked three and allowed six hits, while Johnson struck out five, walked one and allowed five hits.

The closeness of the contest epitomized the season for Johnson and Wood as they finished one-two in six pitching categories. Johnson led in ERA (1.39 to Wood's 1.91), strikeouts (303 to Wood's 258), and strikeouts per nine innings (7.24 to Wood's 6.75) for the second-place Senators, while Wood led in wins (34 to Johnson's 32), complete games (35 to Johnson's 34) and shutouts (10 to Johnson's 7) for the first-place Red Sox.

Wood's 34-5 mark gave him the highest single-season winning percentage (.872) of any pitcher with at least 25 victories. In subsequent years, only Lefty Grove's 31-4 in 1931 and Ron Guidry's 25-3 in 1978 would surpass it. What finally set Wood and Johnson apart that year were Wood's three World Series victories and his defeat of Johnson in their epic face-to-face confrontation. For at least one bright summer Smoky Joe Wood was as good (or better) than the greatest right-handed pitcher of all time. He was not yet twenty-three years old, and even though he did not know it at the time, his pitching career was effectively finished.

In spring training the next season, Joe Wood slipped on wet grass while attempting to field a bunt and broke his right thumb. His hand remained in a cast for three weeks, but Wood pitched on the day the cast was removed. He felt soreness in his shoulder after the game; the soreness would remain with him for seventy-two years. After pitching 35 complete games in 1912, he returned after the injury to complete only twelve in 1913.

He went on to three more winning seasons in 1913-1915 and won the league ERA title in 1915 with a 1.49 mark, but his importance to the staff diminished as his innings decreased. As Wood himself described the agony: "After a game I couldn't even lift my arm. If I put my right hand in my pocket, I'd have to take it out with my left hand."

By 1916 it appeared that Wood's career was over. With the disbanding of the Federal League, owners were no longer worried about losing their players nor were they willing to pay the high salaries of a few years earlier to keep them. When Joe Wood became involved in a salary dispute after the 1915 season, he discovered how dramatically his value had dropped: "Nobody wants Joe Wood. The Red Sox announced yesterday that all major clubs had 'waived claim to Joe Wood, pitcher.' Not so long since he was Smoky Joe. . . . The owner of the Red Sox can send Wood to the minors, now, if he has a mind to."

The Red Sox did not send him to the minors. Joe sent himself home to Shohola, Pa., where he sat out the entire 1916 season. The Red Sox did not miss him much as they won the American League title and the World Series behind the pitching of a young left-hander named Babe Ruth who won 23 games along with the ERA title.

For Wood, the 1916 season was filled with pride and bitterness. The strain on his arm had strained his relationship with the ball club's management. Even though the Red Sox had been paying him to pitch when he was frequently unable to pitch, Wood resented his treatment. "I think they thought I was fooling or something, telling them my arm was bad," he explained in an interview with Lawrence Ritter. "But I was so crazy about baseball, I loved to be in there, but I just couldn't, that's all there was to it."

But fate intervened once again in 1916 in a way that would eventually turn Wood's fortune: the Red Sox traded Tris Speaker to Cleveland. After the 1916 season, Wood contacted his friend Speaker to get him on the Cleveland ball club. The Cleveland management thought that maybe Joe could help their ball club, and Joe took the chance, though he suspected his pitching days were over. He only appeared in five games as a pitcher for the Indians in 1917 and laid to rest any misconceptions about his pitching ability. For the only time in his career, he had an ERA above 3.00 (3.45), a losing record (0-1), more hits allowed than innings pitched (17 to 15), and for only the second time had more walks than strikeouts (7 to 2). Joe Wood could not pitch.

The discovery did not cost the Indians a penny. From July 1, 1917, to June 15, 1918, Wood stayed with the club but refused to draw his salary. He "would not accept money under false pretenses." He stayed, knowing he could not pitch but feeling that he might help on coaching.

In 1918, Cleveland did not even offer Wood a contract, but he showed up at their spring training camp in New Orleans, paying his own way. During the first road trip of that season, the Indians ball club found itself ravaged by the flu which reduced its roster of available players. When left fielder Jack Graney threw his arm out, manager Lee Fohl was forced to try reserve first baseman Ed Miller in left. The next day, he dug deeper for another journeyman first baseman, Eddie Onslow, who made his only major league appearance in the outfield that day. Finally, Joe Wood convinced Fohl to put him out in left field. By this point, it was an easy sell. Five years earlier, a sore arm had forced him out of the game, and now another sore arm (Graney's) was opening his way back in.

Not being able to pitch did not mean he could not play ball. As early as 1916, Wood had considered moving to another position, but even then, there were doubts about him as damaged goods: "Joe (Wood) says he hopes to play the outfield, but he may have trouble in convincing a manager that he can hold up that end, with a lame arm to handicap him."

For Wood, it was a much simpler proposition: "I wanted to show them I was a ballplayer." In 1918, he got that opportunity when a combination of injuries, illness, and a world war opened a regular spot in Cleveland's outfield. In 422 at bats that year, Joe Wood batted .296 and led his club with 5 home runs and 66 RBI. Not the Hall-of-Fame caliber numbers he had produced in his early years as a pitcher, but more than good enough to show he was a ballplayer. In June, Jim Dunn, the owner of the Indians, made it official. "Joe," he said, "I understand you are paying your own way. . . . I wish you would come up and we will fix up a contract."

For the next four years, Joe Wood remained a ballplayer, primarily as a reserve outfielder in close to one-half of the games from 1918 to 1922. He even showed up at second base and first base and twice on the mound—whenever and wherever they needed a player. He did not pack the stands any longer on the legend of his reputation. He was no longer the biggest draw in town. But he was still playing the game and still playing it better than most.

There was more than a little satisfaction in this accomplishment. F. C. Lane, writing in *Baseball* magazine in 1920, termed Joe Wood's reincarnation unparalleled and called his "the most remarkable career of any member of the Cleveland Club." Wood, quoted in the same article, remarked that "the thing which gave me the greatest satisfaction is the thought that after I was read out of baseball as a poor old pitcher who was all through, I was able to make myself over into an outfielder at least good enough to stick with a winning club."

The fans and writers also accepted his transformation into a more than capable outfielder and hitter. Perhaps it was the poetic license of the time that called attention to "Wood's steaming drives, the incomparable grace with which he catches fly balls, the wonderful manner in which he scoops up grounder after grounder to his left or right and the brilliancy of his throws to second, third, or home." But a prosaic note would also sound, calling Wood the "best utility man on the club . . . capable of playing any position except catcher." Regardless of the tone, contemporary newspaper accounts repeatedly referred to his value to the team.

On occasion, he would again grab the headlines as he did with a nineteenth-inning home run, his second of the game, in a contest against the Yankees in 1918. The home run won the game for the Indians, 3-2, in what was then the longest major league game played in the Polo Grounds. Typical of Wood's role as a complete ballplayer, that homer was not his only contribution to the victory. He also made a game-saving catch in the ninth inning that robbed Elmer Miller of a home run and forced the game into extra innings.

In 1920, he played once again on a World Series champion team, though his two hits in ten at bats could not match the glory of his three pitching victories in 1912. In 1922, his final year, he became the Indians' full-time right fielder and in 505 at bats batted .297 and once again led his team in RBI with ninety-two.

He would retire after that year to take a coaching job at Yale, where he stayed for the next twenty years. He had lived three lives in professional baseball—the phenom, the wash-up, and the player—and was not yet thirty-three when he retired. In the final years of his life he found himself a legend once again. He would occasionally appear at Fenway Park to throw out a ball—left-handed—the pain in his right arm still haunting him after all those years. He appeared in Lawrence Ritter's *The Glory of Their Times* and was featured in one of Roger Angell's finest baseball essays, "The Web of the Game." For a time, he was the oldest living former major leaguer. He died in 1985 at the age of ninety-five.

Few men have led lives that were so long and deeply rooted in the landscape of the game. In 1916, it appeared that Joe Wood would have to withdraw from that landscape forever. But, as he told Lawrence Ritter, he drew back to a smaller scene instead: the attic of the house he built on his family homestead in Shohola where he dangled from a trapeze to stretch out his arm, hoping for a miracle to finally end the pain.

That miracle would never occur, but a more lasting one did, one that arose not merely from the starry-eyed dreams of a child, but from a child's unyielding love for a game. He left the dream in the attic but came down with the passion intact. That and his ability would finally bring him back up to the major leagues. He was a player again; it was what he had always been. It is all that a game really needs.

# 33

# DO IT FOR CHAPPIE

MAJOR LEAGUE BASEBALL had been played for forty-nine seasons, and it had never happened. An additional seventy seasons have been played (at this writing), and it hasn't happened since. Only once in the century and a half that big league ball has been around has a man died because of injuries inflicted by a pitched ball. There have, of course, been many other serious injuries due to the so-called beanball. Mickey Cochrane had his career ended by one; Tony Conigliaro had his career curtailed by one; and more recently Dickie Thon was nearly blinded by a Mike Torrez fastball. But only one man lost his life, and he was Ray Chapman.

Raymond Johnson Chapman was born in Beaver Dam, Ky., on January 15, 1891. His family moved to the small town of Herrin, Ill., where Chapman grew to be the town's sports idol. His professional baseball career began on the Mississippi River with Davenport, Iowa, at the age of nineteen. In the short span of a season, however, Chapman jumped to Springfield and then to the Toledo Mud Hens, one of the finest teams in the old International League. Before he reached his twenty-first birthday, in July of 1911, he was sold to the Cleveland club in the American League.

Although he only appeared in 31 games in that rookie season, Chapman hit a solid .312 and dispelled any doubts about his ability to handle major-league pitching. Cleveland believed it had a steady shortstop for at least the next decade. With veteran

Napoleon Lajoie at second, the young Chapman solidified the middle of Cleveland's infield. He led AL shortstops in putouts three times, assists once, and chances per game, the range factor, three times. This is not to imply that Chapman was "good field no-hit." According to contemporary Harry Grayson, Chapman "was the ideal second-place hitter." In 1917 he set a major-league record of 67 sacrifice hits, and he finished second only to Ty Cobb in stolen bases. In fact he was widely considered one of the fastest men in baseball and once won a loving cup for circling the bases in a scant fourteen seconds. In the war-curtailed season of 1918 he led the AL in runs scored with 84, and three years earlier he scored 101 runs.

As for "intangibles," teammate Tris Speaker called him a "wonderful field general, a quick thinker, and a tireless worker." No less an authority than Bill James wrote in his *Historical Abstract*, "Though his statistics were not eye-catching, Chapman was a tremendous offensive and defensive player, probably destined for the Hall of Fame had he lived."

The 1920 season looked especially bright for Cleveland collectively and for Chapman in particular. Ray had married in October of 1919, and his bride Kathleen was expecting their first child throughout the summer of 1920. The Indians were coming off two consecutive near misses for the AL pennant, being nosed out by the Babe Ruth led Boston Red Sox in 1918, and falling short to the Chicago White Sox by three-and-a-half games in 1919. (One wonders how different baseball history would be if the Indians could have only pulled that pennant out.) Indian fans felt in their bones that 1920 was their turn.

They certainly had reason, for the 1920 Cleveland team was very good indeed. They were led, literally, by player-manager Tris Speaker, who hit .388 with 50 doubles and complemented his offense with his usual superlative center field play. The ace of the pitching staff was Jim Bagby who won 31 games with a 2.89 ERA. Stan Covelski added 24 wins, and Ray "Slim" Caldwell rounded out the deep starting staff by chipping in 20 victories. Chapman's partner at the keystone sack was second baseman Bill Wambsganss, who that October became the first and only player to turn an unassisted triple play in World Series competition. At short was Ray Chapman. He was having a solid season, scoring 97 runs in the first 111 games.

When Cleveland came to New York in mid-August, the 1920 pennant chase had come down to three teams: the defending "champion" White Sox, the New York Yankees, and, of course the Indians. In the first game of the series, on August 16, the Yankees sent their ace, Carl Mays, to face the Indians at the Polo Grounds. Mays had developed a reputation for ruthlessness on the mound, and he was renowned for his submarine style delivery. His most effective fastball had a tendency to move toward a right-handed batter—what was then quaintly called an "in-shoot."

Ray Chapman led off the top of the fifth for what seemed to be an uneventful 3,786th career at bat. Mays's battery mate was Muddy Ruel, and Tom Connolly was the home plate umpire. The third pitch came inside and hit Chapman "with such force," Connolly said later, "that some of the players believed it had struck Chapman's bat." One such player was Carl Mays, who fielded the bouncing ball and threw to first baseman Wally Pipp for what he thought to be an out. But at the plate was a crumpled Ray Chapman. Within minutes, six physicians from the Polo Grounds' crowd were milling about home plate attempting to revive Chapman. At first he responded to treatment, and he even began walking under his own power toward the clubhouse in right center field. However, in the vicinity of second base, the base he had helped man so well, he collapsed again and had to be carried from the field. Harry Lunte became the answer to a macabre trivia question when he went in to run for Chapman.

Tris Speaker later spoke about that fateful pitch. "Chappie was able to get out of the way of pitches thrown to his head. But on this occasion he seemed to be in a daze. He just stood there and made no effort to pull away from the pitch." In the clubhouse Chapman was joined by roommate Jack Graney. "I wasn't in the lineup that day," Graney said in November 1962. "He was conscious in the clubhouse. He looked at me and tried to speak but the words wouldn't come out. I knew by the look in his eyes that he wanted desperately to tell me something, so I got a paper and put a pencil in his hand. He made a motion to write but the pencil dropped to the floor."

There is an apocryphal tale that Carl Mays also made a visit to the Cleveland clubhouse. According to one source, Chapman turned to Mays and said, "It's all right, Carl; everything will be all right." It is a beautiful, touching story but it never happened.

In reality, Chapman was rushed to St. Lawrence Hospital in Manhattan where Dr. J. M. Horan began emergency surgery in an attempt to save Chapman's life. The major problem was that Chapman had received a skull fracture. The surgery, which lasted about an hour, was a seeming success as Horan was able to remove a piece of bone and Chapman was given a fair chance at full recovery. However, this would not be the case. His condition worsened almost immediately and irreversibly. By 5:30 A.M., on August 17, 1920, a mere eighteen hours after the beaning, the unthinkable had happened. Ray Chapman was pronounced dead at the age of 29.

The "Chapman Incident," as it was called, had many consequences, some of them quite far reaching. On an individual level, Carl Mays never got over the notoriety of the pitch. Two teams, Boston and Detroit, branded Mays a killer, clamored for his banning, and publicly stated they would forfeit rather than play against him. Even before this, Mays was, as one outraged sportswriter put it, "notorious for his addiction to the beanball." Jack Graney said in 1962, "People ask me if I still feel Mays threw at Chappie. My answer has always been the same—yes, definitely."

But Mays denied any responsibility. In an article for *Baseball* magazine of November 1920, Mays wrote, "Chapman crowded the plate with his head and hands over it." He also believed that the ball that killed Chapman was discolored and ragged and should have been replaced by the umpires. Mays added that he was "disliked" and "unpopular" among ballplayers for unnamed reasons, and it was this unpopularity that made him the target of "malicious statements." "From some of these statements the public would be entitled to gather that I was continually hitting opposing batters . . . On the contrary, aside from Chapman, I have hit only five batters all season and not one of them in the head." During the 1920 season, Mays continued, "There were several pitchers in the league who have hit more batters than I have, some of them twice as many."

However, Mays was never able to clear his name, and many believe the pitch has kept him out of the Hall of Fame. That one pitch, then, dramatically altered the makeup of the Hall: it may well have kept two players out while giving a third player [Joe Sewell, who became the Cleveland shortstop and later reached Cooperstown] his first opportunity to play. Just before Mays died, in 1971, he said, "It was the most regrettable incident of my career and I would give anything if I could undo what has happened." He added bitterly, "Nobody remembers anything about me except one thing—that a pitch I threw caused a man to die."

The death of Chapman also directly altered the way baseball was played. Combined with the breaking of the Black Sox scandal, the Chapman incident led to a strict enforcement of the new rules banning all "freak" or doctored pitches, such as the spitball, as baseball frantically tried to prove to America that it was a legitimate enterprise. Umpires were required to change balls much more frequently in the course of a game. The inflated offensive production of the 1920s is better explained by these changes than by the so-called "lively ball" myth. Hitters who until now were desperately lunging for dingy, sharply breaking spitters were teeing off on clean, uncurving pitches.

Finally, Chapman's death had a marked effect on the pennant race of 1920. The initial reaction of the Cleveland club was disillusion and disunity. A fierce schism formed between Catholic players, led by catcher Steve O'Neill, and Protestant players, led by Speaker, over the issue of Chapman's final resting place. O'Neill stood behind Chapman's wife Kathleen who was striving to bury Chapman in a Catholic cemetary, while Speaker supported Chapman's parents who were attempting to inter him in a Protestant one. O'Neill and Speaker came to blows, with O'Neill sustaining a vicious beating. Even after that issue subsided, Cleveland was still fading from the race. As sportswriter Wilbur Wood wrote on August 30, "But so stunned was Cleveland fandom by the death of its popular idol that in the shadow of his loss the sinking of the Indians in the pennant race has aroused little comment. There is no longer the interest in the games there was before the disaster."

But then the ball club and the city seized on a rallying cry: "Do it for Chappie!" Two memorial funds were initiated; one fund presented a beautiful bronze tablet in Chapman's honor which the club set in center field of old League Park, their home ball field. The other memorial was a floral offering that had

20,623 separate contributors. Spurred on by this show of community support and love, the Indians raced to the pennant by two games over Chicago and by three over the now arch-enemy Yankees. The poor Brooklyn Dodgers had no hope of stalling this juggernaut which quickly dispatched the Dodgers 5 games to 2 in the World Series. It was Cleveland's first World Championship.

Some Cleveland players stated that the Series victory was not the same without Ray Chapman to share it. To those players something died along with Chapman on August 17, and even a world title seemed insignificant when compared with that loss. Nevertheless, one thing is indisputable. The city of Cleveland and their beloved team of 1920 had, indeed, done it for Chappie.

# 34

# PEERLESS

WHEN BASEBALL AFICIONADOS MILL AROUND the proverbial hot stove to discuss the greatest players of all time by position, probably the easiest decision is at first base. Almost all learned experts and casual fans agree that Lou Gehrig is the standard by which we measure such luminaries as Don Mattingly, Keith Hernandez, Eddie Murray, Willie McCovey, Gil Hodges, et al. However, if he had not been afflicted with a rare eye condition that hampered an otherwise brilliant career, the standard might very well be George Sisler. Sisler was so great that Branch Rickey could describe him only in terms of a Platonic ideal: "If all major leaguers were shaped from a model, George Sisler would be that model." But even with all he accomplished, Sisler's career, in the final analysis, is a question mark, a might-have-been.

George Sisler was born on March 24, 1893, to Cassius and Mary Sisler, two staunch members of northeastern Ohio's professional class. In fact, Sisler was an oddity among ballplayers of his era in that both his parents were college educated and well-to-do. One of Sisler's uncles was the mayor of Akron, so the Sislers moved there about the time George was ready for high school. Sisler was the star pitcher for Akron High School, a southpaw known primarily for his fastball, and professional scouts were expressing interest as early as his sophomore year. He signed a contract upon graduation in 1910 with the Akron club in the Ohio-Penn League, but his father voided the contract on the grounds that George was a minor at the time of the signing. Instead, Cassius Sisler insisted George receive a college education. Unknowingly, Mr. Sisler set into motion a series of events that would culminate five years later and reverberate as late as 1920.

Sisler next pitched for the University of Michigan. Also at Ann Arbor at the time was the then little-known Branch Rickey, who was completing his law degree while coaching baseball on the side. Rickey was in the coach's office on May 11, 1911, when word came to him that a Michigan freshman hurler was setting down the opposition with astonishing ease. By the time the seven-inning game was over, George Sisler would record 20 of the 21 outs by strikeout. Thoroughly impressed, Rickey sought and received verbal assurance from Sisler that upon receiving his degree, Sisler would play for the St. Louis Browns. Rickey was privy to inside information that he would become the Browns' manager by that time.

Simultaneously, Sisler's signed contract was being bandied about the country. Akron had sold it to Columbus of the International League who in turn had sold it to Barney Dreyfuss, the owner of the Pittsburgh Pirates. When Sisler attempted to join the Browns in June 1915, Dreyfuss called foul and brought the issue before the National Commission, the three-member judicial panel that oversaw baseball at this time. This panel was composed of the American and National League presidents and the owner of the Cincinnati Reds, Garry Herrmann. The decision seemed to be a mere formality for Dreyfuss: the AL and NL presidents would split their votes according to league partisanship, and most observers believed Herrmann, a close, long-time friend of Dreyfuss, would throw the deciding vote Pittsburgh's way. But Herrmann crossed up Dreyfuss by siding with the Browns. Dreyfuss was so outraged by the betrayal that he refused to speak to Herrmann for the rest of their lives. A much more important consequence was that the authority of the National Commission was undermined, thus paving the way for a single commissioner, a post eventually filled by Kenesaw Mountain Landis.

In any event, George Sisler joined the St. Louis Browns on June 28, 1915, without spending a single day in the minor leagues. For a brief period he remained a pitcher, and it was on the mound later that season that Sisler had what he called his "greatest thrill." On an extremely hot Sunday afternoon in late August in the second game of a doubleheader, Sisler was pegged to pitch against the immortal Walter Johnson of the Washington Senators. The scene was Sportsman's Park in St. Louis. "The first thing you should know," Sisler recounted in 1969, "was that Walter Johnson was my idol. He was not only a great pitcher but as fine a gentleman as I have ever known." In this particular game Johnson was at his usual proficiency, but unbelievably, Sisler was matching him frame for frame. The Browns eked across two runs, one of them knocked in by Sisler, and they hoped Sisler could make them stand up. Remarkably, he did, and the Browns walked away with a 2-1 win. Sisler's pitching career was already heading for oblivion, and he would win only five of eleven games in his entire career. But against Johnson, he won two of three starts, a fact of which he was extremely proud. "I never stopped admiring him," Sisler said of Johnson, "so I suppose you'd say he was forever my hero."

Branch Rickey was well aware that Sisler's career would go nowhere fast as a pitcher, so the Mahatma began experimenting with Sisler in the outfield and at first base to take advantage of his hitting prowess. And it was at first that Sisler finally settled. The transition to the position was not without its struggles, though. In a game in September 1915, Sisler was unable to corral a high but catchable throw from one of the infielders. St. Louis pitcher Bob Groom began to insult and curse Sisler when the team returned to the dugout between innings. "Listen, college boy," Groom reportedly said, "you run harder for those balls." Many expletives have been deleted. Sisler's face blanched, and he approached Groom without sayng a word. No one had ever spoken to him that way in his life, and after one Sisler punch had decked Groom, no one ever spoke that way to him again.

Sisler's career proper began the following season, and from that 1916 season on, his offensive and defensive skills reached astounding levels. After hitting a mere .305 in his first full season, Sisler's average jumped to .353 in 1917. The average slipped back a tad in 1918 to .341, but he led the league in stolen bases and had the longest hitting streak of the year, 26 games. If his baserunning was considered superlative and his hitting awesome, it was his defense that set him apart from all others. "He was lightning fast and graceful," said Branch Rickey. "Effortless. His reflexes were unbelievable. His movements were so fast you simply couldn't keep up with what he was doing."

Two plays in particular which seem so stunning as to be apocryphal may be used to illustrate. In a game in 1921, Sisler fielded a ground ball to his right, and, assuming the pitcher was covering first, he tossed the ball toward the bag. As soon as he let go of it, however, he realized that the pitcher had failed to cover. Sisler dived for his own throw, caught it, and landed on the bag for the out. The second play may be even greater. In 1922, against Washington, the Senators had a runner, Joe Judge, on third with Roger Peckinpaugh batting. Sisler had a hunch that the squeeze play was on, so he started inching toward the plate with the pitch. Sure enough, Peckinpaugh bunted the ball toward the first base line where Sisler fielded it, tagged Peckinpaugh and threw home all in one motion. Judge was tagged out for a double play.

At the plate, Sisler had two of the greatest seasons of all time. There is still a debate whether the 1920 or 1922 season was the better. Rickey tended to support 1922. "There never was a greater player than George Sisler in 1922," he said often. "That year he was the greatest player that ever lived." Rickey's argument has convincing support. Sisler's batting average in 1922 was .41979, the second highest in American League history. Considering the record, Napoleon Lajoie's .422, was achieved in the questionable initial season of the AL in 1901, Sisler's .420 can be considered the highest of all time. He also set the AL record at that time for hitting in consecutive games, forty-one, breaking Ty Cobb's previous best of forty. Sisler's character is shown by the way he surpassed Cobb. In September of 1922, Sisler injured his shoulder early in the forty-first game of the streak, but he taped it up, stayed in the game and doubled, essentially with one arm, to set the record. In addition, Sisler led the league in hits, triples, runs scored and stolen bases. His 246 hits is the eighth highest total in baseball history. And of course, he played his usually incomparable defense at first. For all these accomplishments, Sisler was named the Most Valuable Player, the first one in history.

But Sisler himself was more partial to the 1920 season. "I

was meeting the ball better," he said much later. "The averages don't tell the whole truth." In 1920, Sisler set a record that may never be broken—257 hits. He also stole 42 bases, had 12 four-hit games, fielded a league-leading .990, and struck out only 19 times in 631 at bats. He went 8 for 8 at one stretch, hit for the cycle, hit safely in 131 of 154 games, batted .401 overall, and hit a blistering .473 in his home park.

Perhaps 1920 was greater on an individual level, but 1922 was the closest Sisler would come to a World Series. That year the Browns fell only one game short to the powerful New York Yankees, who were just beginning to piece together their mono-lithic forty-three-year dynasty. The pennant hinged on a three-game series in St. Louis starting on Saturday, September 15. The two teams were in a flatfooted tie going into that weekend, and they split the first two games. In the final meeting of the season between them, on Monday, September 17, the Browns held a 2-0 lead after seven. But the Yanks scored one in the eighth, and the ninth proved to be Sisler's most disappointing moment.

"Gee, it was tough," he said in 1932. "Wally Schang was up first and he singled off of [pitcher] Dixie Davis's glove." After a passed ball pushed the tying run into scoring position, St. Louis manager Lee Fohl brought in lefty Hubert Pruett to face the lefty-hitting Elmer Smith. But Yankee manager Miller Huggins "was using some strategy himself," said Sisler. "When Pruett went to the mound, Hug replaced Smith with Mike McNally." McNally attempted to sacrifice, but Browns' catcher Hank Severeid slipped trying to field the bunt and all hands were safe. Everett Scott followed with a walk, and the bases were filled with Yankees with no one out. After another pitching change, Joe Bush forced a runner at the plate. There was a slight glimmer of hope that the Browns could get out of the jam. But the next batter, Whitey Witt, sent the Brownies down to defeat. Sisler recounted, "When I saw his line drive sail out to center for a single, scoring two runs, why, my heart ached. That was the blow that beat us, and I don't think the Browns ever recovered from that shock." They never contended again during Sisler's tenure with them, and many call Sisler the greatest player never to appear in a World Series.

Most of all, 1922 was the turning point of Sisler's career,

for it was the beginning of the end. Something had gone haywire with his vision at the tail end of the year. "I didn't quite realize what was happening," Sisler said, "until one day when I was driving I thought I saw two cars in the other lane. There was only one, and I knew something was drastically wrong." A sinus condition had affected Sisler's optic nerves, giving him double vision. He struggled through the end of the 1922 season, and he was doctored throughout the winter of 1922-1923. But he was forced to sit out the entire 1923 season in the hopes that rest and a less strenuous routine would correct his vision. In 1924 he returned to the majors, now as player-manager, but he would never see perfectly again. Because of the nerve condition, his two eyes did not always function together.

Nevertheless, by anyone else's standards, Sisler was still a tremendous ballplayer. In 1924 he hit .305, tying his career low, but he then went on to top the 200-hit plateau three more times, and he hit as high as .345 in 1925. Also in that season he knocked in seven runners in two successive at-bats. But these were only flashes of his past brilliance. Even though many ballplayers would have been proud of the numbers, Sisler himself said, "I didn't consider that real good hitting." He never was able to again sustain the level he established in the early twenties. Before 1924, his career average was .367; afterwards, it was .320. And Sisler's average was falling while most other major league averages were rising.

After the 1927 season the Browns sold Sisler to the Washington Senators for a paltry $25,000. But he lasted only until the end of the season with the Senators, who sold him to the Boston Braves in early 1928 for the insulting sum of $7,000. Only four years earlier, the mighty Yankees had offered St. Louis $200,000 for Sisler, and when the Browns turned them down, they handed the job to a young kid from Columbia named Gehrig. Sisler hung on with the Braves for a few more seasons, hitting .309 in 1930, which sounds impressive only until one realizes that the entire National League batted .303.

So we can only surmise how great Sisler could have been. Branch Rickey lamented, "I shall always wonder just how great a batting record Sisler might have left behind if illness hadn't shortened his career." *The Sporting News* wrote in January 1933, on the day of Sisler's announced retirement, that "eye trouble cut far into performance at the peak of his career." Baseball writers remembered his greatness, however, for Sisler was voted into the Hall of Fame in 1939, the first first-baseman to be so honored.

Perhaps Branch Rickey, who essentially discovered and groomed Sisler should have the last word on him. Rickey considered Sisler the greatest player he ever coached not because of what Sisler could do with his bat or glove but because of Sisler's "high qualifications as a man. He never criticized a teammate and never criticized an opponent. He was always thinking. He was a student of the game and devoted to his profession." At the profession of playing first base, George Sisler still has few peers.

# 35

# NO PLACE
# LIKE HOME

IN "A SWEEPING REVIEW of the Major League Season" in the December 1929 issue of *Baseball* magazine, James M. Gould gave halting praise to a Detroit rookie named Alexander, "a great hitter but not so good a fielding first baseman." That Detroit rookie played in all 155 games his team played that year. He batted .343 with 25 home runs, 43 doubles, 15 triples, 110 runs, and 137 RBI. His 215 hits led the league and made him the first American League rookie since Joe Jackson in 1911 to get 200 hits in a season. His offensive numbers put him in the top five of the league in home runs, RBI, hits, slugging, and total bases. It was a year of many outstanding rookie performances, and throughout the winter months, *Baseball* featured a succession of articles on these new stars. But it wasn't until April that the magazine finally found this rookie's accomplishments worthy of a feature article. It would become the mark of his major league career that recognition would come for the most part begrudgingly when it came at all.

His name was Dale Alexander, though he was more often called "Moose" or "Ox." He lasted only five years in the major leagues, but two of those years were outstanding. He was compared to Babe Ruth and dismissed as a clumsy oaf (in one instance by the same person). He won a batting crown, and most people wished that he hadn't. And he was finally forced out of the majors by an injury suffered not on the playing field but in the trainer's room.

Alexander's path to the major leagues was a familiar one for his time. Raised on a tobacco farm near Greeneville, Tenn., he began his professional career in 1924 by playing on his hometown team in the Appalachian League. After batting .331 that year, Charlotte in the Sally League purchased his contract for $500. After two years in Charlotte, where he batted .331 and .323 and knocked in over 200 runs, Toronto of the International League paid $5,000 for him. In two years, his value had increased tenfold.

He had two outstanding years in Toronto culminating with his .380 average, 115 runs, 31 home runs, 144 RBI, and 401 total bases in 1928. He led the league that year in games, hits, doubles, home runs, RBI, and batting average. Following his big year in Toronto, the Detroit Tigers bought Alexander and pitcher Augie Prudhomme for $100,000. Count only half of that amount for Alexander, and it still makes another tenfold increase in two years.

The succession of those early years showed Alexander's rise to be one of increasing promise and reward, both athletic and financial. He delivered immediate payoffs at the major league level as well. His new manager, Bucky Harris, had no doubts about his ability to play in the American League as he told reporters "that big farm boy over on first base is going to be one of the great stars of baseball—perhaps another Ruth." By the end of Alexander's record-setting rookie year, Harris was joined by others in his comparison to the Babe, among them F. C. Lane in *Baseball* magazine: "And now, in the American League, appears a husky young slugger who seems destined to trail Babe Ruth through the upper strata of extra bases. His name is Dale Alexander."

Alexander's next year gave the pitchers little relief. Again, he played in all of his team's games, batting .326 with 196 hits, 20 home runs, and 135 RBI. Admittedly this was the year of inflated offensive numbers when Hack Wilson had 56 home runs and 190 RBIs, and Bill Terry batted .401. But Alexander's .326 average still outdistanced the league average of .288 by thirty-eight points. He led his team in home runs and RBI, and only future Hall-of-Famer Charlie Gehringer had more hits (201) and a higher average (.330) among the Tigers.

In 1931, after the game made some adjustments to give the

pitchers a fighting chance again, Alexander's power production dropped off, but he still batted .325, hit 47 doubles, and led his team in RBI with 87. Through his first three years with the Tigers he had collected 579 hits, 123 of them doubles; scored 271 runs while knocking in 359; and batted at a .332 clip. He had proven without a doubt that he could hit in the major leagues.

But despite these numbers, Alexander's value as a major league player was placed into doubt when the 1932 season got underway. Bucky Harris, who three years earlier had seen Ruth in Alexander, suddenly couldn't see Alexander in his lineup. As sportswriter Daniel M. Daniel recalled it: "The first base situation became an obsession with Harris. He was convinced that with a fielder like Alexander, the Tigers could make no headway. The other players—especially the infielders—also developed that psychology. Something had to be done."

And something was done. First, Harris benched Alexander in favor of the better fielding rookie, Harry Davis. Through the first two months of the season, Alexander appeared in only two games as a first baseman and had only 16 at bats. After seeing his value increase tenfold every two years in the minors, Alexander now found himself on waivers after only three full seasons in the majors. Finally, on June 12, he was traded along with his fellow 1929 rookie sensation, Roy Johnson, to the last-place Red Sox for outfielder Earl Webb.

The fall of Alexander, even faster and more decisive than his rise, seemed final. As sportswriter Daniel pointed out, "Newark [the minor leagues] perhaps would have been better." But in Newark, Alexander could not have won the American League batting championship as he did for Boston with a .367 average in that year of the trade. Harry Davis, Alexander's replacement in Detroit, batted only .269 with 74 RBI. And Davis' defensive statistics, particularly his 16 errors and .989 fielding average, resembled the numbers Alexander produced in his three years at Detroit.

They did not, however, resemble Alexander's play in Boston where his defensive statistics suddenly improved in 1932. His .992 fielding average tied him for second-best at his position in the league and no one topped his 11.2 total chances per game. It appeared that manager Harris lost both offense and defense in the trade. Nonetheless, Detroit did improve its record, from 61-93 in

1931 to 76-75 in 1932, while Boston went from 62-90 to 43-111; so Harris was at least vindicated in the standings.

Alexander, unfortunately, was not vindicated by his performance. Rather than being honored as the man who won the batting championship, he was disparaged as the man who stole that crown from Jimmie Foxx. There was some evidence for that judgment.

In 1932, Jimmie Foxx produced one of the greatest single-season hitting performances of all time. His 58 homers not only led the league but drew added attention as he challenged Ruth's 60. With 169 RBI to also lead the league, he needed only the batting title to win the Triple Crown—and become the first American Leaguer to do so since Cobb in 1909. As he led in batting average virtually all year, it seemed probable he would win that as well, particularly with his .361 mark on September 1. Though he raised it three points in the final month to finish at .364, it was still three points too few to beat Alexander's .367.

To most observers, it didn't seem right. By today's standards it would not even be accepted (and isn't by *Total Baseball*). With only 392 at bats and 61 walks, Alexander falls short of the required 477 plate appearances—but not by much. Still, Alexander had appeared in only 124 games and had nearly 200 at bats and 70 hits fewer than Foxx. While Foxx was second in hitting on May 1 and first at the beginning of June, July, August, and September, Alexander's name didn't enter the picture until the final weeks. And Foxx played on the powerful Athletics who had appeared in the three previous World Series, while Alexander was buried in the cellar with the hopeless Red Sox.

Yet Alexander's performance had real merit. He batted .360 for the Sox in June, .371 in July and August, and .383 in September. In 101 games for the Red Sox, he went hitless in only nineteen of them and had three hits in thirteen. On the final day of the season, his two hits earned him the batting crown.

In March 1933, *Baseball* magazine printed an article that took a closer look at "The Leading Five Batters of the Major Leagues." From the beginning, its tone unmistakably reveals its intention to belittle Alexander's achievement while pitying Foxx. In retrospect, the irony of the article's claims sounds humorous: "There is an obvious injustice here. As the years go by, the time will come when Alexander will be the only batter of the American League membership in 1932 who will be remembered. His championship assures him that recognition. He will take his place among those other immortals: Ty Cobb, George Sisler, Tris Speaker, and Napoleon Lajoie. Few will remember that Jimmy [sic] Foxx, who made far more hits to far greater purpose, was thrust rudely into the background because he failed by three batting points to equal Alexander's mark."

The article then lays out the statistical evidence to prove its point that Foxx, not Alexander, was the true batting champion of 1932. The argument rests on the relative position of the top five batters at the start of each month in the season. Since Foxx appears at the top in every month except May when he's second to Gehrig, and Alexander doesn't appear at all until the season's close, the article asserts that Alexander was a thief who came in the back to take the title. But comparing Alexander's monthly performance to Foxx's, starting with Alexander's move to Boston, shows Alexander on top every time: .360 to .345 in June, .371 to .308 in July, .371 to .362 in August, and .383 to .382 in September.

Alexander's batting crown was not a sneak or a cheat but a well-deserved and rightfully earned prize. That he accomplished it on such a hapless team from what should have been the ignominious end to his career only enhances the achievement. And justice, for those who clamored for it, was soon in the coming. Jimmie Foxx would win his Triple Crown the next year, and Alexander would be gone from the major leagues.

On May 30, 1933, in a game against the Athletics in Philadelphia, fate, not fielding, intervened to decide Alexander's future. In the first game of a doubleheader, Alexander injured his knee sliding into home. The injury was serious enough to require diathermy treatment in the clubhouse between games. Diathermy uses electric currents to produce heat in body tissues. The trainer must have considered it relatively harmless. After putting Dale in for the treatment, he went out to get something to eat and forgot about him. But something went wrong as Alexander himself recalled it several years later: "It was a new method of treatment and not too much was known about it. I noticed my left leg felt awfully hot. Anyway, I ended up with third degree burns and a gangrene infection and I almost lost my leg. I was finished in the majors."

It was typical of this "quiet, good-natured chap" to sit un-complaining as his leg was severely burned and his major league career effectively ruined. It was also typical of him to go un-complaining to the minor league team in Newark when the Red Sox dumped him at the end of the season. Ironically, his unas-suming nature had as much to do with ending his career as his poor fielding or lack of speed.

Not that his fielding wasn't flawed. In his first three years, he led all first basemen in errors twice and his fielding average never rose above .988. One manager despaired enough at these numbers to give up on him completely, and contemporary base-ball accounts, even complimentary ones, seldom mentioned Alexander without mentioning his clumsy glove and fractured footwork. When *Baseball* magazine printed F. C. Lane's article on Alexander in April 1930, they didn't conclude it with a reci-tation of his impressive rookie statistics or finish it with further comparisons to Ruth. Instead, they quoted Alexander's own as-sessment of his fielding prowess: "I know I look bad at first base . . . I had the bad habit of getting my legs crossed at first. That's a serious difficulty, but I've had some good coaching and I'm getting so that I can reach for a ball without falling down."

Because of this slapstick perception, partly based in fact and partly in stereotype, teams found it easier to give up on Alexander as Detroit did in 1932. With the leg injury in 1933, Alexander's batting average fell to .281 and the Red Sox felt he lost the one ability he had in the game. Apparently, the rest of major league baseball agreed because no team picked him up then or in subsequent years. Still, he continued to play profes-sional ball and excelled at the minor league level for the next eight years. His numbers during that time attest to the fact that he never lost the ability to hit:

| YEAR | CLUB | LEAG | AB | R | H | 2B | 3B | HR | RBI | AVG |
|------|------|------|-----|-----|-----|-----|-----|-----|-----|------|
| 1934 | Newark | Int | 545 | 89 | 183 | 35 | 2 | 14 | 123 | .336 |
| 1935 | Kan Cty | A.A. | 461 | 84 | 165 | 29 | 6 | 16 | 95 | .358 |
| 1936 | Kan Cty | A.A. | 612 | 81 | 193 | 30 | 9 | 5 | 100 | .315 |
| 1937 | Nashvl | South | 567 | 91 | 181 | 42 | 1 | 15 | 109 | .319 |
| 1938 | Chattan | South | 518 | 49 | 160 | 24 | 1 | 8 | 85 | .309 |
| 1939 | Sanford | FlaSt | 374 | 72 | 129 | 27 | 2 | 6 | 80 | .345 |
| 1940 | Thomasv | GaFla | 330 | 78 | 128 | 31 | 5 | 14 | 96 | .388 |
| 1941 | Selma | SoEas | 64 | 14 | 28 | 9 | 0 | 1 | 23 | .438 |

In 1942, Dale Alexander finished his playing career where it began eighteen years earlier—at home in Greeneville, Tenn. He remained in baseball for the next twenty years as a minor league manager and scout, never straying far from the Appalachian home where he was born, married, raised his family, and died. That home was more important to him, and more enduring, than any laurels that baseball could bestow. His family had lived there since 1836, and his son Steve lives there today.

At home, Dale seldom spoke of his own career as a major leaguer. His son Steve remembers him not mainly as a ballplayer but as a practical joker with a great sense of humor. And as a man of few words. "You could ride from here (Tennessee) to California with him and never know he played baseball," said Steve. "He didn't talk about himself. He did his job and went home."

We don't think of Dale Alexander now when we remember Cobb and Sisler and Speaker and Lajoie and Foxx. His time among the giants was shadowed and brief, and when it ended, the end was quiet and quick. Yet he did not boast of his accomplishments nor bemoan his fate. "I just didn't have the ability," Alexander was quoted as late as 1970, "I couldn't run or field."

But he could hit the ball. The man who was lumbering on the bases and awkward on the bag found it easy to stand at home. It was the place he belonged. It was where he played the game.

# 36

# A Leg
# To Stand On

THE NAME OF MONTY STRATTON is still remembered today, over fifty years since he last played in the majors, mainly because Jimmy Stewart portrayed him in a movie. But from the beginning, his career could have been fashioned in Hollywood. It has all the elements of a sentimental script.

Monty Stratton was a gangling farmboy (6 foot 6 inches, 190 pounds) from the small community of Celeste, Tex., about fifty miles northeast of Dallas. His father died when he was still a boy, leaving Monty as a young man to help his mother operate the farm. The only ball he played was for the Celeste town team, and then it was strictly for fun, filling in wherever needed.

One day, he filled in as a pitcher and threw a shutout. He won the game, a permanent position, and a nickname, "The Celeste Whirlwind." As his local fame grew, Stratton was encouraged to go to a neighboring town to meet a scout for the Chicago White Sox. He signed a professional contract not long after that.

The White Sox brought him along steadily during his first two years in the minors, 1934 and 1935. To this point, his advance has been almost casual in its ease. Then, a sore shoulder hampered him slightly in the second half of 1935. It was the first sign of trouble, but trouble would visit him repeatedly through the rest of his career.

An appendectomy and tonsillectomy sidelined him for several weeks in 1936, his first year as a White Sox regular. In 1937, a twisted ankle kept him out of the All-Star game, and then an arm injury knocked him out of action again in August. He pitched only three and a half innings after July 31. An arm injury again delayed his start of the 1938 season by several weeks.

Despite these setbacks, Stratton led his team in victories in both 1937 and 1938. At the age of 25 in 1937, he had his best year with 15 wins against only 5 losses. His 2.40 ERA was second in the league to Lefty Gomez's 2.33. He was also second to Gomez in shutouts with five and in fewest hits per nine innings with 7.76. He led the league with only 2.02 walks per nine innings, and his winning percentage of .750 was second-best. In one seven-game stretch starting on June 22, he won seven games in a row with three shutouts.

His 1938 season was not quite as good as 1937, but he still won 15 games and showed a .625 winning percentage on a White Sox team that won only 44 percent of its games. But Hollywood did not buy his story on the basis of that winning percentage. It was what happened after that season's end that put him in the movies.

In November, he was hunting rabbits with a .22 caliber pistol near his mother's farm in Celeste, Tex. The gun was in his holster with a safety on, or so he thought, until he pulled it out with his hand on the trigger, and the gun fired. The bullet cut through his right thigh and severed the large artery behind his knee. Stratton crawled toward his mother's house for half an hour before one of his brothers found him. He was taken to a hospital in Greenville ten miles away and later rushed fifty miles to another in Dallas.

The severed artery cut off all the blood supply to the lower part of the leg. Gangrene set in quickly and Stratton's leg was amputated. Dr. A. R. Thomasson, the operating surgeon, emphasized the role of bad luck in Stratton's tragedy: "It was the craziest sort of accident. Monty couldn't have hit that artery if he aimed at it. It probably wouldn't happen more than once in a hundred times. But it did, with a measly little .22, too."

Afterwards, Stratton was fixed with a wooden leg. On May 1, 1939, a benefit game between the Cubs and White Sox raised

$28,000 for Stratton, as even the players, umpires, and sports writers paid their way into the park. Stratton pitched the first ball and retired to the bench.

J. Louis Comiskey, the White Sox owner, offered him a lifetime job with the team for as long as he wanted it. Stratton accepted the offer and spent the 1939-1941 seasons as a coach with the White Sox. It was a lifetime job, but it was not the job he wanted. He was not yet thirty years old. He wanted to pitch.

In 1942, he became the manager with the Lubbock team in the West Texas League, where he inserted himself into the lineup three times as a relief pitcher. In 1945, he starred in a Houston semipro team and on the basis of that performance signed to pitch with the Sherman Twins in the Class C East Texas League in 1946. He won 18 games that year.

It was nearly eight years since his accident, but Stratton was still only thirty-four years old and "still clinging to the hope that he would return to the big leagues." The East Texas League made a special rule allowing for a substitute runner whenever Stratton reached base. Otherwise, he handled the demands of his position without incident. As reported in a local paper at the time, his "only difficulty [was] running out base hits . . . The artificial leg [didn't] handicap him afield. Bunt balls [were] his dish."

Still, he was far from the majors, much farther than he had been when he first played in Texas as a sixteen-year old farm boy. In 1947, he pitched for Waco in the Class B Big State League, but that's the highest level he achieved on his comeback trail. He retired from baseball the next year to assist Jimmy Stewart in portraying him in the movie, *The Stratton Story*. After the movie, he returned to his farm and occasional pitching appearances in the minor leagues through 1953. By that time, he was forty-one years old and finally ready to quit playing the game. It had been nearly fifteen years since his career seemed tragically cut short. It had been a long and eventful career after all.

# 37

# St. Jude's Boy

AS HERB SCORE lay on the pitcher's mound on the night of May 7, 1957, with blood streaming down his face, he said a short prayer. About a second or two earlier, Gil McDougald had smashed the twelfth pitch of the game directly into Score's right eye. The prayer was simple, directed to the Catholic saint of impossible cases: "St. Jude, stay with me," Score thought to himself. At that moment Score had no idea if he would lose the eye or if he even might die from a skull fracture. Perhaps it was not a miracle of saintly intervention, but Score did retain his right eye, and against all odds he even pitched in the major leagues again. But he would never regain the nearly miraculous effectiveness he possessed before that moment. In the half-second it takes for a ball to travel 60 feet 6 inches, something was lost to Score and all lovers of baseball forever.

St. Jude was not asked for help on this one occasion only. Score's full name is Herbert Jude Score, and he was so named because his mother, Ann, had prayed to St. Jude for a boy when she first discovered she was pregnant. Then, at age three in Rosemont, Long Island, young Herb was involved in a serious accident, having both legs crushed when a bakery truck backed over them. It was doubtful that Herb would walk again, and after deliberation doctors decided only a difficult operation to implant plates had any chance of restoring Score's mobility. "That night before the operation," Score told *Look* magazine in 1957, "a priest brought a relic of St. Jude to the hospital. Next morning,

225

X-rays showed that the bones had worked apart and no operation would be needed.''

But Score's physical problems continued periodically throughout his youth. When he was ten he was bedridden with rheumatic fever for over eight months, and in high school in Lake Worth, Fla., Score fractured an ankle. All of this might have hindered another athlete, but Herb Score was not another athlete.

He was signed out of high school as a $75,000 bonus baby by the Cleveland Indians and began his professional career at Reading, Pa., in 1952. Birdie Tebbetts, then a catcher for the Tribe and later a manager for three major-league teams, was sent to Reading to give the left-handed throwing Score a "look-see." After a few blinding pitches, Score announced to Tebbetts, "Here comes a fastball." "Fastball?" Tebbetts replied. "What have you been throwing?" Score answered, "Oh, that was just loosening up." Tebbetts removed his glove and handed it to another catcher, Joe Tipton. "You catch him," Birdie said. "If that was just warming up, his fastball will go right through me."

And it would be that blazing fastball, along with a sharply breaking but uncontrollable curve ball, that would catapult Score through the Indian minor-league system. At Indianapolis of the American Association in 1954, Score dispelled any doubts about his ability to pitch on the major league level. Score's record was a phenomenal 22-5 with 330 strikeouts, and he was named both the American Association Rookie of the Year and its Most Valuable Player. Ex-pitcher Art Nehf exclaimed that Score was "the best young southpaw I've seen since Lefty Grove." Hall of Famer Tris Speaker added, "This kid is going to be one of the great ones."

Score made the jump to the big club the following spring joining the defending American League champions, and he proceeded to have one of the most impressive rookie seasons a pitcher has ever had. He led the AL with 245 strikeouts, a rookie record that stood almost thirty years. He was fourth in the league in ERA (2.85), tied for third in wins (16), and was in the top ten in innings pitched. For these achievements he walked away with Rookie of the Year honors. And he was all of twenty-two years old.

There were two blights on this otherwise sensational season, and each set an unfortunate pattern that would repeat itself for the next eight years. One was injury, or in this case a virus, that sidelined Score briefly. The other was his control problem— he walked a whopping 154 batters. These two problems would haunt Score incessantly his entire career.

As unbelievable as it might sound, Score improved tremendously in 1956. In that season Score led the AL in four key categories: strikeouts (263), shutouts (5), fewest hits allowed per nine innings (5.85), and strikeouts per nine innings (9.49). He was second in wins (20), winning percentage (.690), and ERA (2.53). He even reduced his walk total to 129. In a scant two seasons he had struck out 508 batters, and he had established himself as the dominant pitcher of the AL.

Yet even this stellar season had its down side. In June Score was hospitalized after he complained of abdominal pain. He was suffering from a spastic colon, a largely psychosomatic ailment which, said Dr. Erwin E. Mayer, rarely affects athletes but is common among tense high-level management businessmen. "He (Score) doesn't show it outwardly," said Dr. Mayer, "but he worries about everything being just right. He's a perfectionist, and this temperament undoubtedly is the basis for his spastic condition." This was the first time that Score's physical ailments were somehow connected to his psychological makeup. It would hardly be the last.

Nonetheless a healthy Herb Score reported to spring training in 1957. His potential seemed unlimited. In an interview in February, Mickey Mantle (who was coming off his Triple-Crown season) flatly stated that Score was the best pitcher in the league. "Everyone knows he's fast, but he's got a good curveball," said Mantle. "And when Herb learns a little more control, brother, he's going to be even tougher to hit."

Most American League teams were interested in landing Score from the pitching rich Indians. On March 18, 1957, Boston general manager Joe Cronin half-jokingly said to his Cleveland counterpart Hank Greenberg, "Hank, would you take a million dollars for Score?" Greenberg hesitated for a moment but responded, "Joe, I could not let you have Score." If a million dollars sounds like a pittance today, one should remember that the estimated value of the entire Cleveland team in 1957 was $3 million. Cronin later related the incident to Hal Lebovitz of *The Saturday Evening Post* and said, "I don't want to belittle the ball club, but maybe Score is worth one-third of the franchise."

The season started for Score as beautifully as could be expected. By early May he was 2-1 with 39 strikeouts in 36 innings. His fifth assignment of the season was the Tuesday night game of May 7. The defending world champion New York Yankees were visiting Cleveland's Municipal Stadium. The leadoff hitter of the game was Hank Bauer, who was retired easily on a ground ball. That brought up Gil McDougald. After McDougald had worked the count to 2-2, Score and catcher Jim Hegan decided to come in with a fastball. Afterwards, McDougald recounted his thoughts before that pitch was thrown. "I had to swing, and I was surprised when he gave me a fastball without much on it." Gil did indeed swing and smashed a sizzling liner back toward the box. It hit Score with full force in his unprotected right eye. "After I crossed first," McDougald said, "I ran to the box. He was such a mess I almost threw up. If I could only have that swing back."

It was 8:05 P.M. Score has retold the story of that pitch innumerable times. "When the ball struck me, I wasn't aware of acute pain," he said in a 1959 interview with Herb Kamm. "I fell, but never lost consciousness. I remember saying 'St. Jude'—he's the saint of impossible cases—'stay with me.' " Other thoughts were fighting with the prayer for his attention. "I thought about being blinded for life, that my teeth were knocked out, that my nose was broken. I was afraid to open my eye, afraid I wouldn't be able to see."

Score was removed from the field by stretcher and rushed to Cleveland's Lakeside Hospital where he was treated by eye specialist Dr. Charles I. Thomas. Meanwhile, the ball game at Municipal Stadium was completed under an atmosphere of gloom. After the game a disconsolate Gil McDougald was shielded from the media by manager Casey Stengel. But reporters were still able to clearly discern McDougald's incessant moaning to teammate Hank Bauer: "If he loses his sight—and you hear me Bauer—I'm going to quit this game. It's not that important when it gets to this."

All anyone could do was wait. The following day, Dr. Thomas stated in a news conference that Score had suffered a broken nose, a cut right eyelid, a contusion of the right cheekbone, and considerable swelling combined with hemorrhaging in the right eye. McDougald made a point of visiting Score that day. In typical fashion, Score immediately exonerated McDougald from any blame. "Don't worry. It's not your fault," he said. Still, McDougald felt tremendous guilt. That same night Score's mother, Ann, told the press, "What I would like to do now is to see Gil McDougald. My heart aches for him. It wasn't his fault and I'm sure everything will be all right."

But Score's pain and progress were more on the mind of the public than McDougald's guilt. On May 9 Dr. Thomas reported that the broken nose distorted his ability to determine how extensive the eye damage was, and he would have to wait for the swelling around the nose to abate.

Eerily, one of the feature articles in the May 11 issue of *The Saturday Evening Post* was about Herb Score. *The Post*, of course, had gone to press before the injury. In the article, Hank Greenberg confidently stated that "Herb is to pitching what Mantle is to hitting," and that Score "may become the greatest pitcher in the game's history." Greenberg paused and then added, "Provided nothing happens to him."

Details of Score's condition were released on a daily basis. On May 13, his peripheral vision returned, and the following day he was fitted with pinhole black sunglasses. "He can't get too much light through these tiny pinholes," explained Dr. Thomas, "so we don't have to be so careful about the light hurting him anymore." Thomas added on the 16th that Score was "progressing nicely" and that "an accurate evaluation will soon be possible." And the best news of all was reported on May 17: Score's retina was not detached while "the hemorrhage in the right eye has cleared." Dr. Thomas was cautiously optimistic, but he believed Score's sight would return to nearly 100 percent.

Score held his first news conference on May 23. "Everything is hazy," he told reporters. "Now I can see the walls and everything. It's better than seeing blackness." Score then heard Dr. Thomas say, "I am certain Herb will regain his vision. I feel sure Herb will pitch again." Less than a week later, Score was released from Lakeside.

Around the first of June, Score was setting a possible comeback date of mid-July, but this proved overly optimistic. He was still languishing on the disabled list on August 16, and when he attempted to pitch on September 4, he realized that the comeback would be more difficult than he had anticipated. "I feel all right and I can see pretty well," he said that day. "But when I am on the mound I have trouble picking up the ball as soon as it leaves the bat." He spookily added, "Sometimes I reach for it and it isn't there." The next day Cleveland announced that although Score's depth perception had improved, it was not at a level that would allow him to play. Consequently, the 1957 season for Score was officially over.

Possibly the hottest topic of spring training, 1958, was the comeback attempt of Herb Score. Teammates and foes alike were rooting for Score to put the horror of May 7 behind him. Score himself treated the moment with typical good humor. "I'm sure I'm not going to do any flinching even though I don't expect to be a good fielder. I never was anyhow." Veteran baseball writer Joe Williams wrote that Score's fastball delivery naturally threw him off balance and made him lose sight of the plate. In the same article, Early Wynn, who was Score's teammate at the time of the injury added, "When a pitcher transfers his weight to the other foot, the sudden jarring impact throws his focus out of line." In Score's case, Wynn said, "He never saw the ball at all, so, of course, he had no chance to block it with his glove, or even duck."

Score basically agreed with Wynn's assessment. In an interview with writer Gay Talese, Score said, "Every once in a while you lose the ball. Very seldom is a batter hit by a pitch unless he loses the ball. I think I heard Gil's hit. But it was too quick and—just like that . . ." Talese asked Score what he expected from 1958. "My eye is fine now," Score responded, "but people this season will wonder if I'm gun shy."

Score's comeback was momentarily interrupted on March 7 by a sprained ankle. That same day Gil McDougald said, "I read about Score's three innings with those six strikeouts [in a Cleveland intra-squad game] and was glad that he came back so convincingly." He also said, "Naturally, we all take calculated risks in baseball, and I certainly did not aim for Score's eye. But the accident made me feel terrible. Now I am able to forget it."

Both Score and McDougald, then, were seemingly able to put the incident behind them as the regular season began. In his third start, Score hurled a 2-0 shutout with 13 strikeouts against the White Sox. This put his early season record at 2-1 with 48 strikeouts in only 41 innings. But once again disaster struck, this time in a less dramatic but no less devastating manner. During a night game in Washington in late April, Score experienced pain in his left elbow and forearm. All of a sudden he could not reach the plate. A specialist prescribed rest, and Score was again on the disabled list, this time for three weeks. He returned to action on May 27 in a relief role, striking out five and ending the game on a pop-up. "But I hurt my arm on that pitch," he said. "After that pitch I was never the same again." The diagnosis was an inflamed elbow, and yet again, Score was sidelined.

Score did not return to action until mid-September. His manager, Joe Gordon, began to doubt Score's resolve. According to Gordon, Score had a "mental block which prevents him from cutting loose." Score was dismayed and hurt by Gordon's comments, and he denied the charge in his typical gentlemanly manner.

But when all was said and done, the 1958 season was as much a washout as the 1957 season. Score's final record was 2-3 with a 3.95 ERA. He realized that 1959 might prove to be his last chance to prove he was still a major-league pitcher. "The chips are really down now," he told Herb Kamm. "My confidence, my hope, my prayers are as strong as ever, but I know, too, that I have to face the possibility that the arm may never be as strong as it used to be." Score won a job on the staff as a spot starter and reliever—a turn of events unthinkable merely two seasons earlier.

On opening day, 1959, Cleveland held a 6-3 lead heading into the ninth. Manager Gordon motioned for Score to relieve. He proceeded to walk his first batter on four pitches, wild pitch a run home, walk a second batter, also on four pitches, and fell behind 2-0 to his third hitter when Gordon mercifully replaced him. Luckily, this inauspicious start was soon forgotten as Score finally began to piece together a decent season. His record stood at 9-4 in July. Then, Score went into the worst slump of his career, a painfully frustrating string of eight ineffective starts. When the White Sox came to Cleveland for a series in late August, the 1959 pennant was on the line. Gordon showed no faith in Score at all; he did not pitch one inning. Chicago swept the series and crushed all hopes for a Cleveland pennant.

Immediately after that series, a thoroughly confused Herb Score said, "If I knew what the trouble was I'd have it fixed in a minute. But I don't . . . I just don't." His dilemma was compounded by the concern of teammates, friends and fans. "Everybody wants to help me," he said, "and they can't and they don't know what to say." Even Joe Gordon seemed sympathetic. "Poor Herb. All the guy needs is one good game. Then he's back in the routine. But he just can't get started. It's slightly crazy." Gordon added wistfully, "I know he's still got what he had when he was the best, and some day he's gonna prove it to a lot of people." However, the season ended with Score dropping his last seven decisions to finish at 9-11.

Trade rumors concerning Score began to circulate as early as October of 1959. To quell these, Cleveland club president Nate Donlin stated unequivocally that Score was not on the trading block. But Donlin was sending mixed signals. Immediately after that vote of confidence, Donlin placed the blame for Cleveland's losing the pennant squarely on the shoulders of Herb Score. "Had Herbie come through we would have won the 1959 pennant and world championship," said Donlin. "But he ran into serious control trouble. He was 9-4 and we were four games in front. Then he lost it and we blew the pennant."

The next spring Donlin went back on his word and traded Score to the White Sox for little known right-hander Barry Latman. Score was pleased about the new beginning. "Joe Gordon doesn't like me," Score said. "He gives me no sympathy." Indian general manager Frank Lane raised the by-now-familiar bugaboo: "Herb's trouble was more psychological than physical. He was always complaining of aches and pains, but he did that when he was winning 20 and striking out 14 a game. I think he still hasn't gotten over the accident that nearly robbed him of his sight three years ago."

For the second time in his career, Score was beginning with a defending AL champion. And for the second time he was under manager Al Lopez who was his first major league skipper back in 1955. In fact, Bill Veeck, then president of the White Sox, traded for Score primarily because of the relationship between him and Lopez. "Two of his finest years he had with Cleveland when Al Lopez was there," said Veeck. With Lopez, Score had the sympathy he felt Gordon withheld. Lopez told reporters, "I told Score to abandon two pitches, the sidearm and the slider. The sidearm delivery was unnatural for him and the slider could hurt his arm and was not needed. I said 'Herb, your fastball and your curve, coming straight overhand, are all you need, at least until you re-establish yourself. Then we'll have another talk.' "

At first it seemed Lopez's pep talk had worked. In early May of 1960 Score threw six "beautiful innings," giving up only three hits and more importantly, walking only two, in a win over the Senators. There was a lengthy period in the season where he seemed the Score of old—in one span of 56 innings he had an ERA of 2.08, five complete games, 36 strikeouts and only 25 walks. Score gave all the credit to Lopez for having confidence in him. But the numbers for the whole season were less than impressive. His record was 5-10 with a 3.71 ERA in only 113 innings. One could not be overly optimistic looking toward 1961.

Score's first start of the 1961 season was not until May 10, and although he ended a two game Chicago losing streak with a two-hit effort, he also walked nine. In his next start, he could not retire any of the six men he faced. On May 27 he was sent to Chicago's Pacific Coast League team in San Diego, and he did not return to the big club until the September call-up.

Nineteen sixty-two began auspiciously when Score made the White Sox, but he was demoted after pitching only six innings. Ironically, Score was sent to Indianapolis, the American Association team with which he set all those records in 1954. This demotion occurred on May 7—five years to the day of the McDougald incident. Score would never pitch in the majors again.

After an ineffective spring in 1963 Score was optioned to Indianapolis again. His first reaction was to call it quits, but after four days he reconsidered. But even at Indianapolis, Score could not find home plate. He was a disastrous 0-6, and he retired from baseball permanently in November. He was thirty years old.

The thirty-year anniversary of that frightful eye injury passed in 1987. When reminded about it, Score insisted once again that the arm trouble of 1958 was more responsible for ending his career than the line drive to the eye. "I know people think it was the McDougald line drive," he said in 1987, "but I don't really think so. Oh, it's possible the long layoff, the medication—

I was on cortisone for ten months to reduce the swelling on the right side of my head—might have altered my muscle tone, and that may have affected my windup somehow. But I've really never been able to make a connection."

Most other pitchers would have been finished by the eye injury. Many have been finished by arm problems. Not even someone as courageous as Herb Score could overcome this tandem of disaster. His first two seasons seemed to be harbingers of a charmed career, but misfortune dogged him mercilessly. Through it all, though, Score never felt alone. After all, when you're an impossible case named Herbert Jude Score, it's good to have a saint along for the ride.

# 38

# THE GOOD
# OF THE GAME

IF BASEBALL were in fact played only on the idyllic fields we imagine, then perhaps we would remember Curt Flood only for his unsurpassed grace in patrolling those fields, his flawless fielding in 1966 when he led all outfielders with 391 putouts and no errors, his .300-plus batting average from 1961-1968 and his key role in the Cardinals' championship teams of 1964, 1967, and 1968. We would see him always as he appeared on the cover of *Sports Illustrated* on August 12, 1968: "Baseball's Best Center Fielder." But when we recall him now, we think first of how he did not play the game, how he refused to play it until the rules were reconsidered and he was given some choice in where he would play.

From the beginning of Flood's career as a professional ballplayer two things stand out: his exceptional talent and his unflinching pride. In 1956, when he first broke in, the struggles of integration were still being fought not only on the major league level but in the minors as well, with even more hostility and less solace. Flood's first assignment as a professional ballplayer was with the High Point-Thomasville club in the Class B Carolina League. Like Bill White, Vada Pinson, Leon Wagner, and other contemporaries, Flood experienced the Jim Crow indignities of playing ball in the South as "a matter of life and death." And like those other ballplayers, Flood asserted his pride on the diamond. "I completely wiped out that peckerwood league," Flood remarked in his autobiography, *The Way It Is*, "I led it in everything but home runs—although I hit twenty-nine. I played in all 154 games. I batted .340, driving in 128 runs with 190 hits. The better I did, the tougher I got."

He was promoted to Savannah of the Class A South Atlantic League in 1957, where he produced a .299 average on 170 hits and made the league All-Star team. He was at this time the property of the Cincinnati Reds, which also had two other rising star outfielders named Frank Robinson and Vada Pinson. However, in the cockeyed calculus of the time, an outfield of Frank Robinson and Vada Pinson and Curt Flood did not equal a pennant—it equalled an all-Negro outfield, which could not be tolerated.

The Reds' first solution was to convert Flood to a third baseman or a second baseman, but that did not work. So they traded him to the St. Louis Cardinals. Flood began the 1958 season with the Cards' minor league affiliation in Omaha. He was batting .340 when the Cards called him up. For the next twelve seasons, he was their regular center fielder.

While Flood played regularly and respectably in his first three seasons, it was not until 1961 that he blossomed into the outstanding offensive and defensive player that would mark his play throughout the sixties. Flood's .322 batting average in 1961 placed him among the top ten in the league. Over the next eight years, he would regularly appear in this company. In 1963, his .302 average again placed him with the top ten and his 401 put-outs and 2.6 chances per game led National League center fielders. He also delivered 200 hits and scored 112 runs. More importantly, the Cardinals won 93 games that year and came in second to the Dodgers.

The next year the Cardinals again won 93 games, but this time it was enough to win the National League pennant. Flood led the league with 211 hits, and his .311 average and 97 runs scored again placed him among the league leaders. His World Series play was less than remarkable—.200 batting average—but he scored five times and his triple in game one drove in what proved to be the winning run. The Series was finally won by the Cardinals in seven games over the Yankees, with Bob Gibson picking up two victories, including the finale, and striking out thirty-one.

Curt Flood came back in 1965 with another typical year for him: .310 average, 191 hits, 90 runs scored, 349 putouts.

But the Cardinals tumbled to an 80-81 record and a seventh place finish. In 1966, Flood's average dipped to .267, but he again led all outfielders with 391 putouts and committed no errors. The Cardinals record improved slightly to 83-79. The next year they improved even more to 101-60 and won the National League pennant. Curt Flood enjoyed the highest batting average of his career (.335) that year to place fourth in the league, but again disappointed with only a .197 mark in the World Series.

The Cardinals repeated their National League success in 1968. Curt Flood's .301 average—high enough to win the batting title in the American League—placed him fifth in the National League and team high on the Cardinals. He again led the league in putouts and total chances per game. With Willie Mays turning thirty-seven and the Cards established as the premier team in baseball, Flood's star was rising. Midway through the season, *Sports Illustrated* dubbed him "baseball's best center fielder."

His bat did not completely abandon him in the World Series that year as he batted .286. By game four of the Series, the Cards again held a three-games-to-one Series lead and looked ready to claim their second straight championship. But the Tigers won the next two games to set up a seventh game with Gibson on the mound versus Mickey Lolich, both of them looking for their third victory of the Series. The game was scoreless through six. Lolich helped preserve his shutout in the sixth by picking Flood off first just after doing the same thing to Lou Brock.

In the next inning, Flood would make an even more costly blunder. With two Tiger runners on base, Jim Northrup lined a fly to center field. Flood later said he did not see the ball, then he tripped. Two runs scored on the play and the Tigers went on to win 4-1. Flood was the goat.

In fifteen months, he would make the headlines again. But this time he would not be a goat; he would be a sacrificial lamb. On October 8, 1969, Curt Flood received a phone call from Jim Tooney, assistant to Cards' general manager, Bing Devine. He was telling Flood he had been traded to the Phillies. Flood had spent a dozen years with the Cardinals. He was making $90,000 a year. The phone call did not please him. His response was simple and direct: "There ain't no way I'm going to pack up and move twelve years of my life away from here. No way at all."

At that time, a player had little choice. Flood chose to contact Marvin Miller, executive director of the Players' Association, who had gradually been making gains for the players since 1966 through collective bargaining agreements. Miller advised Flood to think about it. By early December, Flood had finished thinking. He wanted to challenge the "reserve clause," which bound a player indefinitely to one team and which was about to send him to Philadelphia.

Flood brought his case before the executive board meeting of the Players' Association to get their support. They were skeptical at first, thinking he might just be using the threat as a bargaining chip with the Phillies. It was also thought that the reserve clause could best be challenged by a minor leaguer or second stringer, who would best exhibit the infringement on livelihood caused by being the exclusive property of one team.

But Flood convinced them of his commitment, and the Association decided to back his case completely. On Christmas Eve, 1969, Flood sent a letter to Baseball Commissioner Bowie Kuhn which began: "After twelve years in the Major Leagues, I do not feel that I am a piece of property to be bought and sold irrespective of my wishes." Kuhn replied, "I certainly agree with you, that you, as a human being, are not a piece of property to be bought and sold. . . . However, I cannot see its applicability to the situation at hand."

Kuhn's response was measured and legalistic; the league presidents, owners, and assorted newspapers supplied the venomous attacks. American and National League presidents Joe Cronin and Chub Feeney issued a joint statement from their winter draft meetings which warned that "professional baseball would simply cease to exist" if Curt Flood won his lawsuit: "As Presidents of the two major leagues, we regret that Curt Flood, a highly paid star who has contributed much to and obtained from baseball, has decided to refuse to honor the assignment of his contract by the St. Louis Cardinals to the Philadelphia Phillies and has demanded that he be permitted to play major league baseball where he pleases."

Flood's lawsuit engendered visions of chaos and destruction that struck at the integrity of the game. Many attacked Flood and his alleged motives. He was accused of being ungrateful to baseball and the Cardinals. They found it ironic and offensive for a

$90,000-a-year player to complain of slavery and peonage. Dick Young, writing for the *New York Daily News*, dismissed Flood as "a man of rather impulsive action," and dismissed his case as "superficial rhetoric, a sickness of the times." But for Flood, it was a matter of principle (not principal, as his detractors complained). As he explained to Howard Cosell, "A $90,000 slave is nonetheless a slave."

Flood was not the first to raise the matter of principle, nor was he the first to couch it in the language of slavery. (Lee Lowenfish and Tony Lupien have detailed its long history in *The Imperfect Diamond*, their book-length study of baseball's reserve system.) In 1887, John Montgomery Ward, architect of the Players' League in 1890 (and perhaps the most intriguing figure the game has ever produced), compared the reserve rule to the Fugitive Slave Law. Around the same time, Jim "Orator" O'Rourke likened its grasp to a "white slave trade." As recently as 1948, Judge Jerome Frank, who served on the three-man panel hearing the appeal of Danny Gardella's lawsuit against the reserve clause, said that "excusing virtual slavery because of high pay is only an excuse for the totalitarian-minded."

The case dragged through the courts for two-and-a-half years. Flood was forced to sit out the entire 1970 season after being denied a preliminary injunction in Federal District Court in February 1970 which would have enabled him to play. It was not only the injunction that kept him off the field; there was a principle involved too. In May 1970, Flood turned down an offer from Commissioner Kuhn's office which would have enabled him to make a deal with any National League club and not damage his lawsuit. He felt the freedom of contract would invalidate his case in court.

The first major decision came on August 12, 1970, from Judge Irving Ben Cooper in Federal Court, Southern District of New York. He ruled against Flood when he stated that "the preponderance of credible proof does not favor elimination of the reserve clause." Flood was not present at the ruling; in fact, he was no longer in the country. He had gone to Denmark to escape the publicity and pressures of the case.

In October, 1970, Flood was offered a contract ($110,000) with the Washington Senators. His lawyer, Arthur Goldberg, advised him that accepting the contract would not hurt his appeal since he had already suffered financial losses by missing the 1970 season. With his businesses failing and bankruptcy on the horizon, Flood accepted the offer.

It lasted less than a month. On April 27, 1971, after appearing in only 13 games for the Senators and suffering from a sore arm and a lack of hits, Curt Flood flew out of JFK airport on a one-way flight to Barcelona. His explanation, received by Senators' owner Bob Short in a telegram from Kennedy Airport, stated simply: "I tried. A year and a half is too much. Very serious personal problems mounting every day."

On June 19, 1972, the Supreme Court finally ruled on the Curt Flood case. The decision was 5-3 in favor of baseball's immunity from the antitrust laws and against Flood's challenge to the reserve rule. The basis of the decision was "stare decisis," or let the old doctrine stand. But the times were changing and the old doctrine was already wobbling. Flood had given it a push. It would not stand much longer. In November, 1975, when Peter Seitz's arbitration panel ruled against the reserve rule in the Messersmith-McNally Case, the final push had come. The next decade was one of increasing free-agency and escalating salaries.

The slow gains players had been making since the late sixties suddenly accelerated in the mid-seventies with the onset of free agency. Curt Flood reaped none of these profits. Quite the opposite, the seventies proved to be a trying decade for him. Business ventures failed for him. He spent five years, from 1971 to 1975, running a bar in Majorca, off the coast of Spain, out of sight of baseball and America. In 1976, he returned to Oakland to be near his ninety-year-old mother, but he was still out of sight and out of mind. He basically did nothing for the rest of the decade. Occasionally news reports would crop up about his sorry plight, the forgotten man. "What can you do?" he remarked to one reporter. "You sit in Alameda and think about all the things you should have done."

But as time passed, things gradually improved. In 1981, he took a Civil Service job with the Department of Sports and Aquatics in Oakland. He became the first commissioner of the sandlot leagues which brought organized baseball to over 3,000 ten- to fifteen-year-olds in Oakland. Flood even got the major leagues involved, convincing the Oakland A's and its players and coaches to contribute money and time.

By the mid-1980s he was even more actively involved in public life and baseball. He started doing public relations work, revived his commercial art career, appeared at fantasy baseball camps and played in Equitable Old-Timers' games. For the first time in nearly fifteen years, Curt Flood could again be seen patrolling center field, which no one had ever done better. Just a few years earlier, Flood had remarked that "people forget that I played some pretty good baseball." For anyone who had ever seen him play, the memories were still intact.

Of course, other memories lingered as well, though less bitterly and with good-natured irony after the passage of twenty years. When the Senior League, comprised predominantly of former major leaguers between the ages of thirty-five and fifty, was formed in 1989, it looked for an experienced hand to serve as commissioner—someone who understood the authority and responsibility of the office and who would look out for the good of the game. Curt Flood gladly accepted the offer. Was there any other choice?

# 39

# HARDBALL

NOT MANY BALLPLAYERS reach the major leagues when still teen-agers. The ones who do stand out in memory: Ty Cobb, Bob Feller, Al Kaline, Robin Yount, Dwight Gooden. There are, of course, others; Tony Conigliaro among them. But Conigliaro did not simply make the majors while in his teens; he hit 24 home runs before he reached the age of twenty. That was his first year in the majors, 1964, and he did it in only 111 games. No one has ever hit more major league homers as a teenager. The next year, at the age of twenty, he led the league with 32 home runs. He was a proven star almost before he had the time to prove himself.

If success seemed easy for Conigliaro in those early years, it was still not without incident. In 1963, he started his first season of professional baseball with Wellsville of the New York-Penn League. During the few days off between the end of spring training and the season opener, Tony flew to Boston to pick up his car. While at home, he tried to stay sharp by taking some batting practice with his uncle Vinnie Martelli. According to a story circulated at the time, one of his uncle's pitches hit Conigliaro's hand. Tony revised this tale some years later in his autobiography, *Seeing It Through*, when he admitted that he actually injured his hand punching out a new girlfriend's former boyfriend. The unorthodox hitting practice delayed his debut as a professional ballplayer for a month.

The freak accident was not serious enough to threaten his career, but it did temper his accomplishments. While he went on to pace the league with a .363 average that year, he was not awarded the batting title because he lacked the necessary at bats. That combination of tough luck and remarkable recovery would form a bittersweet pattern for the rest of his career.

One year in the minors was enough. In 1964, Tony stayed with Boston. In his Fenway Park debut, Conigliaro hit the first pitch of his first at bat over the "Green Monster" (Fenway's left-field fence) for his first major league home run. On May 5, he was hit on the left hand by a pitch from Moe Drabowsky of the Athletics. He missed eight games. On July 26, Pedro Ramos of the Indians hit Tony on the right arm with a pitch that fractured his ulna bone and sidelined him for six months. Nonetheless, he managed to hit his 24 home runs that year to break Mel Ott's record of 19 homers for a teen-ager. Tony hit the homer that gave him the new record only hours before Ramos interrupted his season.

An observation by Carl Yastrzemski in 1964, as quoted in an article by sportswriter Larry Claflin, takes on an ominous tone in light of Tony's subsequent career: " 'I was in the on-deck circle and I was watching Tony's face,' said Carl Yastrzemski. 'He never saw the ball. He froze. All he had to do was drop his arm, but he never moved . . . I don't believe Tony ever saw the pitch that hit him.' "

In 1965, Conigliaro played the entire season except for twelve games he missed due to, you guessed it, a broken wrist suffered from a pitch delivered by Wes Stock of the Athletics. This was the year his 32 homers led the league (making him the youngest player ever, at twenty, to win a home run title), but people were beginning to notice his ability to get hit as much as his ability to hit.

The next year, Tony played his first injury-free professional season. His 28 home runs did not come close to leading the league (Frank Robinson hit 49 en route to the Triple Crown), but along with his 26 doubles, 77 runs and 93 RBI, it was good enough to be named Most Valuable Player of the Red Sox. At the age of twenty-one, it seemed he finally stilled his critics and proved that he not only belonged in the major leagues but was also capable of staying there. Charlie Finley, the owner of the Athletics, believed enough to offer $500,000 for Conigliaro following the season.

After his strong showing in 1966, 1967 promised great things for Conigliaro. That promise was broken—not too surprisingly by a pitched ball—before the season began. In spring training, Tony suffered a broken shoulder when his teammate Johnny Wyatt hit him with a hard fastball in the batting cage.

Sidelined during spring training, Tony struggled to get back in form as the regular season started. Just as he was coming around, the Army called him away for two weeks of reserve duty. After the first thirty-one games of the season, he had hit only two home runs, and the success of 1966 seemed a distant memory.

But then he went on a hitting binge. Ten home runs in his next 22 games (10 in 81 at bats). For the first time in his career, he was named to the All-Star team. And for the first time in almost twenty years, the Red Sox were seriously involved in a pennant race.

On August 18, the Red Sox started a four-game weekend series with the California Angels. Ninety thousand fans would attend the series which the Red Sox swept. In the second game of Sunday's doubleheader, the Red Sox rallied from eight runs behind with Carl Yastrezemski leading the way with six RBI on two home runs. The game and the sweep did not clinch the pennant for the Red Sox, but it gave them a dramatic boost for the final six weeks and became emblematic of what would be termed their "Impossible Dream" season.

But that weekend series in Anaheim is not remembered for that drama or for Yastrzemski's last-game heroics. It is remembered instead for an incident that happened before the first game was even decided—an incident that decided the course of the rest of Conigliaro's career. Jack Hamilton, the California right-hander, threw a pitch that hit Tony Conigliaro in the face. The ball hit Conigliaro with as much impact as the ball that killed Ray Chapman or the ball that ended Mickey Cochrane's career. Conigliaro suffered a triple fracture of his cheekbone, a dislocated jaw, and was rendered blind for two days. "When he was released from the hospital eight days later," *Time* magazine reported in 1969, "the imprint of the baseball's stitches were still visible on his brow, and the vision of his left eye was hopelessly blurred."

But unlike Chapman who never had a chance to come back, or Cochrane, who was old enough to not bother trying, Tony Conigliaro would struggle to return. He was only twenty-two years old. Weeks earlier, he had become the youngest player in history to hit 100 major league home runs. After a slow start, he was enjoying the finest season of his career and his team was on its way to the World Series.

The beaning left Conigliaro with a hole in his retina and no depth perception, but there were indications that he might make it back. In December of 1967, Tony had his first public work-out and reported no blurs. In January 1968, the Red Sox were reportedly satisfied that Tony would be okay in spring training and would be ready to play full time in right field. On March 11, 1968, *The Bradenton Herald* had good news for Red Sox followers: "It looks like Boston's Tony Conigliaro is seeing just one baseball again—and seeing it well."

But this was just the optimism that comes with spring. As the early weeks of spring training passed, the papers reported Conigliaro missing pitches by a foot and striking out constantly. When the regular season started, he was not nearly ready to join his teammates. He was finally forced to sit out the entire 1968 season, and it looked like his career was over.

In June of 1968, Tony's nightclub act, "The Tony Conigliaro Review," appeared at Sonny's disco in the St. George Hotel at Kenmore Square—within singing distance of Fenway Park. Tony admitted he had not been to a game all year, but it was also about this time that he thought he found his way back "either as an infielder or as a pitcher." By August he was seriously pursuing the pitching option, and his prospects looked hopeful.

A miracle seemed about to happen as Tony reported to the Florida Instructional League following the 1968 season to work as a pitcher. But his line scores from that experiment were less than impressive. On November 6, against the Phillies, he pitched three innings and gave up two hits, two walks, and three runs. On November 10 against the Twins in two-and-one-third innings, he gave up six walks and eight runs. On November 15, things got better, but he still gave up three runs in five innings.

Despite the Red Sox's optimism, the other clubs weren't convinced of Conigliaro's comeback. Following the 1968 season, Conigliaro could have been purchased in the American League expansion draft by either the Seattle Pilots or the Kansas City Royals, but both teams passed him up. The Red Sox didn't place him on the forty-man roster, so any other team could have picked him up for a mere $25,000 during the winter meetings. No one bothered.

Tony would go on to prove them all foolish. In 1969 he played in 137 games in right field for the Red Sox and appeared in 141 games overall. In 506 at bats, he hit 21 doubles, 20 home runs, knocked in 82 runs, and batted .255. Nineteen seventy would be an even better year. He played in 146 games in right field that year. In 560 at bats, he delivered 20 doubles, 36 home runs, 89 runs, 116 RBI, and batted .266. His home run total, home run percentage, runs, and RBI were the highest marks of his career. He placed fourth in the league in home runs and second in RBI. That same year, his younger brother Billy joined him as a regular in the Red Sox outfield. Things finally seemed to be going Tony's way once again. He was only twenty-five years old and had 160 career home runs. He would hit only six more.

The rest of his career would last only slightly more than half a season—95 games to be exact. On October 11, 1970, the Boston Red Sox traded him to the California Angels in a six-player swap.

Tony struggled at the plate in 1971, hitting only four home runs in 266 at bats. Finally, in the early morning of July 10, he called it quits. Just hours before, the Angels' had lost a 20-inning, 1-0 game to the Oakland Athletics. Twice in that game, Tony had violent arguments with umpire Merle Anthony. In the nineteenth inning, he was finally kicked out of the game for disputing a strikeout and batting his helmet away. When Tony announced his retirement at a 5:00 A.M. press conference, he remarked, "I have lost my sight and am now on the edge of losing my mind."

Jim Murray of the *Los Angeles Times* offered the best explanation of how Tony C. fell so quickly from the heights of his comeback to the mental and physical breakdown that tortured him in California. The clue was in Conigliaro's perseverance;

there never was a miraculous healing: "He [Conigliaro] had discovered on eye-chart tests that he could read charts by shifting his head to one side to bypass a head-on blind spot. This jerky movement was interpreted as pulling away from the close pitches. He was just trying to get a look at them."

Though Tony made one final abortive comeback with the Red Sox in April 1975, his career as a baseball player effectively ended in the early morning in July 1971. His comeback during 1969 and 1970 was indeed miraculous, but as had been the pattern, even that miracle would be thwarted.

After his playing days ended, Tony pursued a career in broadcasting, but fate dogged him there as well. He worked for some television stations in San Francisco but only achieved moderate success. At one point, he had an opportunity to break in as an announcer with the NBC Game of the Week during a Saturday game in San Francisco when NBC found itself short an announcer. On the day before the game, Conigliaro was playing some pickup basketball when he got elbowed in the nose. True to form, Conigliaro was taken to a hospital where he needed a transfusion. His nose started to hemorrhage, and he spent the night in the hospital. He was unable to do the game.

But that wasn't the end of his troubles. Fate reserved an even harder blow. On January 9, 1982, Tony's brother Billy was driving him to the airport after Tony had auditioned for a position with a television station in Boston to work as an announcer for the Red Sox games. He never made it to the airport. He suffered a massive heart attack that nearly killed him but instead left him in a coma for four months. He had just celebrated his thirty-seventh birthday.

Fifteen years earlier, he lay in a hospital bed, blind, his face smashed by a pitch that very nearly killed him. Now he lay in another bed, just barely brought back from death and left in a coma from which he might never come back. His doctors didn't expect any miracles, though they knew that was what it would take.

For four months, Tony remained in that coma with no sign of recovery and little hope beyond that of his family's, which was immense. For four months, his father, Sal, and mother, Theresa, two brothers, Billy and Richie, and uncle Vinnie Martelli stayed at Tony's bedside waiting for a sign. But the doctors couldn't offer much hope, not for someone whose heart had stopped, leaving him with no oxygen for five minutes.

But finally one day Tony did speak: "Hi, Mom." His cardiologist, Dr. Ramon W. DeSanctis, said it was a miracle. But Tony's physician, Dr. Max Kaulbach, sought an explanation elsewhere—at Conigliaro's bedside. "I don't think I've ever seen a family so continuously at work against the odds," he told reporter Steve Marantz of *The Boston Globe*. "You can't help but wonder that the continuous feedback system between the relatives and Tony might have helped him."

Tony would need that support to resurface and survive. On April 15, 1983, just a year past the day he first came out of the coma, a benefit was held in Boston's Symphony Hall to help defray Conigliaro's $4,000 per week medical costs. His pension fund insurance benefits were running out. When he finally left the hospital, it was to go home to his parents' house in Nahant, Mass., where he required constant care. His brother Billy was named his legal guardian.

Rumors about Tony's condition and possible improvement would surface occasionally in the ensuing years, but for the most part he faded from public view. Then, early in the morning of February 24, 1990, Tony Conigliaro died of pneumonia and kidney failure. Despite the years of struggle and decline, the news still seemed shocking and sudden. He was barely forty-five years old.

Sometimes an accumulation of injuries and frustrations will wear a player out. It just hurts too much to keep putting on the uniform every day. So one day, the player quits. It was never that way with Tony C. Things just never got any better. No matter how often he came back—from broken bones, blindness, death—he would always get hit again, a little harder than before. He could always hit back better than most. He just couldn't escape the knockdowns.

# 40

# Is Something Wrong Here?

IT HAPPENED shortly after the All-Star break but had been developing steadily over the years. J. R. Richard of the Houston Astros finally arrived (in 1979) as the premier pitcher that his team and the rest of the league expected him to be. He was twenty-nine years old and had been in the big leagues for almost nine years.

Not that he hadn't been dominating before. In 1976 he won 20 games and then won eighteen in each of the next two years. His ERA over that time was below 3.00, and he collected over 700 strikeouts. But he also led the league in walks in two of those three years and came in second the other year. That lack of control had always plagued him and detracted from his accomplishments. Earlier in his career, it had delayed his full-time use at the major league level for several years. There was no doubt that he could throw it hard enough; he just couldn't seem to throw it over the plate enough.

But in the second half of 1979, J. R. finally brought his blinding fastball and vicious slider under control. It made him nearly unhittable. On July 24, his record was 7-11 with a 3.84 ERA. He finished the year at 18-13 with a league-leading ERA of 2.71 and a respectable 98 walks in 292 innings (about one-third fewer walks than he had allowed in previous years). Though he had always been a second-half pitcher, his performance at the end of 1979 was especially noteworthy. In the final months of that year, J. R. completed 11 of 15 starts, won 11 games and lost only 2, struck out 151 batters in 128 innings, and compiled an ERA of 1.27. In one six-week period, he completed 9 straight games, allowed only 4 earned runs, never allowed more than 1 run in any start, pitched 40 consecutive innings without allowing an earned run, and won 8 games. His only loss during that time was a 1-0 game against Philadelphia in which he gave up only four hits.

Houston signed him to a four-year contract worth $2.4 million following that season. It had been a watershed year not only for J. R. but for the Astros as well, and both were looking toward greater accomplishments in 1980. J. R. was looking for continued improvement. The Astros were preparing for a World Series appearance.

After years of foundering around .500 in the middle of the Western Division, the Astros won 89 games in 1979 and came within two games of winning the division outright. J. R. seemed to weigh this factor heavily in deciding to sign with the Astros without even testing the free-agency market. "My wife, Carolyn, and I liked Houston and wanted to stay there," Richard said. "My teammates had something to do with the decision. So did the fact that we won this season for the first time." Apparently, J. R. also felt some gratitude and loyalty to the organization and its general manager, Tal Smith, who, as he said, "sorta looked out for me and had faith in me back before I got to this point." And from the vantage of late 1979, with the promise of many successful seasons ahead, perhaps a World Series championship or two, the Astros and J. R. seemed assured of future reward. As Richard's agent, Tom Reich, said after the contract signing, "This will not be his [J. R.'s] last contract. And it will not be his biggest."

Neither was it the Astros' biggest. In December 1979, Houston signed free-agent Nolan Ryan to a three-year guaranteed contract with a fourth option year at more than one million dollars per season. The contract made Ryan the highest paid player in team sports and gave the Astros the two hardest throwing right-handed starters in baseball. If there was still any doubt about the Astros commitment to producing a championship team in 1980, it was dispelled in January when they signed two-time MVP Joe Morgan to provide the leadership and experience he gained in his three previous World Series appearances with Cincinnati.

In the Astros home opener on April 10, 1980, J. R. looked ready to pay back on his team's investment as he pitched perfect ball for six and one-third innings and struck out thirteen in a 3-2 victory. Thirty-two of his pitches were clocked at 95 MPH or better, with eleven at 97 and four at 98. In eight innings, he walked no one. J. R. looked to be in mid-season form.

His stellar performance, which he attributed to hard work in the off-season ("I wore out two or three mirrors just practicing my delivery during the winter"), continued through the early weeks of the season. He was named Player-of-the-Month for April after posting a record of 3-0 with a 1.80 ERA, 40 strikeouts in 30 innings, and only 6 earned runs in 4 starts.

Except for one disastrous start against Montreal on May 5 when he lasted only one-third of an inning while giving up five runs, J. R. remained virtually unhittable throughout May and early June. On June 17 he was working on three straight shutouts and had over 30 consecutive scoreless innings as he started a game against the Cubs. But J. R. left the game after only five innings despite eight strikeouts and only two hits because his arm "went dead." Though his record stood at 9-3 with a 1.51 ERA, it was the first indication that something was wrong.

J. R. didn't pitch again for eleven days. In his next appearance at home against Cincinnati, he left the game after three and one-third innings with a "tired arm." One sportswriter joked that at least his arm was going from dead to tired, so he must be improving. But something serious and strange was happening. Earlier in the season, he had to leave five games early due to arm and back stiffness. On July 3, he lasted only six innings in a 5-3 victory in Atlanta. By the season's halfway point, he had missed several of his turns in the rotation and completed only four of the 17 games he started.

For many pitchers, these developments may not have been too upsetting or even noticeable, particularly in light of the 10-4 record and 1.89 ERA. But J. R. had averaged over 280 innings per year for the previous four years and completed over 40 percent of his starts. Still, no one could determine what the problem was. J. R. himself wasn't sure what, if anything, was wrong.

After being named as the starter for the National League All-Star team, J. R. at first said that he wouldn't be able to pitch. But then he changed his mind, started, pitched two shutout innings and said he could have pitched more. He didn't look like a man with arm trouble.

The All-Star game was held in Los Angeles that year, and J. R. took the opportunity to visit the Dodgers' team physician, Dr. Frank Jobe. Afterwards, J. R. announced that he was "going fishing," that Dr. Jobe told him not to pitch for thirty days. A few days later, Dr. Jobe denied telling J. R. not to pitch and instead stated that he found nothing seriously wrong. J. R. admitted as much and declared his intention to pitch, which he did on July 14, just six days after the All-Star game and only three days since his announced fishing trip. It would be his final regular season appearance on the mound in the major leagues.

The night of July 14 was typical of J. R.'s 1980 season. He started by pitching three overpowering innings against the Atlanta Braves, allowing only one hit and striking out Gary Matthews, Bob Horner and Jeff Burroughs in the second. But at the start of the fourth inning, J. R. was slow getting out of the dugout. All his teammates were in position when manager Virdon finally had to ask J. R. if he was going out. He did, but only lasted for two batters after which he left due to a stomachache. After the game, J. R. ate fried chicken, meatballs, and rice with gravy in the clubhouse as he explained that he felt nauseated probably due to a hamburger that he ate before the game. Suspicions were rising that J. R.'s trouble was in his head, not his stomach, back, or arm.

In any case, the Astros placed J. R. on the twenty-one-day disabled list the next day and scheduled three days of diagnostic tests. Despite the negative speculation in the press, the Astros seemed convinced that J. R. had a physical problem which in turn was affecting his emotional state of mind. As general manager Smith said, "I think people have to understand this is new to J. R. It's the first arm trouble he's ever had."

The tests performed on Richard revealed a blood clot on his right side. Dr. Brelsford, the Astros team physician, conferred with surgeons at the hospital that conducted the tests and concluded that surgery was not required. J. R. he said, "should be allowed to resume activities and work out under close control and observed conditions."

Four days later on July 30, J. R. was throwing easy during a light workout at the Astrodome when he suddenly collapsed. When he arrived by ambulance at the hospital he had no pulse in his right carotid artery. Emergency surgery restored the circulation and saved his life. At the age of thirty and at the peak of his athletic ability, J. R. Richard suffered a stroke that nearly killed him. Now everyone knew what was wrong with J. R.

Apologies appeared in the press as quickly and dramatically as accusations had appeared only days and weeks earlier. Bill Conlin writing for *The Sporting News* in August 1980 looked back on the attacks on J. R. and saw that "it was not a shining hour for men of good will." J. R.'s wife, Carolyn, remembered the attacks with less irony and more anguish: "People did a job on us. . . . It got so bad that I didn't want to leave the house or let the children read the papers. . . . When things got bad, we turned around and nobody was there."

After the stroke, it was easy to second-guess not only J. R.'s accusers but also the way he handled his situation. Was the team wrong in putting J. R. back to work after finding the blood clot? According to Dr. Brelsford, "it was a medical judgment that the clot was a chronic situation." He went on to stress that pitchers often exhibit circulatory problems in their arms." Should another course of treatment have been taken? "I've talked with 50 other doctors," said Dr. Brelsford, "and I can truthfully say that none of us could figure anything to do differently. Something happened between July 25 and July 29. But what that was, I just don't know."

For J. R. Richard it marked the beginning of a new struggle, one that would prove far more trying and of far more consequence than learning to control his fastball. His struggle would not be simply to return to baseball but to return to life as he knew it before the stroke.

In 1981 he returned to learn once again how to play the game. By 1982 he was ready to pitch again, if only at the Class A minor league level. "I'll go to the minors if I get the chance to pitch there," he remarked.

It was a difficult struggle, riddled with disappointments, bitterness, and frustration. When he moved up to Triple-A ball that year, he was completely ineffective. It was becoming increasingly apparent that J. R. was a long way from his old major league form. But he was fully aware of the magnitude of his comeback. "How am I going to be my old self in a matter of months?" he asked.

In spring training 1983, he showed up in much better physical condition than the previous year and even seemed to be throwing better. "I believe I can make this club," he said. "I'm planning to make this club." But before spring training ended, J. R. required further surgery to restore proper circulation in his left leg. He would return to pitch in the minor leagues again that year but would never make it back to the majors.

Late in spring training in 1984, the Astros gave J. R. his unconditional release. His control, reflexes, and peripheral vision never completely returned after the stroke, and the team finally acknowledged that the full exercise of these abilities would never come back. But the Astros did not mistake that for J. R. not coming back. "This was an extremely difficult decision for us," said John J. McMullen, Astros chairman of the board. "J. R. has been an example to everyone whether they be a baseball player or not."

During the course of his comeback, J. R. sued the Astros and its doctors for negligence and incompetence before, during, and after his stroke. He eventually settled out of court for $1.5 million. After leaving baseball, there was talk of a biography and movie based on his life, neither of which materialized. He tried his hand briefly at selling cars, but that didn't work out. In 1987, he was reportedly living on interest.

In 1989, he tried another comeback, this time in the Senior League, comprised primarily of former major leaguers aged 35-50. But he was cut from his team for being overweight and out of shape. On January 9, 1990, he filed for bankruptcy. Half a year later, he was talking about still another comeback in the major leagues. "I won't quit until I get back," he told the *Houston Chronicle*.

The record books supply only part of the story: the high school ERA of 0.00; the fifteen strikeouts in his first major league start; the first right-hander in the National League to strike out 300 batters in a season—303 in 1978 and 313 in 1979.

The record books don't catalog the comeback. There is no category for "opportunities just ceased" which is how J. R. characterized his release. No statistics can measure the life of a man. A towering man, for example, 6 feet 8 inches, 222 pounds, with a fastball and more that you could barely see.

# BIBLIOGRAPHY

## Books

Alexander, Charles C. *John McGraw*. New York: Viking Penguin Inc., 1988.

————. *Ty Cobb*. New York: Oxford University Press, 1984.

Angell, Roger. *Late Innings*. New York: Simon & Schuster, 1982.

Asinof, Eliot. *Eight Men Out*. New York: Holt Rinehart and Winston, 1963.

Cohen, Richard M., David S. Neft, and Roland T. Johnson. *The World Series*. New York: Dial Press, 1976.

Conigliaro, Tony and Jack Zanger. *Seeing It Through*. New York: Macmillan Publishing Company, 1985.

Connor, Anthony J. *Baseball For The Love Of It*. New York: Macmillan Publishing Company, 1982.

Creamer, Robert W. *Babe: The Legend Comes To Life*. New York: Simon & Schuster, 1974.

Dickey, Glenn. *The History of the American League since 1901*. New York: Stein and Day, 1980.

Dickson, Paul. *The Dickson Baseball Dictionary*. New York: Facts on File, 1989.

Einstein, Charles, ed. *The Baseball Reader*. New York: Lippincott & Crowell, 1980.

Fleming, G. H. *The Unforgettable Season*. New York: Penguin Books, 1981.

Flood, Curt and Richard Carter. *The Way It is*. New York: Trident Press, 1970.

Gammons, Peter. *Beyond the Sixth Game*. 1985. Lexington, MA: The Stephen Greene Press, 1986.

Hemingway, Ernest. *The Old Man and the Sea*. New York: Charles Scribner's Sons, 1952.

Honig, Donald. *The October Heroes*. New York: Simon & Schuster, 1979.

Hynd, Noel. *The Giants of the Polo Grounds*. New York: Doubleday & Co., Inc., 1988.

James, Bill. *The Bill James Historical Baseball Abstract*. New York: Villard Books, 1986.

Kahn, Roger. *The Boys of Summer*. 1971. New York: New American Library, 1973.

Kubek, Tony and Terry Pluto. *Sixty-One*. New York: Macmillan Publishing Company, 1987.

Lieb, Frederick G. *The Baseball Story*. New York: G. P. Putnam's Sons, 1989.

Lowenfish, Lee and Tony Lupien. *The Imperfect Diamond*. New York: Stein and Day, 1980.

Mayer, Ronald A. *The 1937 Newark Bears*. New Jersey: Wm. H. Wise, 1980.

Nadel, Eric and Craig R. Wright. *The Man Who Stole First Base*. Dallas: Taylor Publishing Company, 1989.

Neft, David S. and Richard M. Cohen. *The Sports Encyclopedia: Baseball*. 6th ed. New York: St. Martin's/Marek, 1985.

Porter, David L., ed. *Biographical Dictionary of American Sports: Baseball*. New York: Greenwood Press, 1987.

Reichler, Joseph L., ed. *The Baseball Encyclopedia*. 8th ed. New York: Macmillan Publishing Company, 1990.

———. *Baseball's Greatest Moments*. New York: Bonanza Books, 1982.

———. *The World Series: 75th Anniversary Edition*. New York: Simon & Schuster, 1979.

Ritter, Lawrence S. *The Glory of Their Times*. 1966. New York: Vintage Books, 1985.

Ritter, Lawrence S. and Donald Honig. *The Image of Their Greatness*. Updated Edition. New York: Crown Publishers, Inc., 1984.

Robinson, Frank and Barry Stainback. *Extra Innings*. New York: McGraw-Hill Book Company, 1988.

Schlossberg, Dan. *The Baseball Catalog*. Middle Village, NY: Jonathan David Publishers, Inc., 1989.

Seymour, Harold. *Baseball: The Early Years*. 1960. New York: Oxford University Press, 1989.

Siwoff, Seymour, Steve Hirdt, and Peter Hirdt. *The 1987 Baseball Analyst*. New York: Collier Books, 1987.

Society for American Baseball Research. *Minor League Baseball Stars*. Vol. I. 1978.

Sowell, Mike. *The Pitch That Killed*. New York: Macmillan Publishing Company, 1989.

Spinks, J. G. Taylor. *Judge Landis and Twenty-Five Years of Baseball*. New York: Thomas Y. Crowell Company, 1947.

Thorn, John and Pete Palmer, eds. *Total Baseball*. New York: Warner Books, 1989.

Turkin, Hy, S. C. Thompson, and Pete Palmer. *The Official Encyclopedia of Baseball.* 10th Revised Edition. New York: Doubleday & Co., Inc., 1979.

Veeck, Bill and Ed Linn. *Veeck as in Wreck.* 1962. New York: New American Library, 1986.

*The Ol' Ball Game.* Harrisburg, PA: Stackpole Books, 1990.

## Newspapers, Magazines, and Journals

Albany Times Union 1987
Baseball 1911, 1914, 1918, 1920, 1929, 1931, 1932, 1933
Baseball Digest 1949
Baseball Quarterly 1977
Boston Globe 1903, 1978, 1979
Bradenton Herald 1969
Chicago Sun Times 1978
Chicago Tribune 1907, 1929
Cincinnati Enquirer 1907
Cincinnati Post 1986
Cleveland Plain Dealer 1977
Detroit Free Press 1937, 1938
Los Angeles Times 1971, 1981
Louisville Courier-Journal Times 1977
Milwaukee Journal 1961
New York American 1907, 1921
New York Clipper 1884
New York Daily News 1970, 1986, 1988
New York Evening Mail 1907
New York Evening Sun 1920, 1924
New York Herald 1907
New York Telegram 1924, 1927
New York Times 1907, 1912, 1924, 1940, 1941, 1950, 1965, 1969, 1973, 1975, 1977, 1979, 1982, 1983
New York Tribune 1925
New York World-Telegram 1932, 1936, 1946
Newsday 1962
Saturday Evening Post 1957
Sport Magazine 1950, 1952, 1960, 1963
Sporting Life 1900
Sports Illustrated 1968, 1990

The Sporting News 1898, 1899, 1900, 1936, 1962, 1964, 1970, 1972, 1976, 1977, 1979, 1980, 1981, 1982, 1983, 1984, 1986
Time 1969
Toledo News-Bee 1911
Tulsa World 1978

**Archives and Private Collections**

National Baseball Library, Cooperstown, NY
Robert K. Wood, Keene, NH

**Interviews with Authors**

Agganis, Phil, telephone interview, 19 Dec. 1989
Alexander, Steve, telephone interview, 3 Jan. 1990
Gehringer, Charlie, telephone interview, 21 Dec. 1989
Wood, Robert K., Keene, NH, 20 Jan. 1990

# INDEX

261